SOCIAL IDENTIFICATION IN GROUPS

ADVANCES IN GROUP PROCESSES

Series Editors: Edward J. Lawler and Shane R. Thye

Recent Volumes:

SOCIAL IDENTIFICATION IN GROUPS

EDITED BY

SHANE R. THYE

Department of Sociology, University of South Carolina, USA

EDWARD J. LAWLER

School of Industrial and Labor Relations, and Department of Sociology, Cornell University, USA

2005

ELSEVIER
JAI

Amsterdam – Boston – Heidelberg – London – New York – Oxford
Paris – San Diego – San Francisco – Singapore – Sydney – Tokyo

ELSEVIER B.V.
Radarweg 29
P.O. Box 211
1000 AE Amsterdam
The Netherlands

ELSEVIER Inc.
525 B Street, Suite 1900
San Diego
CA 92101-4495
USA

ELSEVIER Ltd
The Boulevard, Langford
Lane, Kidlington
Oxford OX5 1GB
UK

ELSEVIER Ltd
84 Theobalds Road
London
WC1X 8RR
UK

First edition 2005

British Library Cataloguing in Publication Data
A catalogue record is available from the British Library.

ISBN: 0-7623-1223-8
ISSN: 0882-6145 (Series)

∞ The paper used in this publication meets the requirements of ANSI/NISO Z39.48-1992 (Permanence of Paper).
Printed in The Netherlands.

Working together to grow
libraries in developing countries

www.elsevier.com | www.bookaid.org | www.sabre.org

ELSEVIER   BOOK AID
International   Sabre Foundation

CONTENTS

LIST OF CONTRIBUTORS

Christopher Barnum	Department of Sociology, University of Iowa, USA
Peter J. Burke	Department of Sociology, University of California, Riverside, USA
John F. Dovidio	Department of Psychology, University of Connecticut, USA
Naomi Ellemers	Department of Social and Organizational Psychology, Leiden University, The Netherlands
Samuel L. Gaertner	Department of Psychology, University of Delaware, USA
Michael A. Hogg	School of Psychology, University of Queensland, Australia
Matthew O. Hunt	Department of Sociology, Northeastern University, Boston, USA
Bert Klandermans	Faculty of Social Sciences, Vrije Universiteit, The Netherlands
Michael J. Lovaglia	Department of Sociology, University of Iowa, USA
Miller McPherson	Department of Sociology, University of Arizona and Duke University, USA
Adam R. Pearson	Department of Psychology, University of Connecticut, USA
Blake M. Riek	Department of Psychology, University of Delaware, USA
Floor Rink	Social and Organizational Psychology, Leiden University, The Netherlands

Dawn T. Robinson   Department of Sociology, University of
                            Georgia, USA

Richard T. Serpe   Department of Sociology, Kent State
                            University, USA

Lynn Smith-Lovin   Department of Sociology, Duke University,
                            Durham, NC, USA

Jan E. Stets   Department of Sociology, University of
                            California, Riverside, USA

Sheldon Stryker   Department of Sociology, Indiana
                            University, USA

Allison K. Wisecup   Department of Sociology, Duke University,
                            Durham, NC, USA

Reef Youngreen   Department of Sociology, University of
                            Iowa, USA

PREFACE

Several years we began a new trend in the *Advances in Group Processes* series. Our goal then was to publish a set of five interrelated volumes that examine core issues or fundamental themes in the group processes arena. Each volume was to be organized around a particular problem, substantive area, or topic of study, broadly defined to include a range of methodological and theoretical orientations. Volume 22 represents the fourth volume in the series, addressing fundamental issues of *Social Identification in Groups*.

The volume opens with a paper by Naomi Ellemers and Floor Rink, who review and analyze the literature on the causes and effects of identification processes with respect to work groups and group performances. They examine how such processes have both beneficial and detrimental effects, and analyze how normative expectations for group behavior can impact commitment and work motivation. Overall, this paper is an important resource for those interested in social identity, multiple (nested or overlapping) identities, and work-group commitment or identification.

The next two papers take on theoretical and empirical issues in Identity Control Theory. In *"New Directions in Identity Control Theory,"* Jan Stets and Peter Burke offer specific hypotheses regarding the negative emotional reactions that occur when transient situational meanings do not verify the meaning an individual holds in their identity standard. The authors assert that emotional reactions depend on the source of the discrepancy, the relative power and status of the other vis-à-vis the self, and the source of the identity standard. This is an important paper that breaks new ground by examining a phenomenon that, over the past 30 years, has received little theoretical and empirical attention. Next, Michael Lovaglia, Reef Young-reen, and Dawn Robinson undertake the important task of linking identity processes and cognitive performances in *"Identity Maintenance, Affect Control, and Cognitive Performance."* Using *Identity Control Theory* and *Affect Control Theory*, they assert that performance on an academic test can be impaired when high performance is not consistent with a salient identity. This work offers the counterintuitive suggestion that individuals might perform poorly on a test when that test is not consistent with the identity. A number of specific hypotheses are offered that promise to inspire new research on academic performance.

The next three papers address issues of social identity in the context of larger structural forces. In "*Making Good on a Promise: The Impact of Larger Social Structures on Commitments*" Sheldon Stryker, Richard Serpe and Matthew Hunt analyze the impact of social structure on role-related commitments. This is an interesting paper that theorizes three structural levels (large scale, intermediate, and proximate) with connections to interactional and affective commitment. The arguments are examined using data from a telephone survey of individuals in a five county region of southern California. This paper represents an important study of a core identity theory principle – that structural constraints and opportunities shape the development of commitments to social relations. Next, Chris Barnum examines how status processes and group membership combine to yield social influence in task settings. His analysis centers on a theoretical construct termed a *group status typification state*, defined as an understanding of the type of person who is expected to be a good source of information. The paper offers theoretical assumptions that bridge status characteristics theory and social identity theory, and then formally models situations where both status and group membership are salient. Barnum concludes by discussing the broader implications of this work. Finally, Bert Klandermans addresses the emergence and conceptualization of collective identity for political protest. The author offers a theory of collective identity that addresses whether collective identities cause or are caused by participation in social movements, and whether subgroup identities are inversely or positively related to larger group identities. The paper presents evidence bearing on these issues from studies of farmers in Spain and the Netherlands, and South African citizens. A key strength of this paper is that it synthesizes ideas from social and collective identity literatures.

The next two papers address issues of social identification and uncertainty. First, Allison Wisecup, Miller McPherson and Lynn Smith-Lovin examine how the presence of an androgynous person with ambiguous gender identity will affect performance on a cognitive task. In "*Recognition of Gender Identity and Task Performance*," they hypothesize that people will take longer to define the identity of androgynous looking individuals, and that their presence will slow performance on a cognitive task. A new experimental investigation supports both hypotheses. The authors close by considering how their findings fit with prevailing theories of impression formation. Next, in "*Uncertainty, Social Identity, and Ideology*," Michael Hogg describes and analyzes how ideology is sustained using his uncertainty reduction theory. The key argument is that subjective uncertainty with regard to self motivates individuals to identify with high entitativity groups possessing ideological belief systems. An important aspect of this piece is that it distills the relationships among uncertainty, group identification, group prototypes, entitativity, and ideology. Overall, this paper serves as a conceptual bridge and an important foundation for those interested in links between individual processes and group identification.

The volume closes with a well-rounded paper that addresses numerous issues in the identity literature. In *"Social Identities and Social Context: Social Attitudes and Personal Well-Being"* John Dovidio, Samuel Gaertner, Adam Pearson and Blake Riek examine how social identity processes affect perception, personal health, and mental health. Drawing on their Common Ingroup Identity Model, the paper examines (i) how multiple identity standards can be activated simultaneously and (ii) how identity perceptions shift from members of separate groups to members of a single, more inclusive group. Their analysis also, when both subgroup and subordinate group identities are salient, explains how both positive and negative reactions may occur. The paper closes by considering the implications of these findings for personal well-being.

Shane R. Thye
Edward J. Lawler
Volume Co-Editors

IDENTITY IN WORK GROUPS: THE BENEFICIAL AND DETRIMENTAL CONSEQUENCES OF MULTIPLE IDENTITIES AND GROUP NORMS FOR COLLABORATION AND GROUP PERFORMANCE

Naomi Ellemers and Floor Rink

ABSTRACT

This chapter reviews recent theoretical developments and empirical research, to examine the causes and consequences of identity processes in relation to collaboration in work groups and group performance. Our central proposition is that identification in work groups can have beneficial as well as detrimental effects, depending on the nature of the shared identity, and the content of distinctive group norms. First, we examine some of the complications stemming from the fact that identification in work settings typically involves groups that can be defined at different levels of inclusiveness and where people can be seen as having multiple cross-cutting identities. Then, we move on to show that processes of identification affect the way people view their co-workers and supervisors, causing the same objective behavior to be interpreted and responded to in

Social Identification in Groups
Advances in Group Processes, Volume 22, 1–41
ISSN: 0882-6145/doi:10.1016/S0882-6145(05)22001-5

*a fundamentally different way. Finally, we examine how normative ex-
pectations about prototypical group behavior determine group processes
and group outcomes, with the consequence that identification and commitment can affect work motivation and collective performance in different ways, depending on the content of distinctive group norms.*

IDENTIFICATION IN WORK SETTINGS

In the past, scholars examining the origins of work behavior have emphasized that instrumental considerations play an important role in the behavioral choices people make (Ambrose & Kulik, 1999; Pinder, 1998; Steers,
Porter & Bigley, 1996), as they maximize their chances of obtaining desired
outcomes (Vroom, 1964), try to establish equity (Mowday, 1979), or work
to achieve specific goals (Locke & Latham, 1990). In addition to these
instrumental or exchange considerations, however, theory and research have
demonstrated the importance of self-definitional (Brief & Aldag, 1981;
Shamir, 1991) and emotional processes (George & Brief, 1996; Lawler, 2003;
Lawler & Thye, 1999; Lawler & Yoon, 1993) for work behavior. In fact,
given contemporary work conditions, which are increasingly characterized
by service provision (Cascio, 1995; Gutek, 1995) and discretionary efforts
(Brief & Motowidlo, 1986) in work teams (Smith, 1997; Parker, 1993), individual reinforcement mechanisms and instrumental exchange considerations turn out to have limited value (Kohn, 1993; Pearce, 1987) to predict
motivation, effort, and performance of people working in groups (Ambrose
& Kulik, 1999; Erez, Kleinbeck & Thierry, 2001).

In response to this development, *identification* has been proposed as the
key to commitment to team work, collective motivation, and the internalization of organizational norms and values (Albert & Whetten, 1985; Coates, 1994; Haslam, Postmes & Ellemers, 2003; Van Dick, 2004).
Considerable work has been done in this area to define (Albert, Ashforth
& Dutton, 2000; Meyer & Allen, 1997; Van Knippenberg & Ellemers, 2003)
and assess identification as a psychological factor that is distinct from other
related constructs (Mael & Tetrick, 1992; Thye, Yoon & Lawler, 2002;
Van Dick, Wagner, Stellmacher & Christ, 2004). In the literature, the term
identification is used to refer to a broad, multifaceted construct, incorporating the *perceived inclusion* of the self in the group (self-categorization), the
evaluation of one's membership in the group (collective self-esteem), as well
as the extent to which the individual feels emotionally *involved* with the
group (group commitment; Tajfel, 1978; Tajfel & Turner, 1979). Although

these components of identification can be distinguished from each other both in terms of their causes and in terms of their effects, they do tend to covary, and often all three components are included in identification measures (Ellemers, Kortekaas & Ouwerkerk, 1999; Ouwerkerk, Ellemers & De Gilder, 1999). Given that affective commitment to the group turns out to be the component that most reliably predicts group behavior (Ouwerkerk et al., 1999), for our present purposes, we will use identification and commitment as interchangeable constructs (see also Miller, Allen, Casey & Johnson, 2000; Riketta & van Dick, in press).

Starting with the seminal paper by Ashforth and Mael (1989) indicating how insights from social identity theory may help understand behavior in organizations (see also Ellemers, De Gilder & Haslam, 2004; Ellemers, Haslam, Platow & Van Knippenberg, 2003; Haslam & Ellemers, 2004; Hogg & Terry, 2000), research has established that identity processes are relevant to a range of organizational problems, and that identification constitutes an important motivating factor in people's behavior in work groups (for overviews see Haslam, 2001; Haslam, Van Knippenberg, Platow & Ellemers, 2003; Hogg & Terry, 2001). Because the initial aim was to demonstrate the *value* of incorporating insights on identification in an area of research that was traditionally dominated by instrumental approaches, scholars have mainly emphasized the possible *benefits* of identification and commitment for work motivation and work performance. Indeed, it has been established that identification and commitment predict a variety of work-related outcomes, including individual performance, organizational turnover, and organizational success (for overviews see Beal, Cohen, Burke & McLendon, 2003; Mathieu & Zajac, 1990). Accordingly, there is an increasing awareness that "ignoring commitment is costly" (Benkhoff, 1997). At the same time, due to the fact that identification has become such a popular construct among organizational theorists and practitioners, the sometimes routine inclusion of identification as a factor in research or business policy has also revealed that its effects are not always as straightforward as they might seem (see also Haslam & Ellemers, 2004; Haslam et al., 2003; Turner, 1999).

In this chapter, we address the possibility that identification in work groups can have "beneficial" as well as "detrimental" effects for the behavior and performance of group members. A key consideration in doing this, is that the processes and behaviors that are functional for group members to define and maintain the distinct identity of the group, may at the same time result in behaviors or outcomes that are seen as undesirable from the point of view of others (e.g., management or society; Ellemers, 2001;

Rotondi, 1975). In our analysis, we aim to show that the *consequences* of identification for group behavior and performance can vary, depending on the nature of the distinctive traits, goals or values on which a common identity is *based*. Specifically, we argue that it is not always self-evident which of multiple possible identities is relevant to the task at hand, which is the first reason why attempts at enhancing feelings of identification in order to facilitate people's behavior in work groups are not always successful. Subsequently, we review evidence showing that the nature of the traits or behaviors that are seen as characteristic for the group determines whether the behaviors and outcomes that are fostered by identification facilitate or undermine group performance.

MULTIPLE IDENTITIES

Initial theory and research on identification in work contexts focused on the organization as a unitary whole, as it examined the antecedents and consequences of organizational identification (Albert & Whetten, 1985). However, consistent with the notion that (especially larger) organizations typically are made up of people working at different locations, representing different business units, or comprising different functional teams, it has been acknowledged that identification and commitment can have different foci or apply to different organizational constituencies (Becker, 1992; Ellemers, De Gilder & van den Heuvel, 1998; Reichers 1986; Meyer, Paunonen, Gellatly, Goffin & Jackson, 1989). To a certain extent these may be seen as "nested" (Lawler, 1992) as they address different levels of inclusiveness. However, they may also represent cross-cutting or sometimes even incompatible identities (Ashforth, 2001; Ashforth & Johnson, 2001; Hernes, 1997). Thus, to be able to understand how identification affects group performance, we first need to establish the relevant *focus* of identification, and specify how this relates to the *goals* of the work group as well as the organization as a whole.

Levels of Inclusiveness

We will first consider the situation that people work in a system where multiple identities are organized in a hierarchical or nested fashion (Lawler, 1992), so that the individual can think of him or herself in more inclusive (e.g., as an organizational member) or less inclusive terms (e.g., as

a team member). Studies that directly compared the strength of identification at different levels of inclusiveness, generally found that people tend
to identify less strongly at the overall level of the organization than with
lower level entities. For instance, examining Indian and Pakistani managers in a multinational (British) organization, Reade (2001a) observed
stronger identification with the local subunit than with the global organization. In a similar vein, a broad sample of Dutch nationals working in
a variety of organizations revealed that people report stronger feelings
of commitment to their work team than to the organization as a whole
(Ellemers et al., 1998, see also Van Knippenberg & Van Schie, 2000). In
fact, a recent meta-analysis comprising data from 38 independent study
samples (Riketta & van Dick, in press) established that, overall, work
group identification and commitment are stronger than organizational
identification and commitment.

The general pattern that emerges from this research is that identification
tends to become less strong, as the entity people identify with is more inclusive (see also Ellemers et al., 2004). This has been explained from the
assumption that one's work team tends to be the "primary" group in the
organization, as this comprises the people with whom one most frequently
interacts, and with whom interdependence relations are most obvious
(Kramer, 1991). From a social identity perspective too, it can be argued that
in many cases the smaller entity is more meaningful, as it offers a more
distinct and salient identity (Ellemers et al., 2004). However, we propose
that this is not the case by definition. That is, it is well possible for situational considerations to overrule the general tendency to identify with
smaller rather than larger units (Ashforth & Johnson, 2001; Burke, 2003;
Serpe & Stryker, 1987). For instance, when focusing on the competition with
another organization, or when faced with the prospect of an unfriendly
takeover, a social identity analysis would predict that the organizational
identity becomes primary, and differences at lower levels of inclusiveness
(e.g., between different teams or sub-units) will be seen as less meaningful
and important (Haslam & Ellemers, 2004). Thus, we conclude that while a
system of multiple nested identities often leads people to identify most
strongly at the level that is least inclusive and most distinctive, we have to
take into account that other considerations, such as chronic importance of
an identity, or contextual salience and relevance (normative fit) can cause
more inclusive identities to become primary. This is one of the reasons why
it is not always easy to predict which identity people consider self-relevant or
which identity should be addressed in order to impact upon people's collective performance.

Cross-Cutting Identities

When we examine multiple identities that cut across each other, the situation is fundamentally different. That is, in the case of nested identities, even if the larger organization is not the primary target of identification, identification with a specific subunit still ties the individual to the organization as a whole, albeit indirectly (Hornsey & Hogg, 2000a; Van Leeuwen, Van Knippenberg & Ellemers, 2003). In the case of cross-cutting identities, however, people can find themselves in an "either-or" situation, as different identities seem incompatible, and place conflicting demands on their time and efforts. In other words, in this latter case, the consideration of one particular identity will tend to undermine or dilute identification with the alternative identity it cuts across (Herriot & Scott–Jackson, 2002).

As a result, an important issue is to establish how multiple cross-cutting identities are related to each other: whether they represent compatible or conflicting characteristics and demands, or whether they can be seen as reinforcing each other. Both cases are possible. "Dilution" effects were demonstrated by showing that workers in a multinational organization who identified primarily in terms of their nationality showed less identification with the organization (Salk & Shenkar, 2001). Likewise, it was established that organizational identification is less strong for employees who strongly identify with their family role (Lobel & St.Clair, 1992). However, "reinforcement" effects have also been documented, for instance, an investigation of employees of different hospitals who could be characterized in terms of different cross-cutting identities (Hernes, 1997) revealed that whereas the primary source of identification was profession-based, people were most inclined to identify with (and to show pro-social behavior toward) those who shared the same professional identity *and* worked in the same department (see also Lau & Murnighan, 1998; Thatcher, Jehn, & Zanutto, 2003).

Despite the importance of the way different identities are structured and related to each other, we wish to point out that contextual salience effects again play a central role in determining the relative importance of different cross-cutting categories (Ashforth & Johnson, 2001; Van Rijswijk & Ellemers, 2002). In fact, it is often not so obvious what constitutes people's "primary" identity, and in a way cross-cutting categories simply imply that people have complex selves as they can define themselves in terms of multiple possible identities (Smith-Lovin, 2003). As a result, situational factors that affect the relative salience or desirability of one identity rather than the other will cause people to focus on certain aspects of their identity and neglect others.

This can be illustrated with a study among Turkish, Iranian, and Portuguese immigrants in the Netherlands, revealing that the language in which they were approached (native language or Dutch language) affected the degree to which research participants identified with two cross-cutting categories, namely the native and host communities. Furthermore, the nature of the relationship between their immigrant group and the host community, and the identity concerns this raised, determined which of these two identities people emphasized as a result of these manipulations (Barreto, Spears, Ellemers, & Shahinper, 2003). This again indicates that – regardless of the way different identities are structurally related to each other – contextual salience effects and self-expression considerations determine which of their different possible identities is most likely to guide people's responses to a particular situation.

Identity–Behavior Match

Now that we have established that different identities can become salient depending on how they relate to each other as well as to relevant features of the situation, we want to examine why this is relevant when we are interested in the *behavioral consequences* of identification. An important notion that has developed with the accumulation of research distinguishing between different foci of commitment or identification, is that as a construct organizational identification is too broad to be considered as a reliable predictor of more specific work-related outcomes (Mathieu & Zajac, 1990). This is in line with more general notions on the attitude–behavior interface, indicating that *specific* intentions should be more closely related to actual behavioral displays than more general attitudes (e.g., Fishbein & Ajzen, 1975).

Initial efforts to examine how differentially focused commitment relates to behavioral displays established that specific forms represent an additional explanatory value compared to more generic organizational commitment in predicting work-relevant outcomes (Becker & Billings, 1993; Hunt & Morgan, 1994). In a study by Ellemers et al. (1998) a distinction was made between organizational commitment, career-oriented commitment, and team-oriented commitment as potential predictors of work-relevant behavior. Results showed that organizational commitment was mainly related to overall work satisfaction. However, engagement in organizational turnover behavior (taking additional training, performing a job search) depended on the extent to which workers were committed to career improvement. Likewise, the extent to which workers identified with and felt committed to their team of co-workers was the only reliable predictor of work behavior (contextual efforts and overall job performance).

A recent meta-analysis examining studies that distinguished between *work group* identification and commitment versus *organizational* identification and commitment (Riketta & van Dick, in press) confirmed this pattern, showing that specific types of identification are related to particular outcomes. That is, across different studies, it was established that work group identification was primarily related to outcomes that have a work group focus (e.g., work group satisfaction, extra-role behavior in the work group), whereas organizational identification mainly predicted organizational outcomes (e.g., organizational satisfaction, extra-role behavior in the organization). This is a relevant distinction, as even in the case of nested identities the consequences of more specific forms of identification (e.g., work team behavior) are not necessarily beneficial for (or even compatible with) the preferred outcomes of the broader organization. For instance, a strong team identity can cause workers to cover for each other and hide mistakes, whereas from an organizational point of view it might be better to acknowledge and address these problems.

This illustrates the importance of taking into account the multiple identities people have, as we need to understand the *causes* of identification, to be able to predict its *consequences*. That is, attempts to address work behavior by looking at identification as a relevant predictor only make sense if the focus of the identification matches the behavior of interest. Failing to do so is not inconsequential: at best, identification will have no effect on behavior (e.g., when it is specified at an inappropriate level of inclusiveness), but at worst, it might suppress (instead of enhance) the desired behavior (e.g., because it is based on a competing cross-cutting identity).

Influencing Identification

A final question we wish to address in this section then is how we might foster identification at the level that is appropriate for the task at hand. As is the case with behavioral outcomes, each identity has its own specific antecedent conditions. For instance, research in a multinational organization (Reade, 2001b) revealed that the factors that predict identification with the local subsidiary are different from those that enhance identification with the global organization. This would suggest that one can design organizational structures, reward systems, activities, and communications in such a way that they emphasize and enhance the identity that is most relevant to the achievement of desired outcomes (Ashforth & Johnson, 2001; Spears, Doosje, & Ellemers, 1997), for instance, by emphasizing team identity when aiming to enhance team performance, but promoting organizational identity when the goal is to prevent organizational turnover.

Although there seems to be a certain awareness that organizational gains can be increased when managers act as so-called "entrepreneurs of identity" (Pratt & Foreman, 2000; Reicher & Hopkins, 1996), in practice, many such attempts suffer from the fact that they are implemented half-heartedly, or their further consequences are not thought through. For instance, company mottos that are introduced (we are as a family) turn out to be empty phrases when nothing in the business policy or leadership behavior is adapted to reflect this notion. Likewise, a stated emphasis on the importance of team work will only be effective when it is followed through in reward and promotion systems, but will not improve collaborative efforts when team members are only evaluated in terms of their individual performance. Alternatively, the exclusive focus on an overarching identity can be counterproductive when it results in the neglect of other important identities, representing specific qualities (e.g., professional expertise) or special needs of individual workers (e.g., women or minority group members) that have to be addressed to achieve an optimal performance.

Even if these difficulties in defining the identity that is appropriate for the task, and enhancing it in a consistent way can be overcome, influencing identification to manage group outcomes remains a tricky business. For instance, an investigation of three samples of professionals, namely teachers, youth workers, and police officers, revealed that in each case these professionals displayed more resistance to organizational changes to the extent that they were more convinced that this represented a threat to their current identity (Ellemers, 1993). In a more general sense, people want to have a sense of self-determination over who they are and what they stand for (Thoits, 2003). As a result, situations that allow people *more options* as to how to define the self, generally elicit more positive emotions and hence will result in greater commitment (Lawler, 1992; Sheldon & Bettencourt, 2002).

Accordingly, empirical research examining self-stereotyping in a situation involving crossed-category identities revealed that when people were reminded of the identity they *shared* with the other group, they emphasized their group's *distinct* identity, and described themselves in terms of characteristics that defined them as *different* from this other group (Van Rijswijk, Haslam, & Ellemers, in press; see also Jetten, Spears, & Manstead, 1997). Similar observations have been made in field studies examining mergers and imposed organizational change. In a government organization where management attempted to restructure the organization into different units, this resulted in decreased organizational identification and resistance to change, in particular among those who identified strongly with their original work unit (Jetten, O'Brien, & Trindall, 2002). Likewise, attempts to merge different groups into one, focusing on the superordinate identity they had in common, resulted in group members emphasizing their distinct sub-group identities, instead of going along with the intended change (Hornsey & Hogg, 1999, 2000b; Van Leeuwen & Van Knippenberg, 2003). These results show that although contextual features can be manipulated to en-hance the salience of specific identities, people are also motivated to protect identities that are important to them, and tend to resist forces that represent change (Serpe & Stryker, 1987).

Acknowledging Multiple Identities

In view of this evidence showing that emphasizing the properties people share with others, or attempting to restructure the situation in a different way, tend to backfire as they meet with resistance and cause people to reinforce their distinct identity, the question then is how one can successfully influence people's identities. To be able to answer this question, we have to remember that the resistance that has been observed is not a matter of conservatism or rigidity *per se*, but is elicited when people feel they *lack control and self-determination* over their self-definition (Lawler, 2003; Thoits, 2003).

Based on the notion that people have multiple identities, we propose that more than one identity can be salient at the same time, and activation of one does not necessarily detract from the other. Indeed, whereas existing theory and research tend to address the *problems* of having multiple identities and have focused on the stress associated with the ambiguous or conflicting role demands that may arise from this (e.g., Peterson et al., 1995; Williams & Alliger, 1994), we want to emphasize that having multiple identities can have a *positive* impact, provided they are self-chosen (Pietromonaco, Manis & Frohardt-Lane, 1986; Thoits, 1986, 2003).

This reasoning implies that measures attempting to (re)direct people's efforts by requiring them to focus on a specific identity at the exclusion of other identity aspects, do not necessarily achieve the intended effect, and can even be counterproductive. By contrast, contexts that allow people to maintain a more complex and multilayered identity should be more effec-tive. For instance, in a consultancy firm working with highly specialized knowledge workers, it was important for these workers to simultaneously identify as an "expert" and as a "consultant" to be able to function effectively (Robertson & Swan, 2003). In a longitudinal case study of this firm, it was demonstrated that when management enabled workers to sustain their multiple identities, this resulted in the development of loyalty and commitment, and enhanced the performance of project groups (Robertson & Swan, 2003). Similar observations have been made in studies examining how people deal with their dual identities as a parent and a worker, showing that people showed greater work satisfaction, more commitment to the organization, and greater career success when both these relevant identities were supported and acknowledged (Ellemers, Van Steenbergen & Benus, 2004; Van Steenbergen & Ellemers, 2004; Lobel & St.Clair, 1992).

A series of experiments under more carefully controlled circumstances (Barreto & Ellemers, 2002) confirmed that resistance to an externally imposed identity can be alleviated when self-defined identities are respected as well. In their first study, research participants were provided with a description of two groups of people, based on their styles of problem solving, and were asked to indicate to which of these groups they thought they belonged (Barreto & Ellemers, 2002). Subsequently they were subjected to a test that allegedly measured which of the two problem-solving styles was most applicable to them. On the basis of this test, they were either assigned to the group they had selected themselves, or their placement in one of the groups did not reflect their self-choice. As a result of this manipulation, research participants reported less identification with the group, and displayed less group loyalty when the externally imposed identity deviated from their self-choice. This clearly illustrates the resistance that is elicited when people are addressed in terms of an identity that does not converge with their self-choice.

In the second study, however, the group assignment procedure was adapted to introduce a third condition. In this condition, participants were told that although the test had revealed that their actual problem-solving style differed from what they had thought, they would nevertheless be placed in the group they had selected themselves. Results revealed that *respecting* participants' *self-chosen identity* in this way *facilitated* their acceptance of the *externally assigned identity*. That is, participants in this condition were more willing to see themselves as similar to and identify with the externally assigned identity, and were more inclined to collaborate with this group than those whose self-selected identity had not been acknowledged (Barreto & Ellemers, 2002; see also Barreto & Ellemers, 2003). Further experiments confirmed that the acknowledgment of multiple identity aspects resulted in increased motivation and task performance (Derks, Van Laar & Ellemers, 2004).

Thus, the results of different studies indicate that whereas people generally tend to resist externally imposed identities, they are more willing to go along with external views others have of them when they feel that their self-identities are also respected by others. This suggests that the *simultaneous* activation and acknowledgment of *multiple identities* may help resolve the problems that are likely to arise when the optimal performance in a given situation requires the adoption or enhancement of an identity that is not self-selected.

In sum, in this section, we have examined how the multiple identities that people have affect cognitive and motivational processes in self-definition, which in turn impact upon group performance. If we want identification to enhance group performance, we should address that level of inclusiveness or focus of identification that is appropriate in view of the required behavior or effort. However, this is not to say that all alternative identities should be neglected or excluded as a result. Instead, the simultaneous adoption and expression of multiple relevant identities should be facilitated. First, because there is value in enabling people to shift their focal identity depending on the context in order to make them adaptable to different work requirements and help them participate in organizational development and change. Second, because externally imposed identities are likely to backfire as they threaten perceived distinctiveness and identity value and undermine feelings of self-determination and situational control.

PERCEIVING AND INTERACTING WITH OTHERS

Now that we have established the different identities people can have, and examined why this is important, we will assess how processes of identification are likely to impact on the perceptions and interactions with others that are relevant for group performance. In this section, we will focus on the *positive* effects this may have, based on research showing that when people respond to ambiguous behavior of others, they generally endorse more positive expectations and interpretations as they identify more strongly with others. In the next section, we will turn to the *negative* effects that tend to ensue, when it turns out that other people's behavior does not live up to the expectations we have of them.

Research examining how people interpret the behavior of others and interact with them, clearly shows that the same behavior elicits different responses, depending on whether the other person is seen as an ingroup or outgroup member. Importantly, such differential responses to identical behavior do not depend on people's group memberships *per se* (i.e., the extent to which they share specific features), but are elicited by the extent to which they subjectively *identify* with others. As we have seen in the previous section, this is determined by a number of considerations, for instance by the categorizations that are relevant to the task at hand, or the group memberships that are salient in view of the current comparative context. However, for reasons of simplicity, in this section, we will only distinguish between "ingroup" and "outgroup" members when discussing how the responses people display depend on how they relate to those they interact with. We will first show how shared identities may result in ingroup favoring biases with respect to the expectations they hold of others, the attributions they make, and the way they behave toward others. Then, we will address some specific consequences of these processes by examining how they influence the way people interpret and deal with criticism directed toward one's group.

Ingroup Favoritism

Because people's self-views are at least partly determined by the characteristics of the groups they belong to, they are generally motivated to perceive "ingroups" more positively than "outgroups" (Tajfel, 1978; Tajfel & Turner, 1979). Indeed, a large body of research has accumulated to show that people generally display ingroup favoritism in trait ratings and outcome allocations. When the relative merits of the different groups are unclear, they do this by simply claiming that the ingroup is superior to the outgroup, or by allocating more resources to ingroup than outgroup members (e.g., Brewer, 1979).

When so-called reality constraints make it more difficult to credibly do this, for instance because the ingroup is objectively inferior to the outgroup in some specific way, people still favor the ingroup, albeit by using more creative and subtle strategies (Ellemers, Barreto & Spears, 1999; Tajfel & Turner, 1979). For instance, they search for alternative domains of comparison, in which the ingroup compares favorably to the outgroup (e.g., Mummendey & Schreiber, 1983, 1984), they focus on the comparison with a different outgroup in which their group seems superior (Spears & Manstead, 1989), they allocate greater importance to domains that characterize the ingroup than to outgroup domains (Ellemers, Van Rijswijk,

Roefs & Simons, 1997), or they privately maintain their confidence in the superiority of the ingroup, while publicly acknowledging the outgroup's superiority (Ellemers, Van Dyck, Hinkle & Jacobs, 2000). The positive expectations people hold about the behavior of those they identify with, in turn shape how people *explain* the behavior of others as well as the way they *behave* toward others.

Biased Attributions

As a result of the general tendency to find ways to view one's own group in more positive terms than other groups, concrete behaviors also tend to be explained differently, depending on whether or not they pertain to a group that reflects upon the self. This is visible, for instance, in the *attributions* people make to explain the performance of others. Consistent with the desire to believe that the ingroup is superior to relevant outgroups, when an ingroup member is seen to fail at a task, this is seen as exceptional and attributed to bad luck, whereas the same performance shown by an outgroup member is taken as indicating a lack of competence which is characteristic for that group (Pettigrew, 1979; Hewstone, 1990).

These mechanisms come into play when people interpret the interactive behavior of those they work with. To examine how ingroup favoring attributions may emerge in a collaborative interaction, Ellemers, Van Rijswijk, Bruins and De Gilder (1998) designed an experimental procedure where participants had to work together with a supervisor on a stock trading task. This enabled them to assess whether people evaluated identical behavior of their supervisor differently, depending on whether they thought this was an ingroup or an outgroup member. The results of this research showed that people were generally dissatisfied and upset when the decisions they had made were frequently overruled by their supervisor. However, when they were overruled by an ingroup supervisor, they attributed this to external pressures on the supervisor. By contrast, when the same behavior was displayed by an outgroup supervisor, this was seen as typical behavior for members of that group. In other words, the same negatively evaluated behavior was more likely to be "explained away" to external factors in the case of an ingroup member, while it was considered to be more "in character" in the case of an outgroup member.

These results indicate that it can be beneficial for a supervisor to instill a sense of common identity with his/her subordinates, as this will lead subordinates to hold more positive expectations of them (Duck & Fielding,

1999), and helps them to cope with any negative leadership behaviors they may encounter (Haslam et al., 1998). While at first sight this seems consistent with notions from Leader–Member and Team-Member Exchange theory (LMX/TMX, Graen & Scandura, 1987), we emphasize that it is not the quality of the interpersonal relation people have with each other that is key. Instead, we propose that the observed effects are triggered by group-level processes, causing leaders who manage to embody the shared identity of the group, and help differentiate the ingroup from relevant outgroups to receive most support from their followers (Haslam & Platow, 2001; Platow & Van Knippenberg, 2001; see also Ellemers et al., 2004).

The differential interpretations of the behavior of ingroup and outgroup members because of previously held expectations about these groups also emerge in the way people *communicate* about the behavior of others (Haslam, 2001; Postmes, 2003; Postmes, Haslam & Swaab, in press). That is, it has been established that people systematically choose different linguistic terms to convey their behavioral observations to others (Maass & Arcuri, 1996; Maass, Salvi, Arcuri & Semin, 1989). For instance, people tend to describe desirable behavior in more abstract terms when it is displayed by an ingroup member (he is smart) rather than an outgroup member (she found the correct answer), while the reverse is true in the case of undesirable behaviors displayed by ingroup (he forgot his notebook) and outgroup (she is disorganized) members. In fact, this so-called "linguistic ingroup bias" constitutes one of the mechanisms through which a favorable image of the ingroup is *maintained* (Wigboldus, Spears, & Semin, 1999). Thus, biased attributions and the communication patterns these give rise to, help people maintain a positive view of others they identify with, even when they are confronted with seemingly negative behaviors.

Differential Behavior Toward Others

Research examining actual interactive sequences in group settings, has revealed that the positive expectations of other ingroup members and their intentions also cause people to *behave* differently toward ingroup members compared to outgroup members. For instance, further results of the study by Ellemers et al. (2000) described above, showed that attributing the power use of an ingroup member to external pressures not only enabled people to maintain a cooperative attitude toward the other, but also caused them to invest greater *behavioral effort* in helping the supervisor on a subsequent task. By contrast, those who were working with an outgroup supervisor were more inclined to refrain from helping the supervisor on an additional task, as a result of the attributions they had made.

In a similar vein, in the domain of negotiation and conflict resolution it has been documented that – due to differential interpretations of identical messages – behavioral sequences tend to develop differently among two parties who share the same social identity than they do between members of different groups (see also Moore, Kurtzberg, Thompson & Morris, 1999). That is, it was demonstrated that, in anticipation of an actual negotiation, an ingroup negotiation partner was expected to be more trustworthy and cooperative than an outgroup negotiation partner (Harinck & Ellemers, 2004, study 1; see also Brewer & Kramer, 1986; Kramer, Shah & Woerner, 1995).

In a further study where the negotiation was actually followed through (Harinck & Ellemers, 2004, study 2), the initial trust that had developed caused people to not only to *interpret* but also to *respond* differently to the same behavior, depending on the group membership of the person who displayed it. Specifically, when an ingroup partner indicated his/her personal interest in the negotiation this elicited a *cooperative* exchange with mutual concern for both parties' interests. However, when an outgroup negotiation partner showed identical behavior, this led to reduced concern for the other and resulted in more *competitive* negotiation behavior.

Taken together, the results of these studies illustrate that the general tendency to maintain differential expectations about the behavior of ingroup vs. outgroup members and the biased attributions and perceptions these give rise to can have tangible consequences for social behavior. That is, group-based expectations can actually work as self-fulfilling prophecies, in the sense that they make people actually behave more cooperatively toward other ingroup members who are then more likely to respond in kind, and confirm initial expectations. Likewise, negative expectations about outgroup members are more likely to trigger competitive behavior toward others, who will then be more inclined to act out in the expected way.

Tolerance for Criticism of One's Group

So far, we have focused on the ways in which positive expectations about fellow ingroup members can help people respond positively to the behavior of others in general. A special case arises when others are negative about *one's own group*. Here too, awareness of a shared identity can be beneficial for the way people deal with the situation. However, we propose that this is a special case because people do not simply *deflect or ignore the negative information they encounter.* Instead, the awareness that other ingroup members who are critical about the group also have their own identity at stake, helps people to cope constructively with negative comments pertaining to the group.

This issue has been addressed in a programmatic series of studies, which systematically compared how people respond to critical comments pertaining to their group, depending on whether these were voiced by an ingroup or an outgroup member (Hornsey & Imani, 2004; Hornsey, Oppes & Svensson, 2002; Hornsey, Trembath & Gunthorpe, 2004). Across different studies, results consistently revealed that critical comments about the ingroup (e.g., indicating that the group may be intolerant, or too confident about its own expertise) were seen as more acceptable when coming from a fellow ingroup member than when the same comments were made by an outgroup member. Furthermore, it was established that the greater acceptance of ingroup criticism emerged because the ingroup source was seen as more legitimate and constructive (Hornsey et al., 2002), and not because the ingroup source had more experience and knowledge about the group (Hornsey & Imani, 2004). Thus, people establish greater tolerance for criticism of the (group) self, when coming from those whose self is also connected to the same group (Hornsey & Imani, 2004), while they tend to respond more defensively to criticism coming from someone located outside the group.

Additional research examining the way people evaluate their own group in front of different audiences (Ellemers et al., 2000), is consistent with the notion that people are relatively willing to acknowledge group-related problems toward those who share the same identity, while they are inclined to deny the existence of such problems in front of people who have a different identity. That is, in this research it was observed that when confronted with ingroup failure, participants would not admit to the inferiority of their group in front of an outgroup audience. However, they were clearly more willing to acknowledge the suboptimal performance of their group when addressing an ingroup audience (i.e., in front of those who also suffered from this problem). Furthermore, the willingness to admit to their group's problems in front of the ingroup was more pronounced the more strongly people identified with their group (Ellemers et al., 2000). This is consistent with the notion that increased identification with others elicits more constructive responses toward others with respect to problems or deficits of the group.

Taken together, the results of these studies complement our previous conclusion that identification processes elicit favorable expectations and responses toward other ingroup members. That is, when others point out group-related problems, identification with others helps people to admit to their shared inadequacies, and increases chances of addressing these in a constructive way. By contrast, a lack of identification with those who criticize the group leads people to deny that any such problems exist, while they respond defensively to those who point them out. That identification is key in determining whether constructive or defensive responses emerge, is further illustrated by the finding that outgroup members can prevent defensive responses to their criticism by emphasizing a superordinate identity they have in common with the ingroup (Hornsey et al., 2004).

In sum, in this section, we have reviewed research showing that identification can have beneficial effects for the way people perceive and interact with others. These can be very straightforward and direct, in the sense that positive expectations about ingroup members cause people to adopt a positive disposition toward them, and maintain this even in the face of undesirable behaviors. However, this is not to say that identification causes people to view their group and its members in unconditionally positive terms. Indeed, we have seen that identification with others may also facilitate the shared acknowledgment of less desirable features of the group, which is necessary to address these in a constructive way. We think this constitutes a more long-term and less obvious way in which increased identification may ultimately enhance group-relevant perceptions and interactions. In the next section, we will examine how positive expectations of ingroup members can also backfire, as they constitute the (high) standard against which the behavior of others is evaluated.

EXPECTANCY VIOLATION AND GROUP NORMS

In this section, we focus on the conditions under which increased identification may be detrimental for social interaction and group performance. We argue that when group members behave in ways that clearly deviate from group norms or violate the general expectation that other group members should show a concern for the self, increased identification results in a more negative response to the behavior of others, causing them to be rejected and excluded from the group. Furthermore, increased identification can deteriorate the quality of the interaction in the group, when it makes people more sensitive and vulnerable to evaluative judgments of others about the self. Finally, we posit that it is important to take into account the content of group norms to address the possibility that increased identification undermines group performance when distinctive group norms prescribe behavior that is detrimental to the achievement of the task at hand.

Expectancy Violation

In the previous section, we have reviewed research suggesting that identification processes generally cause people to extend the benefit of the doubt to other ingroup members. That is, the positive expectations they have of other ingroup members elicit favorably biased attributions, communications, and behaviors toward them, and cause them to respond constructively to the criticisms they express about the group. To complement this picture, we will now turn to the downside of these positive expectations, and examine the possibility that increased identification causes people to judge others *more severely*, namely when they do not live up to these expectations. That is, whereas positive expectations of other ingroup members dominate people's perceptions and behaviors when information is lacking or is in some way ambiguous (assimilation effect), behavior that clearly deviates from group-based expectations, for instance when people show disloyalty to the group (Levine & Moreland, 2002) will elicit an extremely negative response, resulting in rejection of the individual in question (contrast effect).

Due to expectancy violation processes (Bettencourt, Dill, Greathouse, Charlton & Mulholland, 1996; Biernat, Vescio & Billings, 1999; see also Jussim, Coleman & Lerch, 1987; Jackson, Sullivan & Hodge, 1993), behavior that clearly deviates from previous expectations is rated more negatively when it is performed by an ingroup member than when the same behavior is displayed by an outgroup member. This phenomenon, which has been described as the "black sheep effect," has emerged consistently in a number of studies (Marques & Paez, 1994; Marques, Yzerbyt & Leyens, 1988). The specific implications of this general tendency have been illustrated in a series of experiments where people had to exchange information in dyads to reach a common decision (Rink & Ellemers, 2004a, c). In these studies, it was observed that people implicitly expected their fellow ingroup member to be similar to them in terms of relevant task behaviors. When these expectations were violated during the interaction, because the other turned out to be different from the self, this resulted in negative affective responses, and the experience of conflict. As a result, people were less willing to continue working with the other who had violated their initial expectations.

In addition to examining the effects of implicit similarity expectations, Rink and Ellemers (2004a) also assessed the effects of explicit expectations about the task behavior of the other. Importantly, in doing this, they experimentally induced research participants to expect the other to *either* be *similar* to them in terms of their task behavior, *or* they induced the expectation that the other would be *different* from them. This manipulation confirmed that the negative response that was observed was not due to the realization that the group members differed from each other, but was indeed caused by the fact that initial expectations were violated during the interaction. That is, in line with what we observed in the case of implicit similarity expectations, the explicit expectation that the other would be similar to the self generated a negative response when the other turned out to be different. Additionally, however, those who had expected the other to be *different* likewise showed a negative response when the other turned out to actually have similar task-related characteristics (e.g., work style or work goal).

Further research in this area shows that increased identification can intensify the rejection of those who violate group-based expectations. For instance, Castano, Yzerbyt, Bourguignon and Seron (2002) demonstrated that those who identify more strongly with the group tend to use stricter criteria to determine who is a "real" member of the group, and exclude those who do not meet these criteria. Hornsey and Jetten (2003) investigated how people respond to others who claim membership in the group, while they actually do not meet the criteria for group membership (e.g., claiming to be a vegetarian, but eating meat). These "impostors" were downgraded more extremely by those who identified more strongly with the group in question.

The results of these studies indicate that increased identification makes people more vigilant to those who violate group-based expectations, as they potentially threaten the group's integrity. A study by Hutchison and Abrams (2003) further supports the notion that the rejection of deviant group members is motivated by the desire to maintain a positive view of the ingroup. In their study, they compared how psychology students rated a psychologist who was either described in line with the group stereotype (an empathic psychologist), or a psychologist who violated group-based expectations (an insensitive psychologist). The results of this study revealed that those who identified most strongly with the group showed most extreme responses to these two ingroup members. That is, high identifiers were more positive toward the normative ingroup member (empathic psychologist) but rated the deviant ingroup member (insensitive psychologist) more negatively than did research participants who identified less strongly with the group of psychologists. Furthermore, their negative judgments of the deviant group member also affected the impression they had of the group as a whole. That is, after rejecting a deviant group member, high identifiers expressed a more positive stereotype of the ingroup, compared to the situation where they had been exposed to a normative ingroup member whom they had rated favorably.

Self-Relevant Behavior of Others

A special case of enhanced sensitivity to the behavior of others due to increased identification with others, is when their behavior has evaluative implications for the *self*. This is evident, for instance, from the fact that people respond differently to performance evaluations or behavioral rewards depending on whether these come from an ingroup or an outgroup member (Tyler, 2002). That is, when people evaluate the way they are treated by an outgroup member, they mainly focus on whether or not the behavior of the other is *favorable* for the self, assessing whether they personally benefit from it (distributive justice). This sensitivity to favorability of treatment by an outgroup member is more pronounced to the extent that people identify more strongly with the ingroup (Stahl, Vermunt & Ellemers, 2005). However, when evaluating self-relevant decisions made by an ingroup member people are primarily concerned about the quality of *treatment* of the self (procedural justice), and look for indications that might show the extent to which the other cares for the self (Smith, Tyler & Huo, 2003). As a result, the extent to which people identify with the other, determines the evaluation of self-relevant behaviors displayed by the other. That is, increased identification with the other causes people to be *less* concerned about *instrumental* aspects of the way they are treated (Stahl et al., 2005), but makes them *more* preoccupied with the *relational* implications of the decisions that affect them (Huo, Smith, Tyler & Lind 1996; Tyler & Smith, 1999). This illustrates one of the potentially "detrimental" consequences of increased group identification, as it implies that negative evaluative and behavioral responses of people to the failure of an authority to treat them fairly, are *exacerbated* when people identify more strongly with the group membership they share with this authority.

Similar observations have been made in research examining responses of group members to the way they are evaluated by their peers (Spears, Ellemers & Doosje, in press; see also Branscombe, Spears, Ellemers & Doosje, 2002). That is, in a series of studies examining responses to competence-related and relational evaluations in an ingroup context, relational evaluations turned out to be primary in terms of their impact on emotional responses, and liking for the group. Furthermore, a negative relational evaluation from other ingroup members was not compensated by their appreciation of one's competence. Instead, people seemed to feel compromised when their fellow group members evaluated them positively for their competence, while evaluating them negatively on the relational dimension (Spears et al., in press).

A further series of studies in this research program examined the differential impact of relational evaluations, depending on whether they were conveyed by ingroup or by outgroup members (Ellemers, Doosje, & Spears, 2004). The first study revealed that, although initial emotional responses reflected the favorability of the evaluation regardless of whether it came from an ingroup or from an outgroup, only relational evaluations received from an ingroup source affected the individual's collective self-esteem. That is, the more the individual identified with the source of these relational evaluations of the self, the greater the impact of these evaluations on their self-views.

Furthermore, follow-up studies where research participants were simultaneously exposed to evaluations from ingroup *and* outgroup sources revealed that the negative consequences people suffered when they were evaluated unfavorably by their fellow ingroup members could not be compensated or repaired by a positive evaluation from the outgroup. Instead, the negative emotions and the loss of self-esteem people experienced due to an unfavorable evaluation from the ingroup were *intensified* when they were simultaneously exposed to a positive evaluation from the outgroup (Ellemers et al., 2004). This again illustrates one of the potentially adverse consequences of identification, in the sense that it makes people more vulnerable to negative evaluations they receive from others, and shows that this cannot be easily compensated or redressed (and in fact may even be exacerbated) by positive evaluations coming from a group one does not identify with.

Similarities, Differences, and the Definition of Common Norms

The studies reviewed above indicate that group-based expectations constitute an important standard against which social behavior is evaluated. However, it is not always easy to define or predict which specific attitudes and behaviors will be contained in these expectations. First, as we have argued at the outset of this chapter, this is the case because people usually can be seen as having multiple identities, and one or the other of these identities can become meaningful depending on the situation or the task at hand, and the way it relates to each of these possible identities. Indeed, it has been demonstrated that the nature of the salient identity and the content of what people regard as identity-relevant characteristics tend to vary over time and across situations (Van Rijswijk et al., in press). In fact, in line with our previous argument, we would expect people to *prefer* such ambiguity, as it allows for some scope to choose how to define the self.

Second, even if we know that a particular identity is most relevant in a given situation, the same group can still be defined in terms of different characteristics, depending on the comparative context, and how one's group can be distinguished from other groups featuring in that context (Haslam & Turner, 1992). For instance, in a series of experiments, it was observed that when psychology students compared themselves to art history students, they perceived intelligence (but not creativity) as a group-defining trait. When, however, comparing with physics students, these same psychology students were more inclined to think of creativity (not intelligence) as characteristic for their group (Spears et al., 1997). Again this shows that the properties that can be seen as normative for the group are not fixed, but tend to vary, depending on the other groups that seem relevant in a given situation.

Thus, when aiming to predict which traits or behaviors will be seen as characteristic for the group, we cannot simply infer that the traits or characteristics that all group members have in common will be seen as group defining. That is, although it is possible that the recognition of the fact that one shares certain features with others facilitates the formation of a common identity, the reverse process can also occur (Markovsky & Chaffee, 1995). That is, identification and group cohesiveness are not necessarily based on the recognition of interpersonal similarities, but are *group-level* properties that can foster the *development* of common norms (Barnum, 1997; Markovsky & Lawler, 1994).

This reasoning suggests that when task requirements or other external circumstances (instead of the perception of interpersonal similarities) cause people to identify with a work group, this will induce them to search for ways that allow them to define how they can be differentiated from other relevant groups in that context. Thus, in order to assess which traits or behaviors will be considered normative for the group, we should not limit ourselves to the features members of the same group might share (intra-group similarities), but also take into account the ways in which the group can be defined as different from other groups (inter-group differences). This implies that, in principle, *any* characteristic may come to be seen as group-defining (see also Van Knippenberg & Haslam, 2003), even the fact that group members are different from each other!

The validity of this reasoning was tested in a series of studies, examining whether the formation of a common identity and subsequent performance on a joint task would be facilitated or hindered, depending on whether group members were similar to or different from each other (Rink & Ellemers, 2004b). These studies consistently revealed that when working together with others who clearly have other task-relevant characteristics than the self (as is the case, for instance, in highly diverse multi-disciplinary project teams), team members can come to the conclusion that the fact that they are different from each other defines the distinct identity of the group (Rink & Ellemers, 2004b; see also Robertson & Swan, 2003). In turn, the common identity that is based on the realization of being a *diverse* group, has been shown to enhance commitment to the group, and facilitates task performance (Rink & Ellemers, 2004b).

In sum, we argue that in addition to intragroup similarities, intergroup differences help determine which distinctive group characteristics are relevant in a given context. That is, how the individual relates to other group members, and how one's group compares to other groups *jointly* determine the content of the expectations people have of others based on their group membership, which in turn constitute the normative standard against which their behaviors are rated.

Group Motivation and Collective Performance

One of the reasons why we should acknowledge that the content of norms can differ, is because this is important to be able to predict the effects of identification on group motivation and collective performance. That is, we argue that whereas identification increases the motivation to behave according to group norms, the content of these norms determines whether or not the efforts of group members will be directed at increasing the group's performance (Barreto & Ellemers, 2000; Ellemers et al., 1999).

As we have briefly indicated at the outset of this chapter, by now there seems to be considerable agreement in the literature that identification helps prevent social loafing effects (Jehn & Shah, 1997), can increase group motivation and individual effort to achieve group goals (Ellemers et al., 2004), and can actually enhance group performance (Tauer & Harackiewicz, 2004). However, although it seems intuitively plausible that there should be a direct relation between identification and group performance, in fact empirical evidence to this effect has been mixed, so that researchers have started to look for factors that possibly moderate this effect.

A recent meta-analysis of 64 publications describing 71 independent group-level estimates of the relation between group cohesiveness and performance (Beal et al., 2003) examined whether a more reliable pattern might be observed if the relevant concepts would be more narrowly defined. Indeed, when they focused on the *behavior* of group members (efforts and efficiency) instead of group performance (outcomes and effectiveness) group cohesiveness did emerge as a reliable predictor of group member behavior. Beal et al. (2003) explained this discrepancy between behavioral effects and performance effects by arguing that group performance not only depends on the efforts of group members, but is also determined by external factors that are outside their control (e.g., market developments; see also Benkhoff, 1997; Ouwerkerk et al., 1999; Tyler, 2002; Tyler & Blader, 2000).

However, in addition to the question of which aspects of group performance can be expected to reveal the effects of differential motivation, we think it is important to determine how the *content* of relevant group *norms* determines the *direction* of increased group efforts. That is, the more strongly people identify with a particular group, the more they will try to behave in accordance with specific group norms. Yet, it is important to note that the resulting behavior can be considered either beneficial or detrimental from the point of view of management or society as a whole, depending on the content of group norms and the way these relate to broader organizational or societal norms (Ellemers, 2001).

In the literature, it is assumed that membership in particular groups can help resolve the need to belong with the need to be unique (Brewer, 1991; Hornsey & Jetten, 2004). In line with this reasoning, it has been argued that people should be more inclined to conform to workgroup norms and the social influence of other work group members to the extent that these enable them to define themselves as different from other groups (Moreland & Levine, 2001; Sussmann & Vecchio, 1982). That is, because the work group can provide them with a distinct social identity, people should be motivated to think and behave in line of work group norms and goals (Lembke & Wilson, 1998). This is in line with criticisms on work motivation theory, arguing that performance goals should not be defined in terms of general attitudes, but should refer to specific behaviors (Coates, 1994), and alternative approaches to work motivation proposing that self-expression may constitute an important motivational force (Shamir, 1991). Evidence for the validity of this line of reasoning has been obtained in a study by Christensen, Rothgerber, Wood and Matz (2004), who showed that greater identification with the group elicited more positive emotions when conforming to rather than violating group norms, indicating that increased identification caused group members to feel better when they displayed a work style that was seen as typical for the group.

As we have argued above, which behavior is characteristic for the group depends on how they can meaningfully distinguish their own group from relevant other groups in that context. This implies that the different dimensions of intergroup comparison that play a role will also define the nature of relevant group norms. For instance, research suggests that the reliance on collective performance as a group defining feature mostly applies to groups that are confident that they can show a superior performance (Ellemers, Van Rijswijk, Roefs & Simons, 1997; Fiske, Cuddy, Glick & Xu, 2002; Mummendey & Schreiber, 1983). By contrast, however, groups that have little hope of achieving positive ingroup distinctiveness on the focal performance dimension tend to focus on alternative group features where they aim to excel, such as the quality of intragroup relations (communality), or the superior morality of their behavior (Doosje, Branscombe, Spears & Manstead, 1999; Leach, Barreto & Ellemers, 2004). Thus, when we aim to predict how increased identification will tend to affect group performance, we first need to assess which behavioral dimensions are relevant to distinguish the group from other groups in that context.

The sometimes counter-intuitive implications that such adherence to group norms can have for group performance have been illustrated in empirical research. For instance, a study in a hospital setting revealed that different work groups held different beliefs about acceptable and expected absence behavior, depending on the average level of absence from work in that group (Gellatly & Luchak, 1998). Importantly, these normative beliefs turned out to predict individual absence behavior one year later, demonstrating how adherence to group norms may result in a less favorable work group performance. Likewise, identification with "counter cultures" tends to induce people to behave in ways that are considered undesirable (Ellemers, 2001).

The above examples illustrate how group norms can impede rather than enhance the performance of those who identify with that group. Nevertheless, we argue that this is consistent with the idea that increased identification makes people behave in more "groupy" ways. However, the *implications* of this "groupyness" may vary, depending on the nature of the group or the content of its norms. That is, as we have seen above, under some circumstances, the *individual differences* among group members may come to be seen as the defining feature that distinguishes the group from other groups in that context. Paradoxically, identification with such groups should make group members behave in ways that emphasize how they are *different* from each other.

This phenomenon has been illustrated in a number of recent studies. For instance, in a group decision-making context, when the norm was to be critical, increased identification with the group caused group members to show *less agreement* (instead of more agreement) with each other (Postmes, Spears & Cihangir, 2001). Likewise, is has been established that when the group norm endorses individualistic behavior, increased group identification induces people to act in ways that optimize their *individual* outcomes, making them less inclined to work for the group as a whole (Barreto & Ellemers, 2000; Jetten, Postmes & McAuliffe, 2002). Additionally, it was shown that under these circumstances, increased identification facilitates the acceptance of self-serving behavior and dissenting attitudes displayed by other group members (McAuliffe, Jetten, Hornsey & Hogg, 2003).

In sum, we reason that although increased identification generally tends to affect group performance, this relationship is not as straightforward as it seems. That is, whether group cohesiveness predicts group performance depends on the extent to which this performance is indeed mainly determined by the efforts of group members (instead of by less controllable external factors) as well as by the *content* of the relevant group norms which distinguish the group from other groups in that work context, as these norms direct the individual efforts of those who identify with that group to specific goals.

CONCLUSIONS AND PRACTICAL IMPLICATIONS

In the previous sections, we have tried to empirically substantiate our central proposition that identification in work groups can have beneficial as well as detrimental effects on group collaboration and group performance. We argued that the effects of identification in work settings depend on several complex processes, including the behavioral consequences of identification at different *levels of inclusiveness* and with *cross-cutting identities*, the influence of identification on the *perceptions and interactions with others* that are relevant to group performance, and the perceptual and behavioral consequences of identity- or *group-based expectations* and distinctive *group norms*.

We have first illustrated that it is not always easy to specify how multiple identities are structurally related to each other or to predict which of different possible identities people consider self-relevant. We conclude that which identity becomes salient and how it will likely impact upon people's collective performance is for a large part determined by the *contextual salience* of that identity, and how this relates to group goals.

In the second part of this chapter, we outlined the circumstances under which (work) group identification (and the ingroup favoring expectations this gives rise to) can either have positive or negative effects on the way people perceive and interact with others. The good news is that as a result of increased identification people strive to maintain positive expectations of ingroup members and view their actions in a favorable light. As a result, they tend to explain ambiguous behavior of other ingroup members in a positive way and constructively deal with group-relevant criticism. However, the downside is that people tend to reject ingroup members when they clearly violate group-relevant expectations. Furthermore, strong group identification makes people relatively sensitive and vulnerable to evaluative judgments of other ingroup members about the self. Taken together, we believe this indicates that group identification *can* lead people to respond more constructively to others in their group, but only under the conditions that the others conform to group norms and show concern for the self.

In the final section, we addressed the importance of the social comparative context in which groups have to operate for the way in which a group defines itself in terms of specific characteristics and distinct behaviors. That is, depending on the extent to which it enhances group distinctiveness, in principle any kind of feature that is shared among group members can become a group-defining characteristic. We argued that these distinctive characteristics determine the normative expectations of how to behave within the group and – depending on their nature – also influence the extent to which people are motivated to collaborate with others and focus the direction individual efforts on behalf of the group will take.

One of the main aims of this chapter was to show that increasing identification is not an easy remedy for problems of group motivation and performance. How then should managers or organizations go about it, when they strive to improve group performance by fostering the identification of group members? We think that *four key issues* need to be addressed, to be able to do this successfully. In Table 1 we have specified what these issues are, and which questions need to be answered in order to make sure that the required conditions are met. We will now briefly summarize each of these issues.

1. *Optimizing the identity behavior match*: First, it is important to make sure that the focus of the identity matches the goals of the work group and organization. For instance, if organizations foster identification at the

Table 1. How to Foster the Conditions Under which Increased Identification can Improve Work Group Performance.

1. Optimizing the Identity Behavior Match
   Make sure that the focus of the identity matches the goals of the work group.
   - is identity defined at the appropriate level of inclusiveness?
   - is the focus of the identity relevant to the required task behavior?
   - are there no cross-cutting identities that are incompatible with group goals?

2. Acknowledging Multiple Identities
   Make sure that the needs for situational flexibility and self-determination are fulfilled.
   - can people freely adopt multiple identities?
   - can they accommodate their identity to situational requirements?
   - are people's self-views respected?

3. Adapting to Task Requirements
   Specify what is needed for a successful group performance.
   - does the task require that other group members are given the benefit of the doubt through ingroup favoring biases?
   - does the success of the group depend on its openness to criticism?
   - will crucial task feedback be voiced by ingroup members?

4. Anticipating the Effects of Group Norms
   Determine in which attitudes or behaviors define the group's distinct identity, and how these relate to the group task.
   - in what ways it is important for the group to be distinct from other groups?
   - do group norms foster group performance improvement?
   - does the success of the group depend on the exclusion of those who deviate from group norms?

organizational level this will impact upon the way people behave toward the overall organization (e.g., their turnover behavior), but not necessarily affect their efforts or performance in specific work teams (e.g., willingness to help colleagues). Therefore, the identity should be defined at the level of inclusiveness that relates to the task at hand, and the focus of the identity should be relevant to the required task behavior. Additionally, one has to assess whether there are no important cross-cutting identities that are incompatible with group goals.

2. *Acknowledging multiple identities*: When focusing on that particular identity that is relevant to the task at hand, one has to make sure that the needs for situational flexibility and self-determination are fulfilled. This implies that people should be allowed to sustain multiple identities, instead of trying to replace one identity with another, in order to avoid resistance from those who feel threatened in their own focal identity. For instance, in the case of organizational mergers, people are most inclined

to identify with the new, merged organization when they are not required to completely relinquish all indicators of their previous organizational affiliation. Additionally, people should be able to switch identities to accommodate to situational demands, allowing them to adapt and develop in response to changing circumstances. Finally, one should make sure that people feel they have situational control and are being respected in their self-defined identities, for instance, by introducing arrangements that facilitate the combination of work and childcare to accompany efforts to increase identification with the organization.

3. *Adapting to task requirements*: Third, one needs to specify what is required for a successful group performance. Increasing identification will have beneficial effects when it is important for (sustained) motivation that group members maintain positive beliefs about each other through biased attributions, communications, and behaviors (e.g., in long-term interdependence relations). However, when task achievement depends on the group's ability to acknowledge its problems and improve themselves (e.g., in research and development teams), one should first establish whether the feedback that is crucial for such self-improvement can be expected to come from other ingroup members, or only is available to people outside the group. In the first case, increased identification may be helpful, but not in the second case. Alternatively, to increase the chances that critical feedback that is seen as coming from outgroup source (e.g., higher management) is dealt with in a constructive way, one should emphasize the common identity that group members share with the source of the feedback (i.e., as members of the same organization).

4. *Anticipating the effects of group norms*: Finally, one has to determine which attitudes or behaviors define the group's distinct identity in relation to relevant other groups, and specify how these relate to the group task. This is important because the nature of distinctive group norms and specific group goals may lead group members to behave in ways that seem to serve the interests of the group itself (e.g., maintaining a high level of absence behavior), but are undesirable from the point of view of the organization or society. Therefore, one should verify that distinctive group norms indeed foster those behaviors that are relevant for group performance improvement. Additionally, when task success requires a very strict adherence to group norms, implying that those who deviate from group norms should be excluded (e.g., in the case of security work), beneficial effects can be expected from increased group identification, while identification may undermine group performance when this depends on creative thinking and contributions from atypical group members.

In sum, enhancing the level of identification in work settings can offer a valuable solution to motivation or performance problems in work groups. However, in this chapter, we have reviewed recent theoretical developments and empirical research to show that identity processes can also have negative consequences for group functioning, depending on the nature of the shared identity, and the content of distinctive group norms. Thus, whereas previous theory and research has recognized the importance of identification and commitment for work motivation, we argue that there is no simple one-to-one relationship between identification and group performance, and hence promoting identification should not be seen as a panacea for suboptimal group functioning. Instead, we propose that a more detailed analysis of the causes and consequences of identification will yield more accurate and useful insights, that may help avoid frustration and disappointment about the value of identification as an explanatory construct (e.g., Huddy, 2001; Jost & Elsbach, 2001). It is in this sense that we believe that the application of the social identity perspective to work group behavior offers a highly promising perspective to examine the conditions under which groups function effectively in work settings.

ACKNOWLEDGMENT

This chapter was facilitated by a grant from the Dutch National Science Foundation awarded to Naomi Ellemers (NWO grant no. 261-98-906). The authors would like to thank Ilse de Winne for her assistance with literature search and references.

REFERENCES

Albert, S., Ashforth, B. E., & Dutton, J. E. (2000). Organizational identity and identification: Charting new waters and building new bridges. *Academy of Management Review, 25,* 13–17.

Albert, S., & Whetten, D. A. (1985). Organizational identity. *Research in Organizational Behavior, 7,* 263–295.

Ambrose, M. L., & Kulik, C. T. (1999). Old friends, new faces: Motivation research in the 1990s. *Journal of Management, 25,* 231–292.

Ashforth, B. E. (2001). *Role transitions in organizational life: An identity-based perspective.* Mahwah, NJ: Erlbaum.

Ashforth, B. E., & Johnson, S. A. (2001). Which hat to wear? The relative salience of multiple identities in organizational contexts. In: M. A. Hogg & D. J. Terry (Eds), *Social identity processes in organizational contexts* (pp. 31–48). Philadelphia, PA: Psychology Press.

Ashforth, B. E., & Mael, F. (1989). Social identity theory and the organisation. *Academy of Management Review, 14*, 20–39.

Barnum, C. (1997). A reformulated social identity theory. *Advances in Group Processes, 14*, 29–57.

Barreto, M., & Ellemers, N. (2000). You can't always do what you want: Social identity and self-presentational determinants of the choice to work for a low status group. *Personality and Social Psychology Bulletin, 26*, 891–906.

Barreto, M., & Ellemers, N. (2002). The impact of respect vs. *neglect of self-identities on identification and group loyalty. Personality and Social Psychology Bulletin,, 28*, 493–503.

Barreto, M., & Ellemers, N. (2003). The effects of being categorised: The interplay between internal and external social identities. *European Review of Social Psychology, 14*, 139–170.

Barreto, M., Spears, R., Ellemers, N., & Shahinper, K. (2003). Who wants to know? The effect of audience on identity expression among minority group members. *British Journal of Social Psychology, 42*, 299–318.

Beal, D. J., Cohen, R. R., Burke, M. J., & McLendon, C. L. (2003). Cohesion and performance in groups: A meta-analytic clarification of construct relations. *Journal of Applied Psychology, 88*, 989–1004.

Becker, T. E. (1992). Foci and bases of commitment: Are they distinctions worth making? *Academy of Management Journal, 35*, 232–244.

Becker, T. E., & Billings, R. S. (1993). Profiles of commitment: An empirical test. *Journal of Organizational Behavior, 14*, 177–190.

Benkhoff, B. (1997). Ignoring commitment is costly: New approaches establish the missing link between commitment and performance. *Human Relations, 50*, 701–726.

Bettencourt, B. A., Dill, K. E., Greathouse, S., Charlton, K., & Mulholland, A. (1996). Evaluations of ingroup and outgroup members: The role of category-based expectancy violation. *Journal of Experimental Social Psychology, 33*, 244–275.

Biernat, M., Vescio, T. K., & Billings, L. S. (1999). Black sheep and expectancy violation: Integrating two models of social judgment. *European Journal of Social Psychology, 29*, 523–542.

Branscombe, N., Spears, R., Ellemers, N., & Doosje, B. (2002). Effects of intragroup and intergroup evaluations on group behavior. *Personality and Social Psychology Bulletin, 28*, 744–753.

Brewer, M. B. (1979). In-group bias in the minimal intergroup situation: A cognitive-motivational analysis. *Psychological Bulletin, 86*, 307–324.

Brewer, M. B. (1991). The social self: On being the same and different at the same time. *Personality and Social Psychology Bulletin, 17*, 475–482.

Brewer, M. B., & Kramer, R. M. (1986). Choice behavior in social dilemmas: Effects of social identity, group size, and decision framing. *Journal of Personality and Social Psychology, 50*, 543–549.

Brief, A. P., & Aldag, R. J. (1981). The "self" in work organizations: A conceptual review. *Academy of Management Review, 6*, 75–88.

Brief, A. P., & Motiwidlo, S. J. (1986). Prosocial organizational behaviors. *Academy of Management Review, 11*, 710–725.

Burke, P. J. (2003). Relationships among multiple identities. In: P. J. Burke, T. J. Owens, R. T. Sherpe & P. A. Thoits (Eds), *Advances in identity theory and research* (pp. 195–216). New York: Kluwer Academic/Plenum Press.

Cascio, W. F. (1995). Whither industrial and organizational psychology in a changing world of work? *American Psychologist, 50,* 928–939.

Castano, E., Yzerbyt, V., Bourguignon, D., & Seron, E. (2002). Who may enter? The impact of in-group identification on in-group/out-group categorization. *Journal of Experimental Social Psychology, 38,* 315–322.

Christensen, N. P., Rothgerber, H., Wood, W., & Matz, D. C. (2004). Social norms and identity relevance: A motivational approach to normative behavior. *Personality and Social Psychology Bulletin, 30,* 1295–1309.

Coates, G. (1994). Motivation theories' lacklustre performance: Identity at work as explanation for expended effort. *Educational and Training Technology International, 31,* 26–30.

Derks, B., Van Laar, C., & Ellemers, N. (2004). *Social creativity strikes back: Improving low status group members' motivation and performance by valuing ingroup dimensions* (manuscript under editorial consideration).

Doosje, B., Branscombe, N., Spears, R., & Manstead, A. S. R. (1999). Guilty by association: When one's group has a negative history. *Journal of Personality and Social Psychology, 75,* 872–886.

Duck, J. M., & Fielding, K. S. (1999). Leaders and subgroups: One of us or one of them? *Group Processes and Intergroup Relations, 2,* 203–230.

Ellemers, N. (1993). The influence of socio-structural variables on identity enhancement strategies. *European Review of Social Psychology, 4,* 27–57.

Ellemers, N. (2001). Social identity and group norms. In: A. Van Harskamp & B. Musschenga (Eds), *The many faces of individualism* (pp. 225–237). Louvain: Peeters Publ. Co.

Ellemers, N., Barreto, M., & Spears, R. (1999). Commitment and strategic responses to social context. In: N. Ellemers, R. Spears & B. Doosje (Eds), *Social identity: Context, commitment, content* (pp. 127–146). Oxford: Basil Blackwell.

Ellemers, N., Van Rijswijk, W., Bruins, J., & De Gilder, D. (1998). Group commitment as a moderator of attributional and behavioural responses to power use. *European Journal of Social Psychology, 28,* 555–573.

Ellemers, N., De Gilder, D., & Haslam, S. A. (2004). Motivating individuals and groups at work: A social identity perspective on leadership and group performance. *Academy of Management Review, 29,* 459–478.

Ellemers, N., De Gilder, D., & Van den Heuvel, H. (1998). Career-oriented versus team-oriented commitment and behavior at work. *Journal of Applied Psychology, 83,* 717–730.

Ellemers, N., Doosje, B., & Spears, R. (2004). Sources of respect: The effects of being liked by ingroups and outgroups. *European Journal of Social Psychology, 34,* 155–172.

Ellemers, N., Haslam, Platow, & Van Knippenberg (2003). Social identity at work: Definitions, debates, and directions. In: A. Haslam, D. Van Knippenberg, M. Platow & N. Ellemers (Eds), *Social identity at work: Developing theory for organizational practice* (pp. 3–26). Philadelphia, PA: Psychology Press.

Ellemers, N., Kortekaas, P., & Ouwerkerk, J. (1999). Self-categorization, commitment to the group and social self-esteem as related but distinct aspects of social identity. *European Journal of Social Psychology, 29,* 371–389.

Ellemers, N., Van Dyck, C., Hinkle, S., & Jacobs, A. (2000). Intergroup differentiation in social context: Identity needs versus audience constraints. *Social Psychology Quarterly, 63,* 60–74.

Ellemers, N., Van Rijswijk, W., Roefs, M., & Simons, C. (1997). Bias in intergroup perceptions: Balancing group identity with social reality. *Personality and Social Psychology Bulletin, 23,* 186–198.

Ellemers, N., Van Steenbergen, E., & Benus, J. (2004). *Perceived (in)compatibility of work and home responsibilities, and work commitment: Experimental and field evidence.* Working paper. Leiden University.

Erez, M., Kleinbeck, U., & Thierry, H. (Eds) (2001). *Work motivation in the context of a globalizing economy.* Mahwah, NJ: Lawrence Erlbaum.

Fishbein, M., & Ajzen, I. (1975). *Belief, attitude, intention and behavior: An introduction to theory and research.* Reading, MA: Addison-Wesley.

Fiske, S. T., Cuddy, A. J. C., Glick, P., & Xu, J. (2002). A model of (often mixed) stereotype content: Competence and warmth respectively follow from perceived status and competition. *Journal of Personality and Social Psychology, 82,* 878–902.

Gellatly, I. R., & Luchak, A. A. (1998). Personal and organizational determinants of perceived absence norms. *Human Relations, 51,* 1085–1102.

George, J. M., & Brief, A. P. (1996). Motivational agendas in the workplace: The effects of feelings on focus of attention and work motivation. In: B. M. Staw & L. L. Cummings (Eds), *Research in organizational behavior,* (Vol. 18, pp. 75–109). Greenwich, CT: JAI.

Graen, G. B., & Scandura, T. A. (1987). Toward a psychology of dyadic organizing. *Research in Organizational Behavior, 9,* 175–208.

Gutek, B. A. (1995). *The dynamic of service: Reflections on the changing nature of the service industry.* San Francisco: Jossey Bass.

Harinck, S., & Ellemers, N. (in press). Playing hide and seek: The effects of information exchange in intra- and inter-group negotiations. *European Journal of Social Psychology.*

Haslam, S. A. (2001). *Psychology in organizations: The social identity approach.* London: Sage.

Haslam, S. A., & Ellemers, N. (2004). Social identity in industrial and organisational psychology: Concepts, controversies and contributions. *International Review of Industrial and Organizational Psychology, 20,* 39–118.

Haslam, S. A., McGarty, C., Brown, P. M., Eggins, R. A., Morrison, B. E., & Reynolds, K. J. (1998). Inspecting the emperor's clothes: Evidence that randomly selected leaders can enhance group performance. *Group Dynamics, 2,* 168–184.

Haslam, S. A., & Platow, M. J. (2001). The link between leadership and followership: How affirming social identity translates vision into action. *Personality and Social Psychology Bulletin, 27,* 1469–1479.

Haslam, S. A., Postmes, T., & Ellemers, N. (2003). More than a metaphor: Organizational identity makes organizational life possible. *British Journal of Management, 14,* 357–369.

Haslam, S. A., & Turner, J. C. (1992). Context-dependent variation in social stereotyping 2: The relationship between frame of reference, self-categorization and accentuation. *European Journal of Social Psychology, 22,* 251–277.

Haslam, A., Van Knippenberg, D., Platow, M., & Ellemers, N. (Eds) (2003). *Social identity at work: Developing theory for organizational practice.* Philadelphia, PA: Psychology Press.

Hernes, H. (1997). Cross-cutting identifications in organizations. In: S. A. Sachman (Ed.), *Cultural complexity in organizations: Inherent contrasts and contradictions* (pp. 343–366). Thousand Oaks, CA: Sage.

Herriot, R., & Scott-Jackson, W. (2002). Globalization, social identities and employment. *British Journal of Management, 13,* 249–257.

Hewstone, M. (1990). The ultimate attribution error: A review of the literature on intergroup causal attribution. *European Journal of Social Psychology, 20,* 311–355.

Hogg, M. A., & Terry, D. J. (2000). Social identity and self-categorization processes in organizational contexts. *Academy of Management Review, 25,* 121–140.

Hogg, M. A., & Terry, D. J. (Eds) (2001). *Social identity processes in organizational contexts.* Philadelphia, PA: Psychology Press.

Hornsey, M. J., & Hogg, M. A. (1999). Subgroup differentiation as a response to an overly inclusive group: A test of optimal distinctiveness theory. *European Journal of Social Psychology, 29,* 543–550.

Hornsey, M. J., & Hogg, M. A. (2000a). Subgroup relations: Two experiments comparing subgroup differentiation and common ingroup identity models of prejudice reduction. *Personality and Social Psychology Bulletin, 26,* 242–256.

Hornsey, M. J., & Hogg, M. A. (2000b). Intergroup similarity and subgroup relations: Some implications for assimilations. *Personality and Social Psychology Bulletin, 26,* 948–958.

Hornsey, M. J., & Imani, A. (2004). Criticizing groups from the inside and the outside: An identity perspective on the intergroup sensitivity effect. *Personality and Social Psychology Bulletin, 30,* 365–383.

Hornsey, M. J., & Jetten, J. (2003). Not being what you claim to be: Impostors as sources of group threat. *European Journal of Social Psychology, 33,* 639–657.

Hornsey, M. J., & Jetten, J. (2004). The individual within the group: Balancing the need to belong with the need to be different. *Personality and Social Psychology Review, 8,* 248–264.

Hornsey, M. J., Oppes, T., & Svensson, A. (2002). "It's OK if we say it, but you can't": Responses to intergroup and intragroup criticism. *European Journal of Social Psychology, 32,* 293–309.

Hornsey, M. J., Trembath, M., & Gunthorpe, S. (2004). 'You can criticize me because you care': Identity attachment, constructiveness, and the intergroup sensitivity effect. *European Journal of Social Psychology, 34,* 499–518.

Huddy, L. (2001). From social to political identity: A critical examination of social identity theory. *Political Psychology, 22,* 127–156.

Hunt, S. D., & Morgan, R. M. (1994). Organizational commitment: One of many commitments or key mediating construct? *Academy of Management Journal, 37,* 1568–1587.

Huo, Y. J., Smith, H. J., Tyler, T. R., & Lind, E. A. (1996). Superordinate identification, subgroup identification, and justice concerns: Is separatism the problem? Is assimilation the answer? *Psychological Science, 7,* 40–45.

Hutchison, P., & Abrams, D. (2003). Ingroup identification moderates stereotype change in reaction to ingroup deviance. *European Journal of Social Psychology, 33,* 497–506.

Jackson, L. A., Sullivan, L. A., & Hodge, C. N. (1993). Stereotype effects on attributions, predictions, and evaluations: No two social judgments are quite alike. *Journal of Personality and Social Psychology, 65,* 69–84.

Jehn, K. A., & Shah, P. P. (1997). Interpersonal relationships and task performance: An examination of mediating processes in friendship and acquaintance groups. *Journal of Personality and Social Psychology, 72,* 775–790.

Jetten, J., O'Brien, A., & Trindall, N. (2002). Changing identity: Predicting adjustment to organizational restructure as a function of subgroup and superordinate identification. *British Journal of Social Psychology, 41,* 281–297.

Jetten, J., Postmes, T., & McAuliffe, B. J. (2002). "We're all individuals": Group norms of individualism and collectivism, levels of identification, and identity threat. *European Journal of Social Psychology, 32,* 189–207.

Jetten J., SpearsR., & Manstead, A. S. R. (1997). Distinctiveness threat and prototypicality: Combined effects on intergroup discrimination and collective self-esteem. *European Journal of Social Psychology, 27,* 635–657.

Jost, J. T., & Elsbach, K. D. (2001). How status and power differences erode personal and social identities at work: A system justification critique of organizational applications of social identity theory. In: M. A. Hogg & D. J. Terry (Eds), *Social identity processes in organizational contexts* (pp. 181–196). Philadelphia, PA: Psychology Press.

Jussim, L., Coleman, L. M., & Lerch, L. (1987). The nature of stereotypes: A comparison and integration of three theories. *Journal of Personality and Social Psychology, 68*, 228–246.

Kohn, A. (1993). Why incentive plans cannot work. *Harvard Business Review, 71*, 54–63.

Kramer, R. M. (1991). Intergroup relations and organizational dilemmas: The role of categorization processes. *Research in Organizational Behavior, 13*, 191–228.

Kramer, R. M., Shah, P. P., & Woerner, S. L. (1995). Why ultimatums fail: Social identity and moralistic aggression in coercive bargaining. In: R. M. Kramer & D. M. Messick (Eds), *Negotiation as a social process* (pp. 285–308). Thousand Oaks, CA: Sage.

Lau, D. C., & Murnighan, J. K. (1998). Demographic diversity and faultlines: The compositional dynamics of organizational groups. *Academy of Management Review, 23*, 325–340.

Lawler, E. J. (1992). Affective attachment to nested groups: A choice-process theory. *American Sociological Review, 57*, 327–339.

Lawler, E. J. (2003). Interaction, emotion, and collective identities. In: P. J. Burke, T. J. Owens & P. A. Thoits (Eds), *Advances in identity theory and research* (pp. 135–149). New York: Kluwer Academic/Plenum Publishers.

Lawler, E. J., & Thye, S. R. (1999). Bringing emotions into social exchange theory. *Annual Review of Sociology, 25*, 217–244.

Lawler, E. J., & Yoon, J. (1993). Power and the emergence of commitment behavior in negotiated exchange. *American Sociological Review, 58*, 465–481.

Leach, C., Barreto, M., & Ellemers, N. (2004). *The merit of morality: How ingroups negotiate the meaning of intergroup evaluations.* University of Sussex/Leiden University. Working paper.

Lembke, S., & Wilson, M. G. (1998). Putting the "team" into teamwork: Alternative theoretical contributions for contemporary management practice. *Human Relations, 51*, 927–944.

Levine, J. M., & Moreland, R. L. (2002). Group reactions to loyaly and disloyalty. In: E. J. Lawler & S. R. Thye (Eds), *Advances in group processes*, (Vol. 19, pp. 203–228). Greenwich: JAI Press.

Lobel, S. A., & St.Clair, L. (1992). Effects of family responsibilities, gender, and career identity salience on performance outcomes. *Academy of Management Journal, 35*, 1057–1069.

Locke, E. A., & Latham, G. P. (1990). *A theory of goal setting and task performance.* Englewood Cliffs, NJ: Prentice-Hall.

Maass, A., & Arcuri, L. (1996). Language and stereotyping. In: N. Macrae, C. Stangor & M. Hewstone (Eds), *Stereotypes and stereotyping.* New York: Guilford.

Maass, A., Salvi, D., Arcuri, L., & Semin, G. (1989). Language use in intergroup contexts: The linguistic intergroup bias. *Journal of Personality and Social Psychology, 57*, 981–993.

Mael, F., & Tetrick, L. E. (1992). Identifying organizational identification. *Educational and Psychological Measurement, 52*, 813–824.

Markovsky, B., & Chaffee, M. (1995). Social identification and solidarity: A reformulation. *Advances in Group Processes, 12*, 249–270.

Markovsky, B., & Lawler, E. J. (1994). A new theory of group solidarity. In: B. Markovsky, K. Heimer & J. O'Brien (Eds), *Advances in group processes*, Vol. 11. Greenwich, CT: JAI Press.

Marques, J. M., & Paez, D. (1994). The "black sheep effect": Social categorization, rejection of ingroup deviates and perception of group variability. *European Review of Social Psychology, 5*, 37–68.

Marques, J. M., Yzerbyt, V. Y., & Leyens, J. P. (1988). The "black sheep effect": Extremity of judgments towards ingroup members as a function of identification. *European Journal of Social Psychology, 18*, 1–16.

Mathieu, J. E., & Zajac, D. (1990). A review and meta-analysis of the antecedents, correlates, and conseqences of organizational commitment. *Psychological Bulletin, 108*, 171–194.

McAuliffe, B. J., Jetten, J., Hornsey, M. J., & Hogg, M. A. (2003). Individualist and collectivist group norms: When it's OK to go your own way. *European Journal of Social Psychology, 33*, 57–70.

Meyer, J. P., & Allen, N. J. (1997). *Commitment in the workplace: Theory, research, and application.* London: Sage.

Meyer, J. P., Paunonen, S. V., Gellatly, I. R., Goffin, R. D., & Jackson, D. N. (1989). Organizational commitment and job performance: It's the nature of the commitment that counts. *Journal of Applied Psychology, 74*, 152–156.

Miller, V. D., Allen, M., Casey, M. K., & Johnson, J. R. (2000). Reconsidering the organizational identification questionnaire. *Management Communication Quarterly, 13*, 626–658.

Moore, D. A., Kurtzberg, T. R., Thompson, L. L., & Morris, M. W. (1999). Long and short routes to success in electronically mediated negotiations: Group affiliations and good vibrations. *Organizational Behavior and Human Decision Processes, 77*, 22–43.

Moreland, R. L., & Levine, J. M. (2001). Socialization in organiztions and work groups. In: M. E. Turner (Ed.), *Groups at work: Theory and research* (pp. 69–112). Mahwah, NJ: Lawrence Erlbaum.

Mowday, R. T. (1979). Equity theory predictions of behavior in organizations. In: R. M. Steers & L. W. Porter (Eds), *Motivation and work behavior* (pp. 124–146). New York: McGraw-Hill.

Mummendey, A., & Schreiber, H.-J. (1983). Better or just different?: Positive social identity by discrimination against or differentiation from outgroups. *European Journal of Social Psychology, 13*, 389–397.

Mummendey, A., & Schreiber, H.-J. (1984). "Different" just means "better": Some obvious and some hidden pathways to ingroup favoritism. *British Journal of Social Psychology, 23*, 363–368.

Ouwerkerk, J. W., Ellemers, N., & De Gilder, D. (1999). Group commitment and individual effort in experimental and organizational contexts. In: N. Ellemers, R. Spears & B. J. Doosje (Eds), *Social identity: Context, commitment, content* (pp. 184–204). Oxford: Blackwell.

Parker, M. (1993). Industrial relations myth and shop floor reality: The team concept in the auto industry. In: N. Lichtenstein & J. H. Howell (Eds), *Industrial democracy in America* (pp. 249–274). Cambridge: Cambridge University Press.

Pearce, J. L. (1987). Why merit pay doesn't work: Implications from organizational theory. In: D. B. Balkin & L. R. Gomez-Meija (Eds), *New perspectives on compensation* (pp. 169–178). Englewood Cliffs, NJ: Prentice-Hall.

Peterson, M. F., Smith, P. B., Akande, A., Ayestaran, S., Bochner, S., Callan, V., Cho, N. G., Jesuino, J. C., Damorim, M., Francois, P. H., Hofmann, K., Koopman, P. L., Leung, K., Lim, T. K., Mortazavi, S., Munene, J., Radford, M., Ropo, A., Savage, G., Setiadi, B., Sinha, T. N., Sorenson, R., & Viedge, C. (1995). Role conflict ambiguity and overload: A 21-nation study. *Academy of Management Journal, 38*, 429–452.

Pettigrew, T. F. (1979). The ultimate attribution error: Extending Allport's cognitive analysis of prejudice. *Personality and Social Psychology Bulletin, 5*, 461–476.

Pietromonaco, P. R., Manis, J., & Frohardt-Lane, K. (1986). Psychological consequences of multiple roles. *Psychology of Women Quarterly, 10*, 373–381.

Pinder, C. C. (1998). *Work motivation in organizational behavior.* Upper Saddle River, NJ: Prentice-Hall.

Platow, M. J., & Van Knippenberg, D. (2001). A social identity analysis of leadership endorsement: The effects of leader ingroup prototypicality and distributive intergroup fairness. *Personality and Social Psychology Bulletin, 27*, 1508–1519.

Postmes, T. (2003). A social identity approach to communication in organizations. In: S. A. Haslam, D. Van Knippenberg, M. J. Platow & N. Ellemers (Eds), *Social identity at work: Developing theory for organizational practice* (pp. 81–97). Philadelphia, PA: Psychology Press.

Postmes, T., Haslam, S. A., & Swaab, R. (in press). Social identity and social influence in small groups: Communication, consensualization and socially shared cognition. *European Review of Social Psychology.*

Postmes, R., Spears, R., & Cihangir, S. (2001). Quality of decision making and group norms. *Journal of Personality and Social Psychology, 80*, 918–930.

Pratt, M. G., & Foreman, P. O. (2000). Classifying managerial responses to multiple organizational identities. *Academy of Management Review, 25*, 18–42.

Reade, C. (2001a). Dual identification in multinational corporations: Local managers and their psychological attachment to the subsidiary versus the global organization. *International Journal of Human Resource Management, 12*, 405–424.

Reade, C. (2001b). Antecedents of organizational identification in multinational corporations: Fostering psychological attachment to the local subsidiary and the global organization. *International Journal of Human Resource Management, 12*, 1269–1291.

Reichers, A. E. (1986). Conflict and organizational commitments. *Journal of Applied Psychology, 71*, 508–514.

Reicher, S. D., & Hopkins, N. (1996). Self-category constructions in political rhetoric: An analysis of Thatcher's and Kinnock's speeches concerning the British miners' strike (1984–5). *European Journal of Social Psychology, 26*, 353–372.

Riketta, M., & van Dick, R. (in press). Foci of attachment in organizations: A meta-analytic comparison of the strength and correlates of work group versus organizational identification and commitment. *Journal of Vocational Behavior.*

Rink, F. A., & Ellemers, N. (2004a). *Work value diversity and decision making in dyads: Actual differences, or violated expectations?* (manuscript under editorial consideration)

Rink, F. A., & Ellemers, N. (2004b). *Agreeing to differ: The effects of work style diversity and informational diversity on dyadic decision making* (manuscript under editorial consideration).

Rink, F. A., & Ellemers, N. (2004c). *What can you expect? The effects of demographic differences on expected task-related diversity and dyadic collaboration* (manuscript under editorial consideration).

Robertson, M., & Swan, J. (2003). "Control – what control?" Culture and ambiguity within a knowledge intensive firm. *Journal of Management Studies, 40*, 831–858.

Rotondi, T. (1975). Organizational identification: Issues and implications. *Organizational Behavior and Human Decision Processes, 13*, 95–109.

Salk, J. E., & Shenkar, O. (2001). Social identities in an international joint venture: An exploratory case study. *Organization Science, 12*, 161–178.

Serpe, R. T., & Stryker, S. (1987). The construction of self and reconstruction of social relationships. In: E. Lawler & B. Markovsky (Eds), *Advances in Group Processes*, (Vol. 4, pp. 41–66). Greenwich, CT: JAI Press.

Shamir, B. (1991). Meaning, self and motivation in organizations. *Organization Studies, 12*, 405–424.

Sheldon, K. M., & Bettencourt, B. A. (2002). Psychological need-satisfaction and subjective well-being within social groups. *British Journal of Social Psychology, 41*, 25–38.

Smith, V. (1997). New forms of work organization. *Annual Review of Sociology, 23*, 315–339.

Smith, H. J., Tyler, T. R., & Huo, Y. J. (2003). Interpersonal treatment, social identity, and organizational behavior. In: S. A. Haslam, D. Van Knippenberg, M. J. Platow & N. Ellemers (Eds), *Social identity at work: Developing theory for organizational practice* (pp. 155–172). Philadelphia, PA: Psychology.

Smith-Lovin, L. (2003). The self, multiple identities, and the production of mixed emotions. In: P. J. Burke, T. J. Owens, R. T. Sherpe & P. A. Thoits (Eds), *Advances in identity theory and research* (pp. 167–178). New York: Kluwer Academic/Plenum Press.

Spears, R., Doosje, B., & Ellemers, N. (1997). Self-stereotyping in the face of threats to group status and distinctiveness: The role of group identification. *Personality and Social Psychology Bulletin, 23*, 538–553.

Spears, R., Ellemers, N., & Doosje, B. (2005). Let me count the ways in which I respect thee: Does competence compensate or compromise lack of liking from the group? *European Journal of Social Psychology, 35*, 263–280.

Spears, R., & Manstead, A. S. R. (1989). The social context of stereotyping and differentiation. *European Journal of Social Psychology, 19*, 101–121.

Stahl, T., Vermunt, R., & Ellemers, N. (2005). *Friend or foe? Ingroup identification moderates reactions to outgroup members' allocation behavior* (manuscript under editorial consideration).

Steers, R. M., Porter, L. W., Bigley, G. A. (Eds.) (1996). *Motivation and leadership at work.* (6th ed.). New York: McGraw-Hill.

Sussmann, M., & Vecchio, R. P. (1982). A social influence interpretation of worker motivation. *Academy of Management Review, 7*, 177–186.

Tajfel, H. (Ed.) (1978). *Differentiation between social groups: Studies in the social psychology of intergroup relations.* London: Academic Press.

Tajfel, H., & Turner, J. C. (1979). An integrative theory of intergroup conflict. In: W. Austin & S. Worchel (Eds), *The social psychology of intergroup relations* (pp. 33–47). Montery, CA: Brooks/Cole.

Tauer, J. M., & Harackiewicz, J. M. (2004). The effects of cooperation and competition on intrinsic motivation and performance. *Journal of Personality and Social Psychology, 86*, 849–861.

Thatcher, S. M. B., Jehn, K. A., & Zanutto, E. (2003). Cracks in diversity research: The effects of diversity faultlines on conflict and performance. *Group Decision and Negotiation, 12*, 217–241.

Thoits, P. A. (1986). Multiple identities: examining gender and marital status differences in distress. *American Sociological Review, 51*, 259–272.

Thoits, P. A. (2003). Personal agency in the accumulation of multiple identities. In: P. J. Burke, T. J. Owens, R. T. Sherpe & P. A. Thoits (Eds), *Advances in identity theory and research* (pp. 179–194). New York: Kluwer Academic/Plenum Press.

Thye, S. R., Yoon, J., & Lawler, E. J. (2002). The theory of relational cohesion: Review of a research program. *Group cohesion, trust, and solidarity, 19*, 139–166.

Turner, J. C. (1999). Some current issues in research on social identity and self-categorization theories. In: N. Ellemers, R. Spears & B. Doosje (Eds), *Social identity: Context, commitment, content* (pp. 6–34). Oxford: Blackwell.

Tyler, T. R. (2002). Leadership and cooperation in groups. *American Behavioral Scientist, 45*, 769–782.

Tyler, T. R., & Blader, S. (2000). *Co-operation in groups: Procedural justice, social identity and behavioral engagement.* Philadelphia, PA: Psychology Press.

Tyler, T. R., & Smith, H. J. (1999). Justice, social identity, and group processes. In: T. R. Tyler, R. Kramer & O. John (Eds), *The psychology of the social self* (pp. 223–264). Mahwah, NJ: Erlbaum.

Van Dick, R. (2004). My job is my castle: Identification in organizational contexts. *International Review of Industrial and Organizational Psychology, 19*, 171–204.

Van Dick, R., Wagner, U., Stellmacher, J., & Christ, O. (2004). The utility of a broader conceptualization of organizational identification: Which aspects really matter? *Journal of Occupational and Organizational Psychology, 77*, 171–191.

Van Knippenberg, D., & Ellemers, N. (2003). Social identity and group performance: Identification as the key to collective effort. In: S. A. Haslam, D. Van Knippenberg, M. Platow & N. Ellemers (Eds), *Social identity at work: Developing theory for organizational practice* (pp. 29–42). New York: Psychology Press.

Van Knippenberg, D., & Haslam, S. A. (2003). Harnessing the diversity dividend: Exploring the subtle interplay between identity, ideology and reality. In: S. A. Haslam, D. Van Knippenberg, M. J. Platow & N. Ellemers (Eds), *Social identity at work: Developing theory for organizational practice* (pp. 61–77). Philadelphia, PA: Psychology Press.

Van Knippenberg, D., & Van Schie, E. C. M. (2000). Foci and correlates of organizational identification. *Journal of Occupational and Organizational Psychology, 73*, 137–147.

van Leeuwen, E., & Van Knippenberg, D. (2003). Organizational identification following a merger: The importance of agreeing to differ. In: S. A. Haslam, D. Van Knippenberg, M. J. Platow & N. Ellemers (Eds), *Social identity at work: Developing theory for organizational practice* (pp. 205–221). Philadelphia, PA: Psychology Press.

Van Leeuwen, E., Van Knippenberg, D., & Ellemers, N. (2003). Continuing and changing group identities: The effects of merging on social identification and ingroup bias. *Personality and Social Psychology Bulletin, 29*, 679–690.

Van Rijswijk, W., & Ellemers, N. (2002). Context effects on the application of stereotype content to multiple categorizable targets. *Personality and Social Psychology Bulletin, 28*, 90–101.

Van Rijswijk, W. Haslam, S.A., & Ellemers, N. (in press). Who do we think we are: The effects of social context and social identification on ingroup stereotyping. *British Journal of Social Psychology.*

Van Steenbergen, E., & Ellemers, N. (2005). The work-family alliance: Distinct types of work-family facilitation and outcomes for women and men. (Manuscript under editorial consideration).

Vroom, V. H. (1964). *Work and motivation.* New York: Wiley.

Wigboldus, D., Spears, R., & Semin, G. R. (1999). Categorization, content and the context of communicative behaviour. In: N. Ellemers, R. Spears & B. Doosje (Eds), *Social identity: Context, commitment, content* (pp. 147–163). Oxford: Blackwell.

Williams, K. J., & Alliger, G. M. (1994). Role stressors mood spillover and perceptions of work-family conflict in employed parents. *Academy of Management Journal, 37*, 837–868.

NEW DIRECTIONS IN IDENTITY CONTROL THEORY

Jan E. Stets and Peter J. Burke

ABSTRACT

Identity control theory has long posited that there are positive emotional consequences to identity verification and negative emotional consequences to the lack of identity verification. While some of the positive consequences of identity verification have been discussed, little work has been done to elaborate the variety of negative emotions that result for a discrepancy between meanings held in the identity standard and meanings perceived in the situation. This paper elaborates the nature of this discrepancy and hypothesizes the variety of negative emotions that arise depending upon the source of the discrepancy, the source of the identity standard, and the relative power and status of the actor and others in the situation. In this way, the emotional consequences of identity non-verification are shown to depend upon the context of the social structure in which the non-verification occurs.

INTRODUCTION

Identity control theory (ICT) had its beginnings almost 30 years ago with the development of a theoretically based measurement system to capture the

Social Identification in Groups
Advances in Group Processes, Volume 22, 43–64
ISSN: 0882-6145/doi:10.1016/S0882-6145(05)22002-7

meanings of the self in a role (Burke, 1980). The idea was formulated, based on traditional symbolic interaction views, that people choose behaviors, the meanings of which correspond to the meanings in their identity (Burke & Reitzes, 1981; Burke & Tully, 1977). Over time, the simple theory of correspondence became elaborated and more fully developed based upon a systematic program of research (Burke, 1991; Stets & Burke, 2003), especially with the incorporation of ideas based on perceptual control theory (Powers, 1973). The theoretical development of the idea of an *identity control system* was central in that it provided a way of understanding the motivation underlying the actions of individual identity holders through the incorporation of goals. Essentially, individuals bring self-in-situation meanings into alignment with their self-defining meanings held in the identity standard when there is a discrepancy, and they maintain that alignment when there is no discrepancy.

During the most recent past, researchers have incorporated several important features into ICT. First, the view of meanings was expanded to include not only symbolic meanings with which symbolic interaction had been identified, but also sign meanings as tied to *resources*, that is, things that function to sustain a person, an interaction, or a group (Burke, 1997, 2004a; Freese & Burke, 1994). Second, ICT was extended to include identities that are tied not only to roles (role identities), but also to groups or categories (social identities) and to the person as a unique individual (person identities) (Burke, 1997, 2004b; Stets, 1995; Stets & Burke, 2000). Third, the theory was developed to include the emotional reactions that people have in response to identity confirmation and disconfirmation (Burke, 1991, 2004a; Burke & Harrod, in press; Stets, 2003b, 2004, 2005; Stets & Tsushima, 2001).

A fourth development was bringing the social structure, specifically one's status, into ICT to show its influence on the identity verification process (Cast, Stets, & Burke, 1999; Stets, 2004; Stets & Burke, 1996; Stets & Harrod, 2004). Fifth was the incorporation of the idea from James (1890) that people possess many identities that need verification (Burke, 2002, 2003; Stets, 1995; Stets & Harrod, 2004). These multiple identities are arranged in a hierarchical structure, with the output from an identity higher in the hierarchy being the reference or standard for an identity just below it (Burke, 1997; Burke & Cast, 1997; Stets & Carter, 2005; Stets & Harrod, 2004; Tsushima & Burke, 1999). Researchers also began to discover how individuals take on and lose identities, or more broadly, how identity standards slowly change with changing output of higher-level identities (Burke & Cast, 1997; Cast et al., 1999). Finally, to place more emphasis on interaction in dyads and groups, there was also the inclusion of the idea that in many social settings there are multiple persons, each with their own identities, all seeking to have all of their identities confirmed (Burke, 2005; Burke & Stets, 1999; Cast et al., 1999; Riley & Burke, 1995).

In all of the above developments, what has remained relatively unexamined is the nature of the discrepancy between the perceived self-relevant meanings in the situation and the self-defining meanings in the identity standard. In the present paper, we explore the nature of the discrepancy more fully as it is embedded within the social structural arrangements in which identities exists. We develop some hypotheses about the emotional consequences of variations in the nature and source of a discrepancy, when it exists. First, we briefly review the nature of identities as understood in ICT.

IDENTITY CONTROL THEORY

Identities

Within ICT, an identity is the set of meanings that define who one is in terms of a group or classification (such as being an American or female), in terms of a role (e.g., a stockbroker or a truck driver), or in terms of personal attributes (as in being friendly or honest). For the role identity spouse, for example, the identity would include what it *means to the individual* to be a husband or wife. These meanings, which define who one is, serve as a standard or reference for assessing self-relevant meanings in the interactive situation. They represent what the self-relevant meanings in the situation *should* be.[1] Because these standards are the output of higher-level control processes, they are dynamic and changing, although at a slow rate usually measured in weeks or months. Actual meanings in the situation that are relevant to the self are perceived and compared to the standard by means of a mechanism that has been coined the comparator. The comparator measures the degree of correspondence between the two sets of meanings (those in the standard and those perceived in the situation).

Any differences or discrepancy between the meanings are represented in an error signal that both generates emotion and produces meaningful behavior or activity that changes meanings in the situation so that the error is reduced and the perceptions match the standard. When the discrepancy is large or increasing, people feel bad and they do something about it (Burke, 1991). When the discrepancy is small or decreasing, people feel good and continue to do what they are already doing. We illustrate this

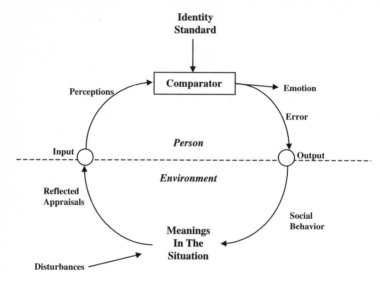

Fig. 1. Basic Identity Model.

negative-feedback control system in Fig. 1. The figure shows a representation of the identity standard, the perceptions of meanings in the situation, the comparator that compares the two sets of meanings, and the error (difference or discrepancy) which influences both emotions and behavior that changes the situational meanings.

In this paper, we discuss the nature of the discrepancy between the identity standard meanings and the actual meanings in the situation in an attempt to further understand and differentiate the various emotional consequences of that discrepancy. Because meaning is at the heart of both the identity standard and perceptions, we begin with a discussion of the nature of meaning in ICT.

Meaning

ICT follows the work of Osgood and his colleagues (Osgood, Suci, & Tannenbaum, 1957) in defining meaning as a bi-polar mediational response of a person to a stimulus. The dimensions along which the response occurs define the underlying dimensions of meaning. Osgood and his associates found that there are three primary dimensions consisting of evaluation (good–bad), potency (strong–weak), and activity (lively–quiet) that account for about 50% of the responses that people have. These primary dimensions cultures share. The other 50% of people's responses involve the multitude of other meanings, which vary across everyday situations but are important for understanding social life.

To illustrate the above, let us briefly discuss what it means to be a male. One might incorporate into his identity standard certain levels of evaluation and potency, but also many other aspects of masculinity and/or femininity, having to do perhaps with levels of assertiveness, drive, emotionality, and other characteristics. In addition to these more symbolic characteristics, being a male also conveys meanings in the resources that a male controls, including the cars, tools, clothes, and the job he has. To be clear, culture provides the relevant dimensions of masculinity/femininity in which the individual exists, but the particular levels on the various aspects that make up masculinity/femininity in the culture are individually determined and vary from one person to another. In this way, all identities have a cultural component (with respect to the relevant dimensions for a particular identity) and an idiosyncratic component (given individual differences).

As mentioned earlier, the definition of meanings has been expanded to include the notion of resources – that which functions to sustain the self and interaction. Recent theorizing has distinguished between active resources and potential resources (Burke, 1997, 2004a; Freese & Burke, 1994). Active resources currently support a person, role, or group such as air to breathe, a car that is transporting one to a destination, or current approval from one's boss on the job. Potential resources may be used in the future to support a person, role, or group such as food that will be later consumed or love that is forthcoming. Tied to active resources are *signs* that are responses to direct experiences that others do not share but allow individuals to control actual resources in the situation. It is through signs that persons perceive active resources. Tied to potential resources are shared *symbols* that are responses to anticipated experiences; these responses are stored in the form of conventional meanings that allow for interaction, communication, thought, and planning.

The distinction between signs and symbols is analytic. Empirically, they are less easily distinguished. For example, a pen is used to write with and is controlled with signs obtained directly through sight and feeling to accomplish that writing – a resource in use. At the same time, the pen may also have symbolic value conveying high status, for example, an expensive Mont Blanc with a gold nib and platinum inlay. All who see it understand that it represents the level of quality enjoyed by the rich and famous.

When the signs and symbols in the situation are congruent with the meanings in the identity standard, identity verification exists; the perceptions of the relevant meanings are the same as those held in the standard, and the error is zero. As mentioned above, the person feels good and continues to act as he or she has been acting. When there is a disturbance in the situation, that is, something changes the perceived meanings in the situation so that they no longer correspond to the meanings in the identity standard, the person feels bad and acts to change the meanings in the situation so that they correspond to those held in the standard. What governs what a person does and how the individual feels is the correspondence between the meanings in the identity standard and the perceived meanings in the situation.

THE NATURE OF THE DISCREPANCY

The above simply discusses the correspondence between meanings in the identity standard and the meanings in the situation, and the effect of that correspondence on the individual's feelings and behavior. It would appear from that discussion that any difference is equivalent to every other difference of the same magnitude and has similar consequences. However, common experience suggests that not all discrepancies are equivalent. As we discuss below, because there is variation both in the *source of the meanings* in the identity standard (self or other) and the *source of the discrepancy* (self or other), different consequences may emerge for the self when these variations occur. In order to understand these potentially differences consequences, we extend ICT by developing a set of hypotheses about such differences.

The Source of Meaning

In thinking about the different sources of identity standard meanings, distinguishing between different types of identity standards is one way of understanding the different discrepancies that can emerge between self-in-situation meanings and identity standard meanings. Higgins and his colleagues (1987, 1989; Higgins, Klein, & Strauman, 1985) have distinguished between "ideal" standards and "ought" standards. As identity standards, the ideal standards contain meanings that one aspires to maintain; ought standards contain meanings that one feels obliged to maintain. According to

Higgins (1987, 1989; Higgins et al., 1985), discrepancies between perceptions and meanings held in an "ideal" standard result in feelings of depression and dejection; one has not lived up to one's aspirations or ideals. Discrepancies between perceptions and the meanings held in an "ought" standard result in feelings of anxiety and agitation; one has not accomplished what one was expected to accomplish. In this way different emotions arise from different kinds of discrepancies (Marcussen & Large, 2003).

Although Higgins frames his work in terms of different types of standards, we think it is more useful to consider the different sources of the meanings held in the identity standard. Keeping in mind that there are many dimensions of meaning for any one identity that is invoked in a situation, we conceptualize these various dimensions of meaning as rooted in the self or in others. When the self is the source of an identity standard meaning, individuals have essentially built a set of expectations that they hold for themselves in the identity. Such meanings may be unique or shared. What is important is that they have the additional meaning of *belonging to the self.* Alternatively, when others are the source of an identity standard meaning, while the meaning is part of the identity standard and therefore protected and verified, it does not belong to the self.

To illustrate the above, let us take the role identity of professor. The identity of professor carries with it many identity standard meanings, some of which are rooted in meanings defined by others and some of which are rooted in how the self defines being a professor. Identity meanings rooted in others, for example, may include keeping an active research program, publishing papers, and maintaining national visibility. Identity meanings rooted in the self may include, for example, being a very caring, helpful, and supportive mentor of students. A discrepancy between perceptions of relevant meanings in the situation and identity standard meanings rooted in the self would occur if the professor reads student evaluations that report that the professor is an insensitive, non-supportive teacher. Alternatively, a discrepancy between perceptions of relevant meanings in the situation and identity standard meanings rooted in others would occur if the professor fails at getting research grants or getting papers accepted for publication.

According to ICT, perceptions of relevant meanings in the situation derive themselves from reflected appraisals or how persons perceive that others see them in the situation. In the example above, this would be the professor perceiving students' feedback on his performance. Relying on reflected appraisals may be a limited view as to the basis of perceptual input because it neglects one's own appraisal as to how one is doing in the situation. Actors can ignore reflected appraisals, and instead, rely on their own perceptions of their performance as feedback. In the above example, for instance, the professor may discount the students' comments that he is a non-supportive teacher by concluding that the students are not privy to all that he does for his students, thus they are not in a position to evaluate the professor on that dimension of meaning. Thinking that one is more qualified than others to judge how he or she is doing in a situation may be one of several reasons as to why a person relies on his own perceptions rather than the perceptions of how he thinks others see him.

The Source of the Discrepancy

Identities locate one within the social structure in terms of the various role positions, group memberships, and personal attributes one has. In this sense, identities are clearly social (Burke, 2004a), orienting not only a person or holder of an identity to maintain certain meanings, but others with whom the person comes in contact so that others know with whom (with what identity) they are interacting. When a person verifies an identity, he or she has altered meanings in the situation to bring them into alignment with his or her identity standard. Since others typically are in the situation, the meanings that a person changes to verify himself or herself may be the same meanings others need to verify their own identities. Thus, self-verification may cause a disturbance in the verification process for others in the situation if those meanings change in a way that no longer confirms their identities. Similarly, others may change meanings that are relevant to the verification of a person's identity and create a discrepancy between situational meanings and the person's identity standard.

One's relationship to others in the situation thus becomes critical for the self-verification process, and the nature of the relationship can change the consequences of any discrepancy that arises. In Fig. 2, we provide a modification of the identity model showing the interaction of two identities in a situation. As the figure reveals, there are two sources of a potential discrepancy between an actor's identity standard and his or her perceptions of self-relevant meanings in the situation: the self and others.[2]

It is easy to see how others can disrupt the identity verification process for a person. Others can alter meanings in the situation such that they no longer correspond with the actor's identity standard, thereby causing conflicting goals (for self and other) in a situation. For example, employees may expect their female boss to be less feminine than how the woman defines herself (in terms of her gender) on the job, and the employees may act on this, thus

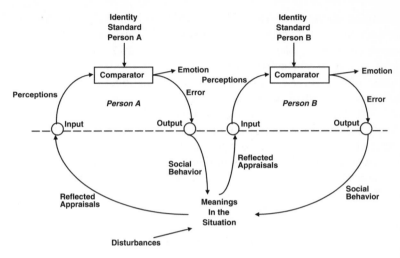

Fig. 2. Identity Models for Two Interacting Persons.

changing situational meanings. However, it is more difficult to see how the self can disrupt its own identity verification process.

There are at least three ways in which the self can act as a disturbance to its own verification process. First, when an individual acts to reduce a discrepancy and verify his or her identity, it is possible that more than one identity is salient in the situation such that the verification of one identity results in a lack of verification of the other identity. The identities are in conflict with each other in the sense that their standards have different levels on some dimension of meaning (Burke, 2002). For example, in an interaction, a young person may be in the presence of both a friend and her parents. While she may want to display her "worldliness" to her friend, she may also want to show her "innocence" to her parents. When interacting with her friend (in the role identity of friend) and with her parents (in the role identity of daughter), acting to verify one identity will necessarily create a discrepancy with the other identity. Thus, the source of the discrepancy is the self in that a person has multiple identities, which are simultaneously competing for verification.

A second way in which the self may create a discrepancy is through accidental or inadvertent actions. The perceived meanings that result from such actions are inconsistent with the identity standard meanings. For example, when one accidentally spills a glass of red wine on a light-colored suit, the person is spoiling the symbolic representation of oneself through the wearing of certain clothes (Stone, 1962). Alternatively, by accidentally tripping, one shows a level of ineptness not held in one's identity standard as a competent person, thereby creating an identity discrepancy.

A third way in which the self is the source of an identity discrepancy is through unintended consequences of intended actions. In general, the self acts in ways to control certain meanings to maintain self-verification. However, sometimes the results of these actions unwittingly negate identity verification. For example, Stets and Burke (2005) have shown that when one member of a couple attempts to increase their control over the other in order to get the other to verify their spousal identity, especially through the use of aggression, the consequence can be a decrease in the level of verification that the other provides.

Emotional Outcomes

Given that both the source of the identity meanings (self or other) and source of the discrepancy (self or other) are important in understanding the nature of identity discrepancies because of the additional meanings they provide, we anticipate that different emotional experiences will result from different combinations of self-other meanings and discrepancies. Table 1 reveals this, and we express it in the following hypotheses:

H1. When the source of meanings is the self and the source of the discrepancy is the self, the self will experience emotions ranging from disappointment to sadness.

H2. When the source of meanings is the other and the source of the discrepancy is the self, the self will experience emotions ranging from embarrassment to shame.

H3. When the source of meanings is the self and the source of the discrepancy is the other, the self will experience emotions ranging from anger to rage.

H4. When the source of meanings is the other and the source of the discrepancy is the other, the self will experience emotions ranging from annoyance to hostility.

In general, actors take responsibility for the identity standard meanings and the discrepancy that may emerge in the situation (an internal attribution), or they do not take responsibility for the identity meanings and discrepancy (an external attribution). Blaming the self for not being able to verify one's identity standards, whether those standards are set by the self or others, usually involves a negative evaluation of the self as "bad," and directs negative feelings inward (row 1 of Table 1). Blaming others for not being able to verify one's identity standards keeps intact the evaluation of the self as "good," and redirects negative feelings outward, onto others (row 2 of Table 1).

Internal attributions that one is responsible usually involves a family of related feelings ranging from the milder emotion of disappointment to the stronger emotion of sadness in not living up to one's own expectations, and from embarrassment to shame in one's own failure to meet the internalized expectations of others. The external attribution that others are responsible involves related feelings that range from anger to rage at having someone else cause the failure to meet one's own expectations, and from annoyance to hostility when someone else is responsible for the actor's failure to meet the internalized expectations of others (Lewis, 2000; Tangney, 2003). In each cell in Table 1, we suggest that there is a range of emotion (from weak to strong) on that dimension.

Earlier theorizing on identity discrepancies and emotion maintained that we should think of emotions in terms of their intensity, with less intense emotions more likely to be felt when a disrupted identity is less prominent to a person, and when a person is not very committed to the identity (Burke, 1991). Alternatively, a disrupted identity that is highly prominent and that a person is highly committed to would generate a more intense emotional response. We think that an improvement on this relationship would be to regard identity prominence and commitment as important because they influence the intensity of the emotions experienced, but to recognize that a less intense emotion feels very different compared to a more intense emotion. For example, a less intense state of sadness is disappointment and this feels very different compared to a more intense state of sadness such as depression. In general, in keeping with recent research that has suggested

Table 1. Emotional Responses by the Source of the Discrepancy and the Source of the Meanings.

Source of Discrepancy	Source of the Meanings	
	Self	Other
Self	Disappointment–sadness	Embarrassment–shame
Other	Anger–rage	Annoyance–hostility

that more work is needed on how social psychological theories can inform us about specific emotions that individuals experience (Stets, 2003a), we are attempting to link particular identity discrepancies to particular emotional states.

We point out that these different emotional states yield outcomes that are conducive to reducing the likelihood of further discrepancies, thereby maintaining self–other relationships. By turning inward when the self is the cause of the discrepancies, the self is motivated to manage identities and behaviors in ways that are less likely in the future to lead to discrepancies. By turning outward and directing negative feelings to others who are the cause of the discrepancies, one makes others more likely to change their identities and behaviors to prevent future discrepancies for the actor.

EXTENDING THE NATURE OF THE DISCREPANCY

The Dimensions of Status and Power

Thus far, we have dealt with generic forms of self–other interactions and the emotional consequences of discrepancies that occur when identities lack verification. We turn now to bring specific social structural features into ICT by extending our analysis on the nature of the discrepancy to discuss how one's position in the social structure, in terms of status (esteem and respect) and power (control of resources), acts to provide additional meanings that influence the emotional consequences of identity disconfirmation. Changes in status and power are at the heart of Kemper (1991), Lovaglia and Houser (Houser & Lovaglia, 2002; Lovaglia & Houser, 1996), and Thamm's (2004) theorizing about emotions. However, unlike Kemper (1991), we do not see an absolute change in status or power in the situation as that which determines one's emotional responses, but rather, a change in status and power meanings *relative to the status and power meanings that are held in the identity standard*. Additionally, following Thamm (2004), we suggest that not only does the source of the discrepancy make a difference in the emotional response to the discrepancy, but also the relative status and power of others that may be present in the situation.

Unlike Thamm, however, who views status and power in absolute terms, we view status and power in relative terms. This is in keeping with the symbolic interactionist perspective of ICT in which the interaction process is understood through the eyes of the actor. Thus, status is relative to the actor's status, and power is relative to the actor's power. A further distinction between our work and the work of Thamm is that Thamm maintains that at the root of the emotional experience is whether, given cultural expectations, one receives rewards or punishments. However, in ICT, rewards and punishments are defined in terms of the actor's identity-verification process. That which aids the identity-verification process is a reward, while that which disturbs or prevents identity verification is a punishment. Thus, rewards and punishments are not exogenous to the process.

Like the work of Lovaglia and Houser, who draw upon Turner's (2000) evolutionary view, we see the emotional responses as primarily integrative in the sense of facilitating identity verification in the present and future. Unlike Lovaglia and Houser, however, we view the emotional reactions not to status or power per se but to the additional meanings that power and status provide when identities are not verified.

In Tables 2 and 3, we identify the different emotional experiences that are a consequence of discrepancies resulting from the actions of self or other, the status of the other in the situation (Table 2), and the power of the other in the situation (Table 3). Consistent with the placement of these emotions in these tables, we offer the following hypotheses:

H5. When the source of the discrepancy is the self, the self will experience shame when the relative status of the other in the situation is higher than the self, embarrassment when the relative status of the other is equal

Table 2. Emotional Responses by the Source of the Discrepancy and the Relative Status of the Other in the Situation.

Source of Discrepancy	Relative Status of Other		
	Higher	Equal	Lower
Self	Shame	Embarrassment	Discomfort
Other	Anxiety	Annoyance	Hostility

Table 3. Emotional Responses by the Source of the Discrepancy and the Relative Power of the Other in the Situation.

Source of Discrepancy	Relative Power of Other		
	Higher	Equal	Lower
Self	Sadness	Disappointment	Displeasure
Other	Fear	Anger	Rage

to the self, and discomfort when the relative status of the other is lower than the self.

H6. When the source of the discrepancy is the other, the self will experience anxiety when the relative status of the other in the situation is higher than the self, annoyance when the relative status of the other is equal to the self, and hostility when the relative status of the other is lower than the self.

H7. When the source of the discrepancy is the self, the self will experience sadness when the relative power of the other in the situation is higher than the self, disappointment when the relative power of the other is equal to the self, and displeasure when the relative status of the other is lower than the self.

H8. When the source of the discrepancy is the other, the self will experience fear when the relative power of the other in the situation is higher than the self, anger when the relative power of the other is equal to the self, and rage when the relative status of the other is lower than the self.

The emotions in Tables 2 and 3 include the feeling states typically associated with internal attributions (row 1 in each table) and external attributions (row 2 in each table) as revealed in Table 1. Also included in Tables 2 and 3 but not included in Table 1 are the emotions of anxiety and fear, which we think emerge when the other is the source of one's identity discrepancy and the other is of high status or power. In each row in Tables 2 and 3, the feeling states become milder as one moves from the other in the situation being higher in status or power, to equal status, to the other being lower in status or power when the self is the source of the discrepancy. Indeed, there is more at stake in a situation when the other has higher status or power than the self than when the self has higher status or power than the other. Thus, the emotions should be stronger. However, when the other is the source of the discrepancy, there are shifts in the tone of the emotion from anxiety to hostility (going from higher to lower status), and from fear to rage (going from higher to lower power) as the feelings become more externalized.

As in Table 1, the emotional states in Tables 2 and 3 are consistent with the idea that the information about the source of the discrepancy and the relative status and power of the other provide additional meanings for the actor. These additional meanings as to the source of the discrepancy and the relative status and power of the other yield emotions and behaviors that reduce the present discrepancy, future discrepancies, and attempt to keep intact the self–other relationship.

Earlier, we argued that identity prominence and commitment influence emotions that range from weak to strong. Here, we maintain that one's status and power relative to another in an interaction also will influence the type of emotion individuals will experience. When we incorporate identity prominence and commitment into a situation that we can distinguish along status and power lines, we can expect a further differentiation regarding the type of emotions that will emerge. For example, if another is the source of one's identity discrepancy, the other is higher in power, and the disrupted identity is of high prominence and commitment, the self may feel terror rather than fear. Alternatively, if the disrupted identity is of low prominence and commitment, the self may simply feel a little scared. Future research will want to test whether the emotions emerge in situations in the manner described above.

The Three Bases of Identity

Another way to extend the analysis of the nature of identity discrepancies is to examine the emotional outcomes that result from identity discrepancies that occur for social (group-based), role-based, and person-based identities. As noted elsewhere (Burke, 2004a; Cast & Burke, 2002), identities formed on each of these bases have different consequences when there is identity verification. Past work has shown that verifying a social or group-based identity signifies that the person is like others in the group and belongs with those others. This leads to acceptance by others in the group as a legitimate member who is like other members (Stets & Burke, 2000). Such results lead to increased feelings of self-worth and solidarity.[3]

Verifying a role-based identity signifies that the person is competent and skillful in the role, meeting the expectations of the self and others (Stets & Burke, 2000). This increases feelings of efficacy and pride in one's accomplishments. Since most roles are embedded in some group or organization, the successful performance of the role also connotes worthiness in the group and thus may increase feelings of self-worth. Finally, verifying a person identity signifies that one is in fact who one claims to be, meeting one's own expectations and aspirations for the self, qua self. Past work has suggested that this leads to increased feelings of authenticity and happiness (Burke, 2004a). What we now need to outline is the emotional responses associated with identity disconfirmation. We offer the following three hypotheses:

H9. Non-verification of a group-based identity will lead to feelings ranging from embarrassment to shame.

H10. Non-verification of a role-based identity will lead to feelings ranging from feeling discomfort to guilt.

H11. Non-verification of a person-based identity will lead to feelings ranging from occasional sadness to depression.

When a discrepancy arises with respect to a social or group-based identity, there is the threat of rejection by the group, especially if the discrepancy occurs in the presence of other group members, or it emerges by other group members failing to confirm the actor's identity in the group. If the identity is low in prominence and commitment, the self is likely to feel embarrassed, but if the identity is high in prominence and commitment, the self is likely to feel shame. The outward focus of these emotions encourages the self to do something about the discrepancy and obtain verification to remain a part of the group.

Since role-based identities have to do more with what one does rather than acceptance as to who one is as in group-based identities (Stets & Burke, 2000), emotions should occur that focus on having done something that disrupts the identity verification process. Whereas feelings of shame (and its family of related emotions) focus on not meeting up to the expectations of others, with the entire person evaluated negatively, feelings of guilt (and its close relatives) address having done a bad thing, thus the person's behavior, rather than their entire self, is evaluated negatively (Lewis, 2000; Tangney, 2003). Therefore, we expect that if the disrupted role identity is low in prominence and commitment, the self should feel discomfort, but if the role identity is high in prominence and commitment, the self should feel guilt. Again, with either result, the actor is motivated to both restore identity verification as well as prevent future discrepancies from arising.

Finally, person identities relate to verifying the "real self." Because they are activated across situations, roles, and groups, they are more likely to be prominent. Further, because more people know the individual in terms of the characteristics of the person identity, there is more commitment to person identities. With the higher prominence and commitment come stronger emotional responses to problems in verification. We anticipate that the lack of verification of person identities will range from occasional sadness for low prominent and committed person identities to depression for high prominent and committed identities. The inward focus of these emotions helps to motivate the changes in identities and behaviors that will results in future success in verification.

Mutual Verification Contexts

A further way in which we examine the nature of identity discrepancies is within mutual verification contexts. In earlier work, Burke (1991) argued that individuals feel more intense emotional arousal when their identities are disrupted by a significant other compared to a non-significant other. According to Burke, significant others are those with whom one has built up a set of mutually verifying set of behaviors and identity standards. Burke and Stets (1999) introduced the term "mutual verification contexts" to recognize these situations in which each of two or more actors mutually support each other by not only verifying their own identities, but in doing so help in the process of verifying the identities of others in the situation. For example, a married couple often develop a mutual verification context in which each partner not only verifies his or her own spousal identity, but in doing so helps to maintain their spouse's identity (Burke & Stets, 1999). Close relationships often result because the meanings and resources controlled by each identity help to reinforce and facilitate the meanings and resources controlled by other identities in the situation. A mutual verification context is very stable and results in positive emotions and feelings of trust and commitment among the members (Burke & Stets, 1999). These emotions and feelings produce a context in which, up to a point, people will work harder to restore mutual verification than they would otherwise. However, beyond that point, as we discuss below, people's emotional reactions may be stronger and have stronger consequences than they would otherwise.

When an identity is not verified by the actions of a close other in a mutual verification context, one is likely to take the view that this is the result of the lack of information on the part of the other, or alternatively, it is an accidental or inadvertent outcome that one initially is not to be very upset about. Individuals seek ways to change meanings or resources to levels that maintain the mutual verification context. This is in the interests of everyone so that all identities are maintained. We thus offer the following hypothesis:

H12. If the discrepancy is not large or not persistent in a mutual verification context, the feeling of annoyance will manifest itself that helps members restore the mutual verification context.

However, if the lack of verification continues or recurs, or if the other is perceived as intentionally disturbing one's own verification process, bewilderment, anger, or even rage may result that is all the more intense for two reasons. It will be intense because the mutual verification situation is a well-established identity process that has become interrupted and the interruption of well-established identity processes is more distressful than interruption of less well-established processes (Burke, 1991). Second, because it is a *mutual* verification context, interruption occurs in the verification process of *all* of the identities in the situation, leading to strong negative reactions. The mutual verification context may become a mutual war and lead to the demise of the verification context. In larger groups, there may develop local mutual verification contexts among subgroups that are at odds with other subgroups, which have their own mutual verification contexts. Such bifurcations develop new in-groups and out-groups as new structures emerge. We thus hypothesize that:

H13. A discrepancy in a mutual verification context that is large or persistent and caused by another will result in feelings of anger.

H14. A discrepancy in a mutual verification context that is large or persistent when caused by the self will result in feelings of depression.

DISCUSSION

During the past 10 years, ICT as a theory has undergone considerable development. We know more about the different bases for the identities individuals hold (group, role, and person), the emotional responses of individuals to identity confirmation or disconfirmation, identity change, and the intersection of multiple identities and multiple persons in situations, with the goal of identity verification for all involved. However, there is still much work to do, and this paper has discussed some new directions for ICT.

While identity processes themselves, within the scope of ICT, are psychological, dealing with the perceptions and emotions of an active agent, these are necessarily set within the context of a social structure of relations between individuals, groups, and institutions, and within a context of an existing culture. The issues we discussed for future research bring the individual, the social, and the cultural together. We propose the examination of the location of individuals within the social structure and the additional meanings that location conveys when those individuals experience identity discrepancy.

At the core of ICT is an identity, which is a set of meanings that define who one is. Meanings are the medium of both communication and interaction and identity verification. Symbolic meanings arise in the culture and reflect characteristics of the social structure and social processes embedded within it. Individuals adapt them to the extent that they allow communication and interaction among persons who share the meanings in common groups, interconnected roles, and socially relevant personal characteristics.

The meanings that define persons as individuals, role players, or group members are identity standards. The identity verification process manipulates these meanings in the social situation to make them congruent with the identity standards. Discrepancies between situational meanings and identity standard meanings generate emotional responses that facilitate behavior. Behavior reduces the discrepancies to bring about identity verification, but it also accomplishes role performances, maintains the groups, or displays appropriate personal characteristics upon which others may rely.

By understanding the nature of the discrepancy and the varieties of emotional response that accompany discrepancies, we have better knowledge about the ways in which identities both reinforce and change the social structure in which they exist. The way identities are embedded in the social structure places "additional meanings" into the situation, which influence the responses and actions people take in response to discrepancies between situational meanings and meanings held in the identity standard. These "additional meanings" locate the actors within the social structure: in groups, roles, and relationships, and modify responses to the discrepancies that help to maintain and sometimes change the social structure.

The first distinction we make is the most basic: between self and other in the situation. We make this distinction both for the source of the meanings held in the identity standard (this is who I want to be or this is who I am expected to be), and the source of the situational meanings that create the discrepancy (the self causes the discrepancy or others cause the discrepancy). Each of these elements, when combined, adds meaning to the situation and changes the emotional reactions to the discrepancy. We predict that these emotional responses motivate the individual to act in ways that protect the actor from further discrepancies, thereby sustaining the interactive setting. For example, the actor might withdraw, rethink the situation, or modify behaviors or identities if the self caused the discrepancy. Alternatively, the person might behave more aggressively to change others, if they were the source of the discrepancy. These reactions are stronger if the source of the standard is the self rather than the other.

We then extend this analysis to consider other structural features of the situation including the status and power of the other, the type of linkage to others (through group memberships, role relationships, or personal characteristics), and the establishment of close bonds through the development of mutual verification contexts. In each case, we hypothesize that the emotions and behaviors result from the combination of the discrepancies and the additional meanings conveyed by the particular structural context in which they occur. We further hypothesize that these emotions and behaviors are particularly suited to both reducing the immediate discrepancies and preserving the structural relationships that help define the identities involved. People do not *just* "feel bad" when there is an identity discrepancy and they do not *just* act to reduce the discrepancy. The particular emotions and actions that they generate are the ones that best serve to reduce the discrepancy *and* preserve the social structural relations within which the identities exist.

NOTES

1. The idea of a "should" is only meant to convey an imperative from the point of view of the individual holding the standard. What is unstated is how the individual acquired the standard.
2. A third source may exist, which we label non-social factors such as situational exigencies and circumstances. For example, unexpected events may arise in a situation such as natural disasters or environmental hazards, thereby disrupting the perceived match between meanings of the self in the situation and identity standard meanings. In this paper, we limit our discussion to the self and other as the source of identity discrepancies.
3. In situations where there is more than one group, verifying a group identity not only makes one like others in one's own group, but also differentiates one from other groups by making clear what is "not me" (McCall, 2003).

REFERENCES

Burke, P. J. (1980). The self: Measurement implications from a symbolic interactionist perspective. *Social Psychology Quarterly, 43*(1), 18–29.
Burke, P. J. (1991). Identity processes and social stress. *American Sociological Review, 56*(6), 836–849.
Burke, P. J. (1997). An identity model for network exchange. *American Sociological Review, 62*(1), 134–150.
Burke, P. J. (2002). *Marital socialization, gender, and identity change.* Vancouver, BC: The Pacific Sociological Association.
Burke, P. J. (2003). Relationships among multiple identities. In: P. J. Burke, T. J. Owens, R. T. Serpe & P. A. Thoits (Eds), *Advances in identity theory and research* (pp. 195–214). New York: Kluwer Academic/Plenum.
Burke, P. J. (2004a). Identities and social structure: The 2003 Cooley–Mead Award address. *Social Psychology Quarterly, 67*(1), 5–15.
Burke, P. J. (2004b). Identities, events, and moods. *Advances in Group Processes, 21*, 25–49.

Burke, P. J. (2005). Can you see what I see? In: K. McClelland & T. J. Fararo (Eds), *Purpose, meaning, and action: Control systems theories in sociology*. New York: Palgrave Macmillan.

Burke, P. J., & Cast, A. D. (1997). Stability and change in the gender identities of newly married couples. *Social Psychology Quarterly, 60*(4), 277–290.

Burke, P. J., & Harrod, M. M. (in press). Too much of a good thing? *Social Psychology Quarterly*.

Burke, P. J., & Reitzes, D. C. (1981). The link between identity and role performance. *Social Psychology Quarterly, 44*(2), 83–92.

Burke, P. J., & Stets, J. E. (1999). Trust and commitment through self-verification. *Social Psychology Quarterly, 62*(4), 347–366.

Burke, P. J., & Tully, J. C. (1977). The measurement of role identity. *Social Forces, 55*(4), 881–897.

Cast, A. D., & Burke, P. J. (2002). A theory of self-esteem. *Social Forces, 80*(3), 1041–1068.

Cast, A. D., Stets, J. E., & Burke, P. J. (1999). Does the self conform to the views of others? *Social Psychology Quarterly, 62*(1), 68–82.

Freese, L., & Burke, P. J. (1994). Persons, identities, and social interaction. *Advances in Group Processes, 11*, 1–24.

Higgins, E. T. (1987). Self-discrepancy: A theory relating self and affect. *Psychological Review, 94*, 319–340.

Higgins, E. T. (1989). Self-discrepancy theory: What patterns of self-beliefs cause people to suffer? *Advances in Experimental Social Psychology, 22*, 93–136.

Higgins, E. T., Klein, R., & Strauman, T. (1985). Self-concept discrepancy theory: A psychological model for distinguishing among different aspects of depression and anxiety. *Social Cognition, 3*, 51–76.

Houser, J. A., & Lovaglia, M. J. (2002). Status, emotion, and the development of solidarity in stratified task groups. *Advances in Group Processes, 19*, 109–137.

James, W. (1890). *Principles of psychology*. New York: Holt Rinehart and Winston.

Kemper, T. D. (1991). Predicting emotions from social relations. *Social Psychology Quarterly, 54*(4), 330–342.

Lewis, M. (2000). Self-conscious emotions: Embarrassment, pride, shame, and guilt. In: M. Lewis & J. M. Haviland-Jones (Eds), *Handbook of emotion* (pp. 623–636). New York: The Guilford Press.

Lovaglia, M. J., & Houser, J. A. (1996). Emotional reactions and status in groups. *American Sociological Review, 61*(5), 867–883.

Marcussen, K., & Large, M. D. (2003). Using identity discrepancy theory to predict psychological distress. In: P. J. Burke, T. J. Owens, R. T. Serpe & P. A. Thoits (Eds), *Advances in identity theory and research* (pp. 151–166). New York: Kluwer Academic/Plenum.

McCall, G. (2003). The me and the not-me: Positive and negative poles of identity. In: P. J. Burke, T. J. Owens, R. T. Serpe & P. A. Thoits (Eds), *Advances in identity theory and research* (pp. 11–26). New York: Kluwer Academic/Plenum.

Osgood, C. E., Suci, G. J., & Tannenbaum, P. H. (1957). *The measurement of meaning*. Urbana: University of Illinois Press.

Powers, W. T. (1973). *Behavior: The control of perception*. Chicago: Aldine.

Riley, A., & Burke, P. J. (1995). Identities and self-verification in the small group. *Social Psychology Quarterly, 58*(2), 61–73.

Stets, J. E. (1995). Role identities and person identities: Gender identity, mastery identity, and controlling one's partner. *Sociological Perspectives, 38*(2), 129–150.

Stets, J. E. (2003a). Emotions and sentiments. In: J. DeLamater (Ed.), *Handbook of social psychology*. New York: Kluwer Academic/Plenum.

Stets, J. E. (2003b). Justice, emotion, and identity theory. In: P. J. Burke, T. J. Owens, P. A. Thoits & R. Serpe (Eds), *Advances in identity theory and research* (pp. 105–122). New York: Kluwer Academic/Plenum.

Stets, J. E. (2004). Emotions in identity theory: The effects of status. *Advances in Group Processes, 21*, 51–76.

Stets, J. E. (2005). Examining emotions in identity theory. *Social Psychology Quarterly, 68*.

Stets, J. E., & Burke, P. J. (1996). Gender, control, and interaction. *Social Psychology Quarterly, 59*(3), 193–220.

Stets, J. E., & Burke, P. J. (2000). Identity theory and social identity theory. *Social Psychology Quarterly, 63*(3), 224–237.

Stets, J. E., & Burke, P. J. (2003). A sociological approach to self and identity. In: M. R. Leary & J. P. Tangney (Eds), *Handbook of self and identity* (pp. 128–152). New York: The Guilford Press.

Stets, J. E., & Burke, P. J. (2005). Identity verification, control, and aggression in marriage. *Social Psychology Quarterly, 68*(2), 160–178.

Stets, J. E., & Carter, M. J. (2005). The moral identity: A principle level identity. In: K. McClelland & T. J. Fararo (Eds), *Purpose, meaning, and action: Control systems theories in sociology*. New York: Palgrave MacMillan.

Stets, J. E., & Harrod, M. M. (2004). Verification across multiple identities: The role of status. *Social Psychology Quarterly, 67*(2), 155–171.

Stets, J. E., & Tsushima, T. (2001). Negative emotion and coping responses within identity control theory. *Social Psychology Quarterly, 64*(3), 283–295.

Stone, G. P. (1962). Appearance and the self. In: A. Rose (Ed.), *Human behavior and social processes* (pp. 86–118). Boston: Houghton Mifflin.

Tangney, J. P. (2003). Self-relevant emotions. In: M. R. Leary & J. P. Tangney (Eds), *Handbook of self and identity* (pp. 384–400). New York: The Guilford Press.

Thamm, R. (2004). Towards a universal power and status theory of emotion. *Advances in Group Processes, 21*, 189–222.

Tsushima, T., & Burke, P. J. (1999). Levels, agency, and control in the parent identity. *Social Psychology Quarterly, 62*(2), 173–189.

Turner, J. H. (2000). *On the origin of human emotions*. Stanford, CA: Stanford University Press.

IDENTITY MAINTENANCE, AFFECT CONTROL, AND COGNITIVE PERFORMANCE

Michael J. Lovaglia, Reef Youngreen and
Dawn T. Robinson

ABSTRACT

A theory of self and the identities it comprises may explain differences in academic and other cognitive performance because successful perform- ances are associated with strong internal motivation. Identity control theory and affect control theory assume that individuals act to confirm identities, even when those actions have negative consequences. Cognitive performance, then, could be impaired if high performance is inconsistent with a salient identity. A developing theory explaining the relationship between identity maintenance and cognitive performance assumes that the effects of identity maintenance combine with other motivations to achieve. Anticipation of a performance relevant to an identity is assumed to put pressure on the identity, motivating performances consistent with it. Un- der some conditions identities may change to reflect different performance standards.

Social Identification in Groups
Advances in Group Processes, Volume 22, 65–91
Copyright © 2005 by Elsevier Ltd.
ISSN: 0882-6145/doi:10.1016/S0882-6145(05)22003-9

INTRODUCTION

The link between identity and role performance is fundamental to theories of identity, an avenue of research that also has important practical implications. For example, Ogbu (1978) observed a culture of opposition among black students in which commitment to a positive racial identity required active opposition to academic success. Steele (1997) observed that top African-American students hold identities with conflicting aspects, as good students and as African Americans. That internal conflict, he proposed, impairs their performance on standardized tests. Identity theories address this problem by seeking to explain how individuals manage multiple identities that vary in importance to them (Stryker, 1968). We extend existing identity theories to explain the relationship between identity and cognitive performance.

Several major identity theories assume that individuals are motivated to perform identities by behaving in ways that tend to confirm those identities: structural identity theory (Stryker, 1968, 1980; Burke & Reitzes, 1981; Stryker & Serpe, 1982), identity control theory (Burke, 1991, 1997; Burke & Stets, 1999; Stryker & Burke, 2000), and affect control theory (Heise, 1979; Smith-Lovin & Heise, 1988; MacKinnon, 1994, Smith-Lovin, 1987). The counterintuitive implication is that individuals highly motivated to do their best will nonetheless score low on standardized tests when a high score is inconsistent with a salient identity. We further propose that anticipation of a performance capable of altering an identity puts pressure on that identity, motivating the behavior that reaffirms the identity.

Achievement and identity maintenance can be conflicting goals that interfere with an individual's performance. The following section summarizes existing theory and research that explains how negative stereotypes and associated low status can reduce mental ability test scores when stereotyped individuals expect negative consequences from their performance. Then we develop a theory that explicates the role of identity maintenance in cognitive performance. We propose that identity maintenance may interfere with cognitive performance whenever a performance threatens to disconfirm an established identity, even when the identity is not negatively stereotyped.

EXPLAINING GROUP DIFFERENCES IN COGNITIVE PERFORMANCE

Explanations for group differences in cognitive performance have focused on one of the two contrasting causes, genetics and environment, which might generate differences in mental ability. Recently, however, social psychological theories have sought to explain how test-takers with similar backgrounds but from different groups might score differently on standardized tests despite identical mental ability. The social psychological approach shifts the perspective from *mental ability* as a stable individual trait to *cognitive performance* influenced by the array of factors capable of altering individual performances.

Mental ability is defined as the capacity of an individual to understand ideas, adapt to the environment, to reason and solve problems (Neisser et al., 1996). Despite recent attempts to expand the definition (Damasio, 1994; Gardner, 1983; Sternberg, 1985; Sternberg, Wagner, Williams, & Horvath, 1995), the psychometric approach using standardized tests remains dominant. When mental ability is used to make decisions that matter to individuals, such as admission to college, mental ability is operationalized as a score on a standardized test (Scarr, 1997). That is, as a performance.

Research to determine the social factors that influence mental ability remains at an early stage of development (Neisser et al., 1996). Surprisingly, however, research on heredity's contribution to individual mental ability also demonstrates the importance of the environment, of which social factors are an important part.

Nature and Nurture

Twin studies have been the primary method used to disentangle the relative contributions to mental ability of heredity and environment. Perhaps, the best exemplar is the Minnesota study of twins reared apart, which found a correlation of 0.70 for the mental ability test scores of monozygotic twins reared apart (Bouchard, Lykken, McGue, Segal, & Tellegen, 1990). In contrast, the correlation was 0.80 for monozygotic twins reared together. That comparison may overstate the heredity's contribution, however, because other factors could be responsible for at least some of the similarity between twins reared apart and twins reared together (Eysenck & Kamin, 1981).

Bouchard et al. (1990) conclude from the Minnesota twin study results that heredity contributes 70% to individual mental ability with environment contributing 30%. Other recent studies estimate the role of heredity and environment at about 50% each (Chipuer, Rovine & Plomin, 1990; Loehlin, 1989; Rodgers, Rowe, & May, 1994; Scarr & Weinberg, 1978; Scarr, Weinberg, & Waldman, 1993). Studies of adopted children also indicate roles for both heredity and environment. On the heredity side, Plomin and

Daniels (1987) found that adopted children raised in the same family are about as different from one another as children randomly selected from the population. On the environment side, Schiff et al. (1978) found increased mental ability in children from deprived backgrounds adopted into more affluent families. In sum, we can safely conclude that both heredity and environment make important contributions to an individual's mental ability.

Assessing the contribution of social factors moves the level of analysis from individual differences to group differences in mental ability. Early standardized tests were criticized for test items that advantaged individuals with knowledge of the dominant culture. It may not be possible to construct tests of verbal or even mathematical ability that are completely culture neutral. Some tests of abstract reasoning such as the Raven Progressive Matrices, however, require no language or mathematical background. Cultural bias in tests as an explanation for group differences in mental ability has difficulty accounting for the consistent differences in test scores found for racial and ethnic groups across a variety of tests (Herrnstein & Murray, 1994; Jensen, 1992). And while attempts to control for socioeconomic status and other social factors that reduce the gap, a substantial difference in test scores among racial and ethnic groups remains unexplained (Ainsworth-Darnell & Downey, 1998; Hedges & Nowell, 1998, Loehlin, Lindzey, & Spuhler, 1975; Rodgers et al.,1994).

Individual versus Group Differences in Cognitive Performance

It is important to separate the analysis of individual differences from group differences in cognitive performance. Well-constructed tests such as the Scholastic Achievement Test (SAT) predict individual academic success with some accuracy (Jencks & Phillips, 1998). A white student with a high SAT score will usually have an easier time succeeding in college, than will a white student from a similar background but with a low SAT score. Moreover, the same can be said of two black students from similar backgrounds but differing SAT scores. Further still, black students as a group score lower on the SAT and also do less well in school than do white students. Even after controlling for income and other relevant variables, the black–white test score gap remains (Hedges & Nowell, 1998). When middle-class black students take the SAT test under the same conditions as white students from similar backgrounds who went to the same schools, black students still score lower on the SAT than do white students. Given the consistency of the evidence, it is easy to draw the invalid conclusion that black students have less academic ability than do white students.

The error lies in the assumption that the test scores of black and white students are comparable, when those students come from similar middle-class backgrounds and take the test under identical test conditions. Students from different groups taking a test may have quite different expectations for the consequences of a particular score on the test (and also for the consequences of academic success). Recent social psychological theories explain how those different expectations alter performance on standardized tests.

Expectancies, Self-Esteem, and Self-Efficacy

Rosenthal and Jacobson (1968) demonstrated a Pygmalion effect in the classroom. Researchers led teachers to believe that some of their students were likely to "bloom" intellectually during the coming school year. At the end of the school year, those students whom teachers expected to show greater intellectual improvement did show significantly greater gains on a mental ability test than did "non-bloomers." Hundreds of studies have since reported expectancy effects in various social situations although the size of the effect remains unknown (Rosenthal & Rubin, 1978; Rosenthal, 1994). Moreover, the extent to which teacher expectancies can influence student scores on mental ability tests remains in doubt (Snow, 1995).

The expectations that individuals have for their own performance may also affect scores on mental ability tests. Social disadvantage could lead to lower ability test scores by adversely affecting self-esteem or self-efficacy. Bandura proposed that self-esteem and especially self-efficacy could improve perform-ance by increasing persistence and reducing anxiety (Bandura, 1986). How-ever, researchers have found no effect of self-esteem on achievement test scores (Maruyama, Rubin, & Kingsbury, 1981) and only small self-efficacy effects on standardized test scores in a few studies (Multon, Brown, & Lent, 1991).

The following sections describe recent theories proposing that expecta-tions for self and others about test performance generate patterns of social interaction that facilitate or hamper test performance. Steele (1990) noticed that even the best black students feel ambivalent about academic success. They are as motivated as are white students by the rewards of education, but black students expect more negative consequences as well. Such conflicting expectations could produce both underperformance in school and lower scores on mental ability tests. Mickelson (1990) called it the "attitude-achievement paradox," wherein African-American students are as motivated to succeed academically as are white students, yet black students perform poorly in school and on academic tests. It could be that expectations about the personal consequences of a test score, rather than expectations about personal ability, explain differences in cognitive performance between social groups.

Stereotype Threat: The Expected Negative Consequences of Low Test Scores

Steele (1999) proposed that members of different social groups can experience a situation differently although it appears the same to an outside observer. *Stereotype threat* exists for members of a negatively stereotyped group in situations where others' judgments or their own actions can confirm a negative stereotype (Steele, 1997). For example, black students taking a mental ability test risk confirming the stereotype that African Americans have low academic ability. Steele and Aronson (1995) proposed that the threat of confirming a negative stereotype could distract black students and lower their scores on an academic test.

Steele's (1997, 1999) theory proposes two different ways that expectations can lower test scores of negatively stereotyped students. First, a student can identify with the negative stereotype making it difficult to overcome. Ogbu (1986; Ogbu & Simons, 1998) has a related explanation; a black identity may require opposition to success in school. Little research directly assesses the effect of identity on cognitive performance. Researchers have analyzed data from the National Education Longitudinal Study (NELS), some finding no evidence of an oppositional culture while others using different techniques disagree (Farkas, Lleras, & Maczuga, 2002; Ainsworth-Darnell & Downey, 1998). In this chapter, we develop a theory that explains the process through which identity impacts cognitive performance and propose a method to test that theory.

Most theoretical development and testing of stereotype threat focuses on the negative impact of a stereotype on those students who *do not* identify with the stereotype and who *do* identify themselves as good students. Steele (1997, 1999) proposed that resisting the stereotype creates concern about confirming it. Pressure to succeed then becomes more intense for negatively stereotyped students striving to disconfirm the stereotype. Increased pressure to succeed might then distract students from performing up to their potential.

Research has consistently supported the proposed effects of stereotype threat on standardized test scores. Negatively stereotyped students scored higher when stereotype threat was reduced (Steele & Aronson, 1995, Aronson, Quinn, & Spencer, 1998). A particularly dramatic study compared the performance of Asian-American and European-American women on a math test, because AsianAmericans are positively stereotyped with respect to mathematical ability, but women are negatively stereotyped with respect to math. Shih, Pittinsky, and Ambady (1999) found that making female identity salient lowered women's scores on a difficult math test, while making Asian identity salient increased them.

Stereotype threat is thought to impair test performance by creating anxiety, intensifying frustration with difficult test problems, and distracting students from concentrating on the test (Steele & Aronson, 1995). Thus, stereotype threat predicts lower scores when students know that they are negatively stereotyped and are challenged with difficult test problems. Stereotype threat is situational; it can occur whenever people know that a stereotype applies to them (Steele, 1997). They need not have identified with the negative stereotype nor have experienced it in the past. If students expect that a poor performance on the test will subject them to negative evaluation and confirm the stereotype, then their performance is likely to suffer. That is, expecting negative consequences from poor performance reduces test scores.

Differential Expected Consequences: The Expected Negative Consequences of High Test Scores

In addition to the negative consequences expected by negatively stereotyped students when threatened by poor test performance, they may also expect negative consequences if they score higher than others expect they should (Lovaglia & Lucas, 1997; Lovaglia, Lucas, Houser, Thye, & Markovsky, 1998; Lovaglia et al., 2004). This cognitive double bind could produce mental and emotional turmoil that would be especially distracting to black students caught in it (Steele, 1990).

Negative stereotypes with respect to mental ability are associated with low status. Berger, Fisek, Norman, and Zeldtich (1977) developed the theory that status in groups is related to expectations formed by self and others for the contributions members will make to group goals. Negative stereotypes with respect to mental ability would seem likely to result in reduced expectations for competent contributions to a group and consequently lower status.

The self-fulfilling nature of the status process works to enhance the performances of high-status individuals and detract from the performances of low-status individuals. Those with high status are evaluated more positively for their performances than are those with low status (Berger et al., 1977; Lucas & Lovaglia, 1998). Thus, in test situations, high-status individuals may have higher self-efficacy than low-status individuals. Moreover, status processes produce a social structure that provides rewards based on status (Berger, Fisek, Norman, & Wagner, 1985). Those with high status come to expect high rewards for a competent performance. Those with low status not only expect low rewards, but may anticipate punishment for competent performances that challenge an existing status hierarchy (Berger, Ridgeway, Fisek, & Norman, 1998; Meeker & Weitzel-O'Neill, 1977; Ridgeway & Berger, 1986, 1988). Low-status test takers may consciously try to overcome low expectations and get the highest possible score. Nonetheless, the expectation of negative consequences could distract them from concentrating on the test, impairing their performance (Lovaglia et al., 1998).

Several laboratory studies suggest a role for status processes in the performance of cognitive tasks. Jemmott and Gonzalez (1989) found that grade school children randomly assigned to a low-status condition performed less well on an anagram task than did children assigned to a high-status condition. Lucas (1999) randomly assigned participants to high- and low-status positions in a work group, then participants completed an individual task alone that was expected to be relevant to subsequent group work. Participants assigned high status performed better on the individual task than did participants assigned low status. Lovaglia et al. (1998) proposed that status processes constrain individual performances when those performances are expected to have an impact on the relative status of the performer when working on *future* collective tasks.

Research also suggests that students may be penalized for demonstrating more competence than their low status would lead others to expect. In the Pygmalion study of teacher expectancies, teachers judged students unfavorably who performed above what teachers expected of them (Rosenthal, 1994). In a follow-up to the Pygmalion study, student teachers were given reports of their students' standardized test scores that randomly assigned scores in the "gifted" range to some students. Student teachers were more likely to criticize African-American students they thought were "gifted" but more likely to praise European-American students they thought were "gifted" (Rubovits & Maehr, 1973). Also, a low-status individual may identify with the expectation of poor performance and find the prospect of a high test score distressing (Ralph & Mineka, 1998). In a survey of university student attitudes, Thompkins, Lucas, Thye, and Lovaglia (1999) found that African-American students were as motivated as European-American students, but nonetheless expected more negative consequences to result from academic success than did European-American students.

The theory of differential expected consequences proposes impaired test performance for students who expect negative consequences from a high test score as well as from a low test score. Lovaglia et al. (2004) designed a study with a condition that isolated the expected negative consequences of low test scores consistent with stereotype threat. They found that students randomly assigned to a negative stereotype and associated negative expected consequences scored lower on a standard mental ability test than did students assigned a positive stereotype. Negatively stereotyped students scored even lower in another condition, which added expected negative consequences of a high test score to the design. Thus, the proposed effects of both stereotype threat and differential consequences were found to occur under laboratory conditions (see Lovaglia, 2003).

In the following section, we explicate the role of identity in cognitive performance. Stereotype threat and differential expected consequences explain how test performances that can enhance or reduce an individual's social position affect cognitive performance. In contrast, identity has the potential to explain effects on cognitive performance in situations where a test score will *not* impact an individual's position in the social hierarchy.

RELEVANT IDENTITY THEORY AND RESEARCH

Despite the success of stereotype threat and differential expected consequences in explaining some racial and gender differences in academic performance, they do not tell the complete story. The negative expected consequences of academic performance proposed by both theories are factors external to the individual. Their theoretical scope contains all students who are aware that a negative stereotype applies to them and expect it to shape the consequences of their performances. That is, the stereotype need not have been internalized as part of their self-concept. Internal motivation, however, has long been associated with academic success; optimal academic performance is largely self-motivated (Fair & Silvestri, 1992). Thus theories of the self and especially of the identities that the self comprises may provide a powerful means to understand differences in academic performance.

In summarizing their related programs of theoretical development and research on identity, Stryker and Burke (2000, p. 284) term identity as "those parts of a self composed of the meanings that persons attach to the multiple roles they typically play in highly differentiated contemporary societies." Stryker (1968) used George Herbert Mead's conceptions of self and society to develop a testable theory of identity. Mead (1934) had suggested that society and the individual selves that society comprises form a system in which society shapes the self-concepts of individuals, which then shape their social behavior. Our research question is grounded in this fundamental conception of a self comprising identities that generate behavior with important social consequences for individuals. We ask how identities shape cognitive performance.

The difficulty in formulating a testable theory of self centers on the enormous complexity of the phenomenon. The self changes as individuals' conceptions of themselves vary depending on the shifting social contexts in which they interact. The shifting nature of self makes it difficult to isolate and measure. The multiplex nature of self further complicates investigation because one person's self can comprise many identities. An identity is a facet of the self that becomes evident when an individual enacts a role in a particular social context. Identities depend on the position occupied by an individual with respect to others with whom she interacts. Thus, an individual can have many identities that vary from mutually reinforcing to contradictory (Stryker & Burke, 2000). Each identity can also shift and vary in its importance to an individual depending on the social context while exhibiting considerable stability in similar social contexts over time. The result is self composed of a hierarchy of identities. An identity more important to the self would be more likely to be enacted across situations. Predicting how individuals manage their identities to choose a particular behavior that enacts a role associated with a particular identity in a particular situation became the daunting research problem for identity theory (Stryker, 1968, 1980).

More formally, *identities* are defined as the shared social meanings, internalized by individuals, about themselves and their behavior in their various social roles (Burke & Reitzes, 1991; Stryker & Burke, 2000). *Salience* is the term used for the relative importance of the identity to the self compared to other identities. In the self's hierarchy of identities, an identity ranked higher is more salient and thus more likely to generate behavior that supports it than some alternative identity.

In identity research, an individual's commitment to an identity has been found to be an important component of salience (Burke & Reitzes, 1991). Identity *commitment* "refers to the degree to which persons' relationships to others in their networks depend on possessing a particular identity," and is measurable as the perceived cost of losing meaningful relationships that would occur in the absence of the identity (Stryker & Burke, 2000, p. 286). The more embedded is an individual in a network of relationships that commit the individual to an identity, the more salient that identity is expected to be. The theory also proposes that individuals strive to successfully perform those identities most salient to them and to which they are most committed (Stryker, 1968, 1980; Burke, 1991; Stryker & Burke, 2000).

Identity control theory extends identity theory by specifying a process through which identities motivate actions that sustain the identity (Burke, 1991,1997; Burke & Reitzes, 1991). An identity is composed of an *identity standard*, the internalized self-meanings about what is required for an individual to enact that identity, and *situational meanings*, the interpretations of information coming from the environment that individuals use to compare their role performance of that identity with the identity standard.

Analogous to the thermostatic system that controls home heating and cooling, the identity process operates to maintain stable identities. A home thermostat compares temperature information from a thermometer to the temperature standard that has been set. If the temperature sensed by the thermostat falls below the temperature standard, then a switch activates the furnace which heats the house until the thermometer senses that the temperature is above the temperature standard, at which point the switch deactivates the furnace.

In identity control theory, individuals interpret input from the environment – such as SAT scores – to create situational meanings that they compare with their internalized identity standard, and then behave in ways to reduce any discrepancy between the identity standard and information about the self that they receive from the environment. The more salient is the identity and the more commitment there is to the identity, the more pronounced should be behavior that reaffirms that identity (Burke & Reitzes, 1991). People who see themselves as dominant, for example, when given evidence that they are actually submissive, then act in an even more dominant manner; conversely, submissive people when given evidence that they are dominant, respond with increased submissiveness (Swann & Hill, 1982).

Affect control theory's more general explanation of face-to-face interaction includes an identity maintenance theory based on the same control imagery as identity control theory (Heise, 1979, 1985; Smith-Lovin & Heise, 1988). The control process is modeled in affect control theory by an assumption that individuals behave to maintain meanings associated with their understanding of a social situation. Actors assign meanings to the various elements of a social situation by defining them symbolically. The assumption of affect control – meaning maintenance – implies that once a configuration of labels has been assigned to a situation, an actor will strive to maintain the meanings associated with that configuration of labels and will produce behavior consistent with those meanings. In other words, once an actor defines a situation using symbols that have social meaning, he or she behaves in a way that supports this assigned meaning. Thus, affective meanings associated with the initial definition of a social situation become a point of reference to be confirmed. When social events create new *transient* meanings within the situation, the difference between the *fundamental* reference meanings and these *transient* meanings motivates new behaviors that bring transient meanings back closer to fundamental meanings. This difference between fundamental meanings and situation-induced transient meanings is the motivating state, and is called *deflection*. Deflection represents the amount of disruption in meanings produced by the current interaction. It is experienced by actors as a sense of "unlikelihood" (Heise & MacKinnon, 1988; MacKinnon & Heise, 1993).

Both affect control theory and identity control theory offer the counterintuitive implication that individuals will act to counter feedback that appears to disconfirm an identity, "even if that feedback is more positive than their identity" (Burke, 1991, p. 839). Robinson and Smith-Lovin (1992) used an experimental approach to discover whether individuals choose to interact with partners who confirm or disconfirm their identities. Students in this study were faced with another student who either confirmed or disconfirmed their own self-evaluations on a dispositional identity (sociability). These researchers found that participants who thought of themselves as highly socially skilled chose to interact with partners who agreed with them. Likewise, participants who self-labeled as socially unskilled were more likely to choose partners who evaluated the participant's social skills negatively. That is, Robinson and Smith-Lovin (1992) found evidence that individuals' identities motivated them to create further interactions that would confirm those identities, even when those identities were negative.

Standardized tests are an important setting in which role performances are enacted because failure and success have implications for identity (Burke, 1991). These tests are developed and used to capture ability differences under the assumption that individuals strive for the highest possible score. However, identity maintenance theories predict that when test scores are part of an identity, an individual is also motivated to score not as high as possible, but rather at a level that would optimally affirm the identity.

IDENTITY CONTROL THEORY IN
A PERFORMANCE SETTING

Taking an aptitude test – whether measuring academic ability in general like the SAT or more specific aptitude for a particular occupation – represents a performance with the potential to alter an identity. For example, suppose a senior in high school strongly identifies with being a good student, the identity is important to her compared to her other identities. In identity theory terms, it is highly salient. That salience is reinforced by her commitment to the identity as indicated by her family and friends who have supported and encouraged her academic success. She might have difficulty imagining what her parents might think of her if she brought home a C, an event that has probably never occurred. The prospect of taking the SAT to get into a good college will likely put pressure on her to do well on the test. That is, the test is so important that doing poorly on it might require her to reassess her identity.

We need to specify how an identity might shift in response to performances that fail to reaffirm it. A single performance may not be sufficient to alter the salience of an individual identity in the long term. If our good student does poorly on the SAT, she may respond by entering the best college she can and working hard to get excellent grades. In doing so, her performances would come to coincide once again with her identity standard. In the period between getting her SAT results and her subsequent success in college classes, she would have felt considerable concern over her identity and whether she would be able to sustain it. That concern could motivate her to study harder. But what if, no matter how hard she studied, her college grades remained barely average? Being a good student might well become less important to her. Some other identity might rise in importance to replace being a good student in her hierarchy of identities. She might also find that family and friends continue to support her despite her poor academic performance. That is, being a good student might become less salient and she might become less committed to it.

Individual performances and their results can represent information from the environment that individuals interpret to create situational meanings that are compared to identity standards. Identity control theory suggests that if an individual cannot change situational meanings to match an identity standard, then the standard will slowly change to match those meanings. Both the identity standard and situational meanings are continually adjusted as information flows in from the environment (Peter Burke, personal communication). The identity standard, however, will change less and more slowly than the situational meanings. More specifically, identity theorists also suggest that people become more committed to identities that they perceive as rewarding (Burke & Reitzes, 1991), that provide positive affect for example (Stryker, 2004). The process may also work in reverse, as when a good student performing poorly in school begins to find the good student identity less rewarding and so becomes less committed to it.

Elaborating on Burke's (1991) control system model of identity, we assume that as a disparity between situational meanings and an identity standard grows or endures over time, the identity standard will shift. Moreover, we assume that as the identity standard shifts, it will pull the identity with it through the hierarchy of identities that compose the self.

For example, an individual with a salient good student identity would feel pressure to perform well when faced with an important test. She would know that her test performance will provide information that she will have to interpret as a situational meaning to compare with her good student identity standard. Doing poorly on the test would then increase the pressure to do better in school. The discrepancy between the situational meaning of a poor test score and the identity standard would create a pressure to resolve it. Eventually, however, if the student continues to perform below the expectations prescribed by the good student identity, the discrepancy may be resolved in another way. We propose that the good student identity will become less salient and she will become less committed to it.

The idea of a shifting identity standard has implications for a poor student identity as well. Suppose an individual identifies himself as a C student, he will feel pressure to perform in ways that maintain his C average, even though he values the rewards that come with high grades and is motivated to attain them. If he gets a B on an exam, then he may be delighted with his success but also uncomfortable with himself. The high exam grade puts pressure on his C-student identity. He may then consciously or unconsciously behave in ways that lead to a D on the next exam, reaffirming his identity. If, despite himself, he continues to get As and Bs in school, then his identity as a C student would become less salient. He would be less committed to his C average and might find it easier to behave in ways that produce higher grades.

Would the committed C student be as discomfited when receiving an A grade on a test as would the A student who gets a C? The answer depends on the relative salience of their various identities as well as external factors and the interactions among identities and external factors. For example, the C student might receive encouragement and other social rewards for getting an A that conflict with his C student identity. Or, he may also hold an identity as a generally competent person who usually performs well, resulting in one identity partially counteracting the other. The following section develops a theory to explain how identities shape cognitive performance.

A THEORY OF IDENTITY MAINTENANCE AND COGNITIVE PERFORMANCE

In explicating these ideas, we use several definitions and assumptions to develop a theory of identity maintenance and performance.

We define *identity concordance* as the degree to which an individual's situational meanings accord with her identity standard. For example, if an individual with a highly salient good student identity is asked how well a list of attributes of good students fits her, she likely will respond that they fit quite well. The theory explains how performances and anticipation of performances relevant to an identity might change that assessment. And as in identity control theory, we assume that the degree of discord between situational meanings and an identity standard motivates performances that can increase concordance.

Assumption 1. (*Identity maintenance*). A reduction in identity concordance pressures individuals to behave in ways that increase concordance.

We further assume that anticipation of a performance relevant to a salient identity decreases identity concordance because the outcome of that performance might require reassessment of the identity. For example, when the good student anticipates taking the SAT, she is aware that a poor performance is possible and might jeopardize her good student identity. At least, she would likely consider the consequences of a low score. How would she tell people? What would they think of her? What would she think of herself? Thus, the prospect of an important performance relevant to an identity promotes consideration of a change in that identity. The discomfort produced by that consideration creates pressure to perform in ways that maintain the identity.

Assumption 2. (*Anticipation of identity performance*). Anticipation of evaluation of a performance relevant to an identity reduces identity concordance.

Assumption 3 states that an outcome of a performance relevant to an identity that does not accord with the identity standard would then put additional pressure on the identity. Information from the environment that is difficult to reconcile with an identity standard may cause more intense discomfort than did the mere anticipation of that information. The good student who receives low SAT scores likely feels intense discomfort because it is so difficult to interpret those scores in ways that sustain her good student identity.

Assumption 3. (*Evaluation of identity performance*). Evaluation of a performance relevant to an identity reduces identity concordance to the extent that it fails to accord with the identity standard.

Following Burke and Reitzes (1991), we define *commitment* as the degree to which a person's relationships with others depend on an identity. We assume that the degree of pressure produced by a reduction in identity concordance also depends on the commitment that an individual has to the identity. For example, individuals who are more committed to their identity as a good student will likely feel pressure to work harder to perform well academically than will individuals who are less committed, who may see little interpersonal cost in abandoning the good student role.

Assumption 4. (*Identity commitment*). The more committed an individual is to an identity, the more motivated she will be to maintain identity concordance.

An alternative way to reduce the pressure of a discordant identity would be to reduce commitment to it. Failed attempts to reaffirm an identity, therefore, are likely to weaken commitment to it.

Assumption 5. (*Identity commitment reduction*). Failed attempts to reduce identity concordance weaken identity commitment.

Multiple Identities, Motivations and Performance

An important assumption of identity theory is that the self consists of multiple identities that can mutually reinforce each other, actively conflict, or range anywhere in between (Stryker & Burke, 2000). Motivation to achieve can also be seen in terms of an identity as a competent person. Moreover, achievement can have many desirable social rewards. When a good student takes the SAT, identity maintenance works to enhance performance. The identity is congruent with achievement. Individuals, however, may have conflicting motivations. Even individuals committed to a C-student identity may well want to get the best score they can on a test. Thus, motivation to achieve can be independent of identity maintenance.

Assumption 6. (*Achievement motivation*). Individuals are motivated to perform well when performances have socially desirable consequences.

Further, an individual also may have two identities that call for different levels of performance. Mickelson's (1990) attitude–achievement paradox reflects the idea that African-American students are at least as motivated to achieve in school as are European-American students and yet, a good student identity can conflict with a positive black identity resulting in reduced academic performance. We assume that how individuals resolve conflicting motivations shapes their performances. More specifically,

Assumption 7. (*Conflicting motivations*). The effects of motivation to achieve and motivation to maintain identity concordance combine to affect performance.

Burke and Tully (1977) assume that identities presuppose counter-identities. For example, the parent identity presupposes the child counter-identity. Performances that reinforce the parent identity may weaken the child counter-identity. A grown woman may feel more like a child when visiting her mother, which may interfere with her identity as a parent when she interacts with her own young daughter. The more the woman reinforces her child identity, the less she reinforces her parent identity. Similarly, a high score on an aptitude test that reinforces a counter-identity would necessarily put pressure on an identity. The degree of pressure seems likely to vary depending on the degree of opposition between identity and counter-identity.

Assumption 8. (*Counter-identity*). Identity concordance will decrease following a performance confirming a counter-identity.

Among occupations, for example, the role of social worker runs counter in many ways to the role of businessperson, although the two occupations are not complete opposites. While a businessperson might see herself as pragmatic, assertive and efficient, a social worker might see herself as a builder of relationships, sensitive, and empathetic. We would predict that the more a person identifies with business, the less she might identify with social work. We would expect that a social worker, when surprised by a high score on a business aptitude test, would exhibit reduced concordance with her social work identity. She might at least consider that she is less suited to be a social worker than she had thought.

Affect Control Theory, Deflection, and EPA Ratings of Self-Concept

Affect control theory, like identity control theory, suggests that individuals will behave in ways that maintain meaning, that reduce the discrepancy between their interpretation of events and the meanings they have associated with social situations (MacKinnon & Heise, 1993). For example, university students are expected to study and do well on tests. A high level of academic performance is the reason they were admitted to the university. We assume that university students will experience more deflection, the sense of "unlikelihood," when they do poorly in school or receive a low score on a test. In contrast, doing well in school or getting a high score on a test is likely to be felt as proper and expected rather than as surprising or unlikely.

> **Assumption 9.** (*Affect differential*). To the extent that individuals identify with the role being evaluated, they will experience more deflection when receiving a lower than expected evaluation than they will when receiving a higher than expected evaluation.

Recall the question about the C student who received an A on a test. In our theory, he holds two partially conflicting identities simultaneously, as a student performing the accepted student role working for a high grade but also more specifically as a C student who rarely performs above average. In his case, the theory predicts that he would feel less discomfited by his A grade than would an A student who received a C. In contrast, those students identified by Ogbu (1978, 1986) as dis-identifying with the student role might well feel worse when their academic performances exceed expectations.

Affect control theory has developed mathematical formulae for predicting how transient meanings and behavior interact to maintain established meanings associated with particular situations (MacKinnon & Heise, 1993). Affect control researchers have compiled dictionaries of meanings surveying numerous individuals to elicit their assessment of various situations, individuals, and behavior on the three dimensions considered fundamental by the theory: Evaluation, Potency, and Activity (EPA). Data from the dictionaries can be analyzed with the mathematical machinery of affect control theory using a computer program called INTERACT, available on the Internet. When an event occurs that creates transient meaning disruptive to established meaning associated with a situation, deflection is indicated by a change in the EPA profile of the individual in that setting (MacKinnon & Heise, 1993).

EPA ratings can be collected from individuals with reference to themselves as well as with reference to others. Assumption 9, then, can be used to predict that self EPA ratings made by university students will be deflected more by a low score on an aptitude test than they will by a high score. Moreover, it seems possible to predict the direction of deflection following a performance. A low score on a test, for example, will likely result in lower evaluation and potency ratings on the EPA scales. Other assumptions of the theory can be used to develop various hypotheses that are equally suited to empirical test.

HYPOTHESES

Using identity control theory and affect control theory and the assumptions developed to apply them in a performance context, we developed a number of hypotheses that link identity with the processes of identity maintenance and performance relevant to that identity. Some, like the deflection of EPA ratings predicted above accord with accepted conceptions of student motivation. Others are more counterintuitive and capable of providing more dramatic tests of the theory.

Assumption 2 – the idea that the mere prospect of having one's aptitude for an identity evaluated puts pressure on the identity, deforming it in anticipation of a possible negative evaluation – is a foundational assumption that to our knowledge appears nowhere else in the research literature on identity. We further assume that when a person anticipates an aptitude test relevant to an identity, the pressure on the identity will decrease the identity's concordance. In contrast, anticipating an aptitude test for a role in accord with a counter-identity is unlikely to put pressure on an existing identity unless a person anticipates doing unusually well in the test, which is also unlikely. Thus, identity concordance would decrease more for a person anticipating a test measuring aptitude for an identity than it would for a person anticipating a test measuring aptitude for a counter-identity. Identity concordance could be measured using individual assessments of how well a description of a particular identity accords with their conception of self.

Hypothesis 1. Anticipation of a standardized test score that participants expect to measure aptitude for an identity will decrease identity concordance more than anticipation of a test score that participants expect to measure aptitude for a counter-identity.

Doing poorly on a test measuring aptitude for an identity would likely further decrease concordance (Assumption 3).

Hypothesis 2. A low score on a standardized test score that participants expect to measure aptitude for their identity will decrease identity concordance more than a low score that participants expect to measure aptitude for a counter-identity.

We assume that students' identities will be more pressured by a low score than they will be by a high score regardless of whether measured aptitude was for an identity or counter-identity. Because students desire to maintain a student identity, we also assume that they would consciously desire a high score on the test regardless of the aptitude it measures (Assumption 6). Thus, the self-concept as measured by the EPA ratings of affect control theory would change more for participants who believed they did poorly on the test than it would for participants who believed they did well on the test (Assumption 9).

Hypothesis 3. EPA ratings of self-concept for participants who believe they did poorly on a standardized test will change more than will the ratings of participants who believe they did well on the test.

To the extent that students identify with the role for which a test measures aptitude, a high score on the test would maintain that identity (Assumption 3). In contrast, students who take a test measuring aptitude in a role constituting a counter-identity have no identity at stake, less expectation that they should do well on it, and less motivation to do well. Further, getting a high score in a test measuring aptitude in a counter-identity could potentially undermine an identity (Assumption 8). And, because students desire to maintain a student identity (Assumption 5), we assume that participants have two motivations working together to produce a high test score when they take a test measuring aptitude in their major. In contrast, when taking a test measuring aptitude in a role constituting a counter-identity, students are ambivalent, having one motivation to score as high as possible and another motivation to avoid a high score. By presenting a neutral mental ability test as one that measures aptitude that either accords with an identity or a counter-identity, we could test Hypothesis 4.

Hypothesis 4. Participants will score higher on a standard mental ability test when it is presented as a test of aptitude in accord with their identity than they will when it is presented as a test of aptitude in a counter-identity.

We also expected that the hypothesized difference in test scores would be greater for participants more committed to the major identity (Assumption 4). Commitment can be measured by scales rating how much an individual's relationships depend on performing a role in accord with an identity.

Hypothesis 5. Participants more committed to an identity will score higher on a test presented as measure of aptitude in their identity than will participants less committed to it.

Testing these and other hypotheses will allow us to assess the validity of the theory.

DISCUSSION AND CONCLUSION

To address the role of identity in cognitive performance, we used identity control theory and affect control theory to develop a general explanation that applies to all role performances. A basic assumption is that individual performances are shaped by the degree to which they are expected to conform to existing identity standards. Role performances have social consequences and are evaluated not just by the performer but also by others. The potential for evaluation puts pressure on individuals to maintain their identities with consonant performances. One implication is that students will perform on cognitive tasks at levels that maintain their identities, and not necessarily to the best of their ability. Students may have conflicting motivations, with the motivation to succeed partially or completely overshadowed by the motivation to maintain a consistent identity that calls for a less successful performance.

Perhaps the most important aspect of the theory is that it accommodates identity change. That is, when evaluated role performances consistently undermine an identity, the underlying identity will gradually shift, becoming less salient in the hierarchy of identities. Other identities that require different performances would become more salient or the underlying identity standard would change. For example, a student might identify herself as an athlete, but does poorly academically. Suppose she is transferred to a new school and was unsure about whether she could perform academically at a sufficient level to remain eligible for sports. She might do her best in school at least until she received enough evaluations to gauge her performance level. Usually, we would expect her academic performance to drift lower until it reached a familiar level consistent with her identity as an athlete. If, however, she continued to be unsure of an adequate level of performance for some time, then her strong academic performances might persist, giving her student identity a chance to become more salient relative to her athlete identity. Or, her athlete identity standard might morph into one that encompasses the concept of student-athlete. Predicting the course of identity change in different contexts and under different kinds of performance pressure is one area of future theoretical development.

Future theoretical development could also address the speed with which identities change. Currently, the theory only proposes a gradual shift in identity brought about by consistent evaluations discrepant from an identity standard. Discovering a process that accelerates identity change could be useful for programs aimed at improving performance. The student-athlete example highlights the effectiveness of isolation from peers in promoting identity change. One reason an athlete at a new school might begin to perform at a higher academic level could be that she is cut off from a peer group capable of informing her of the academic performance standards consonant with being an athlete there. Isolation could be one reason for the effectiveness of boot camps to mold a soldier identity relatively quickly. Factors that seem capable of altering the pace of identity change could be systematically investigated.

The concept of a counter-identity (Burke & Tully, 1977) could open an important avenue for future research on identity change to enhance performance. A counter-identity embodies qualities that are discrepant from an identity. Yet, individuals commonly maintain an identity and a counter-identity simultaneously, student and athlete being one example. Mother and business professional is another. Discovering how identities and counter-identities are managed by an individual could lead to ways to increase the salience of particular aspects of identities in situations where those aspects would contribute to enhanced performance. For example, suppose we could demonstrate that a particular kind of athletic training enhanced both athletic and academic performance., A dedicated athlete would embrace the training regimen as consonant with her athlete identity. Perhaps she also would then accept with little resistance the side effect of improved academic performance.

The complex interaction among emotional states and identity formation, maintenance, and change is an understudied but fundamental aspect of group processes (Stryker, 2004). Discovering how emotions and identities interact to affect performance represents an even more difficult research problem. Consider, for example, the relatively simple case of basic arousal as a motivator for cognitive performance. If a student's identity required opposition to academic goals, then he might be bored and lethargic during tests, unable to concentrate long enough to get correct answers. More aroused students would seem likely to perform better. Stereotype threat research, however, has shown that students threatened with confirming a negative stereotype in test situations perform less well precisely because they are more aroused than in the absence of stereotype threat (Croizet et al., 2004). Moreover, there is evidence that manipulating the emotions of students might ameliorate the negative effects of stereotype threat. Researchers found that women who were more likely to use humor as a coping mechanism performed better on a challenging quantitative test in the presence of stereotype threat than did women less likely to use humor to cope (Ford, Ferguson, Brooks, & Hagadone, 2004). They also found that state anxiety moderated the effect. That is, women high in coping humor who were more anxious about the test were more impaired by stereotype threat than those who were less anxious. Perhaps individuals can use humor to manage their emotions in ways that facilitate performance in stressful situations. We might further suggest that humor or other emotional interventions could affect identity formation, maintenance, and change with consequences for the performance of roles associated with identities. These intriguing speculations emphasize the need for more research.

REFERENCES

Ainsworth-Darnell, J. W., & Downey, D. B. (1998). Assessing racial/ethnic differences in school performance. *American Sociological Review, 63*, 536–553.

Aronson, J. D., Quinn, M., & Spencer, S. J. (1998). Stereotype threat and the academic underperformance of minorities and women. In: J. Swim & C. Stangor (Eds), *Prejudice: The target's perspective* (pp. 83–103). San Diego: Academic Press.

Bandura, A. (1986). *Foundations of thought and action*. Englewood Cliffs, NJ: Prentice-Hall.

Berger, J., Fisek, M. H., Norman, R. Z., & Zelditch, M., Jr. (1977). *Status characteristics and social interaction: An expectation states approach*. New York: Elsevier.

Berger, J., Fisek, M. H., Norman, R. Z., & Wagner, D. (1985). Formation of reward expectations in status situations. In: J. Berger & M. Zelditch Jr. (Eds), *Status, rewards, and influence* (pp. 215–261). San Francisco: Jossey-Bass.

Berger, J., Ridgeway, C. L., Fisek, M. H., & Norman, R. Z. (1998). The legitimation and delegitimation of power and prestige orders. *American Sociological Review, 63*, 379–405.

Bouchard, T. J., Jr., Lykken, D. T., McGue, M., Segal, N. L., & Tellegen, A. (1990). Sources of human psychological differences: The Minnesota study of twins reared apart. *Science, 250*, 223–228.

Burke, P. J. (1991). Identity processes and social stress. *American Sociological Review, 56*, 536–849.

Burke, P. J. (1997). An identity model of network exchange. *American Sociological Review, 62*, 134–150.

Burke, P. J., & Reitzes, D. C. (1981). The link between identity and role performance. *Social Psychology Quarterly, 44,* 83–92.

Burke, P. J., & Reitzes, D. C. (1991). An identity theory approach to commitment. *Social Psychology Quarterly, 54,* 239–251.

Burke, P. J., & Stets, J. E. (1999). Trust and commitment through self-verification. *Social Psychology Quarterly, 62,* 347–366.

Burke, P. J., & Tully, J. C. (1977). The measurement of role identity. *Social Forces, 55,* 881–897.

Chipuer, H. M., Rovine, M. J., & Plomin, R. (1990). LISREL modeling: Genetic and environmental influences on IQ revisited. *Intelligence, 14,* 11–29.

Croizet, J., Despres, G., Gauzins, M., Huguet, P., Leyens, J., & Meot, A. (2004). Stereotype threat undermines intellectual performance by triggering a disruptive mental load. *Personality and Social Psychology Bulletin, 30,* 721–731.

Damasio, A. R. (1994). *Descartes' error: Emotion, reason, and the human brain.* New York: Putnam.

Eysenck, H. J., & Kamin, L. (1981). *The intelligence controversy.* New York: Wiley.

Fair, E. M., & Silvestri, L. (1992). Effects of rewards, competition and outcome on intrinsic motivation. *Journal of Instructional Psychology, 19,* 3–8.

Farkas, G., Lleras, C., & Maczuga, S. (2002). Does oppositional culture exist in minority and poverty peer groups. *American Sociological Review, 67,* 148–155.

Ford, T. E., Ferguson, M. A., Brooks, J. L., & Hagadone, K. M. (2004). Coping sense of humor reduces effects of stereotype threat on women's math performance. *Personality and Social Psychology Bulletin, 30,* 643–653.

Gardner, H. (1983). *Frames of mind: The theory of multiple intelligences.* New York: Basic Books.

Hedges, L. V., & Nowell, A. (1998). Black–white test score convergence since 1965. In: C. Jencks & M. Phillips (Eds), *The black-white test score gap* (pp. 149–181). Washington, DC: Brookings Institution Press.

Heise, D. R. (1979). *Understanding events: Affect and the construction of social action.* New York: Cambridge University Press.

Heise, D. R. (1985). Affect control theory: Respecification, estimation and tests of the formal model. *Journal of Mathematical Sociology, 11,* 191–222.

Heise, D. R., & MacKinnon, N. J. (1988). Affective bases of likelihood judgments. In: L. Smith-Lovin & D. R. Heise (Eds), *Analyzing social interaction: Advances in affect control theory* (pp. 133–152). New York: Gordon and Breach.

Herrnstein, R. J., & Murray, C. (1994). *The bell curve: Intelligence and class structure in American life.* New York: Free Press.

Jemmott, J. B., III, & Gonzalez, E. (1989). Social status, the status distribution, and performance in small groups. *Journal of Applied Social Psychology, 19,* 584–598.

Jencks, C., & Phillips, M. (Eds) (1998). *The black-white test score gap.* Washington, DC: Brookings Institution Press.

Jensen, A. R. (1992). Spearman's hypothesis: Methodology and evidence. *Multivariate Behavioral Research, 27,* 225–233.

Loehlin, J. C. (1989). Partitioning environmental and genetic contributions to behavioral development. *American Psychologist, 44,* 1285–1292.

Loehlin, J. C., Lindzey, G., & Spuhler, J. N. (1975). *Race differences in intelligence.* San Francisco: Freeman.

Lovaglia, M. J. (2003). From summer camps to glass ceilings: The power of experiments. *Contexts, 2*(4), 42–49.

Lovaglia, M. J., & Lucas, J. W. (1997). Group processes and individual scores on standardized tests: A theoretical note and basis for investigation. *Current Research in Social Psychology, 2*, 1–13 http://www.uiowa.edu/~grpproc.

Lovaglia, M. J., Lucas, J. W., Houser, J. A., Thye, S. R., & Markovsky, B. (1998). Status processes and mental ability test scores. *American Journal of Sociology, 104*, 195–228.

Lovaglia, M. J., Youngreen, R., Lucas, J. W., Nath, L. E., Rutstrom, E., & Willer, D. (2004). Stereotype threat and differential expected consequences: Explaining group differences in mental ability test scores. *Sociological Focus, 37*, 107–125.

Lucas, J. W. (1999). Behavioral and emotional outcomes of leadership in task groups. *Social Forces, 78*, 747–776.

Lucas, J. W., & Lovaglia, M. J. (1998). Leadership status, gender, group size, and emotion in face-to-face groups. *Sociological Perspectives, 41*, 617–637.

MacKinnon, N. J. (1994). *Symbolic interactionism as affect control.* Albany, NY: State University of New York Press.

MacKinnon, N. J., & Heise, D. R. (1993). Affect control theory: Delineation and development. In: J. Berger & M. Zelditch Jr. (Eds), *Theoretical research programs: Studies in theory growth* (pp. 64–103). Stanford, CA: Stanford University Press.

Maruyama, G., Rubin, R. A., & Kingsbury, G. G. (1981). Self-esteem and educational achievement: Independent constructs with a common cause? *Journal of Personality and Social Psychology, 40*, 962–975.

Mead, G. H. (1934). *Mind, self, and society.* Chicago: University of Chicago Press.

Meeker, B. F., & Weitzel-O'Neill, P. A. (1977). Sex roles and interpersonal behavior in task-oriented groups. *American Sociological Review, 42*, 91–105.

Mickelson, R. A. (1990). The attitude-achievement paradox among black adolescents. *Sociology of Education, 63*, 44–61.

Multon, K. D., Brown, S. D., & Lent, R. W. (1991). Relation of self-efficacy beliefs to academic outcomes: A meta-analytic investigation. *Journal of Counseling Psychology, 38*, 30–38.

Neisser, U., Boodoo, G., Bouchard, T. J., Jr., Boykin, A. W., Brody, N., Ceci, S. J., Halpern, D. F., Loehlin, J. C., Perloff, R., Sternberg, R. J., & Urbina, S. (1996). Intelligence: Knowns and unknowns. *American Psychologist, 51*, 77–101.

Ogbu, J. U. (1978). *Minority education and caste: The American system in cross-cultural perspective.* Burlington, MA: Academic Press.

Ogbu, J. U. (1986). The consequences of the American caste system. In: U. Neisser (Ed.), *The school achievement of minority children: New perspectives* (pp. 19–56). Hillsdale, NJ: Erlbaum.

Ogbu, J. U., & Simons, H. D. (1998). Voluntary and involuntary minorities: A cultural-ecological theory of school performance with some implications for education. *Anthropology and Education Quarterly, 29*, 155–188.

Plomin, R., & Daniels, D. (1987). Why are children in the same family so different from one another? *Behavioral and Brain Sciences, 10*, 1–16.

Ralph, J. A., & Mineka, S. (1998). Attributional style and self-esteem: The prediction of emotional distress following a midterm exam. *Journal of Abnormal Psychology, 107*, 203–215.

Ridgeway, C., & Berger, J. (1986). Expectation, legitimation, and dominance behavior in task groups. *American Sociological Review, 51*, 603–617.

Ridgeway, C., & Berger, J. (1988). The legitimation of power and prestige orders in task groups. In: M. Webster Jr. & M. Foschi (Eds), *Status generalization: New theory and research* (pp. 207–231). Stanford, CA: Stanford University Press.

Robinson, D., & Smith-Lovin, L. (1992). Selective interaction as a strategy for identity maintenance: An affect control model. *Social Psychology Quarterly, 55*, 12–28.

Rodgers, J. L., Rowe, D. C., & May, K. (1994). DF analysis of NLSY IQ/achievement data: Nonshared environmental Influences. *Intelligence, 19*, 157–177.

Rosenthal, R. (1994). Interpersonal expectancy effects: A 30-year perspective. *Current Directions in Psychological Science, 3*, 176–179.

Rosenthal, R., & Jacobson, L. (1992[1968]). *Pygmalion in the classroom.* New York: Irvington.

Rosenthal, R., & Rubin, D. B. (1978). Interpersonal expectancy effects: The first 345 studies. *Behavioral and Brain Sciences, 3*, 377–386.

Rubovits, P., & Maehr, M. L. (1973). Pygmalion in black and white. *Journal of Personality and Social Psychology, 25*, 210–218.

Scarr, S. (1997). Behavior-genetic and socialization theories of intelligence: Truce and reconciliation. In: R. J. Sternberg & E. Grigorenko (Eds), *Intelligence, heredity, and environment* (pp. 3–41). New York: Cambridge University Press.

Scarr, S., & Weinberg, R. A. (1978). The influence of 'family background' on intellectual attainment. *American Sociological Review, 43*, 674–692.

Scarr, S., Weinberg, R. A., & Waldman, I. D. (1993). IQ correlations in transracial adoptive families. *Intelligence, 17*, 541–555.

Schiff, M., Duyme, M., Dumaret, A., Stewart, J., Tomkiewicz, S., & Feingold, F. (1978). Intellectual status of working-class children adopted early into upper-middle-class families. *Science, 200*, 1503–1504.

Shih, M., Pittinsky, T. L., & Ambady, N. (1999). Stereotype susceptibility: Identity salience and shifts in quantitative performance. *Psychological Science, 10*, 80–83.

Smith-Lovin, L. (1987). Impressions from events. *Journal of Mathematical Sociology, 13*(1–2), 35–70.

Smith-Lovin, L., & Heise, D. R. (Eds) (1988). *Analyzing social interaction: Advances in affect control theory.* New York: Gordon and Breach.

Snow, R. E. (1995). Pygmalion and intelligence? *Current Directions in Psychological Science, 4*, 169–171.

Steele, C. M. (1997). A threat in the air: How stereotypes shape intellectual identity and performance. *American Psychologist, 52*, 613–629.

Steele, C. M. (1999). Thin ice: 'Stereotype threat' and black college students. *Atlantic Monthly, August*, 44–54.

Steele, C. M., & Aronson, J. (1995). Stereotype threat and the intellectual test performance of African-Americans. *Journal of Personality and Social Psychology, 69*, 797–811.

Steele, S. (1990). *The content of our character.* New York: St. Martin's.

Sternberg, R. J. (1985). *Beyond IQ: A triarchic theory of human intelligence.* New York: Cambridge University Press.

Sternberg, R. J., Wagner, R. K., Williams, W. M., & Horvath, J. A. (1995). Testing common sense. *American Psychologist, 50*, 912–927.

Stryker, S. (1968). Identity salience and role performance. *Journal of Marriage and the Family, 4*, 558–564.

Stryker, S. (1980). *Symbolic interactionism: A social structural version.* Menlo Park, CA: Cummings.

Stryker, S. (2004). Integrating emotion into identity theory. In: J. H. Turner (Ed.), *Advances in group processes*, (Vol. 20, pp. 1–23). New York: Elsevier.

Stryker, S., & Burke, P. J. (2000). The past, present, and future of an identity theory. *Social Psychology Quarterly*, *63*, 284–287.

Stryker, S., & Serpe, R. T. (1982). Commitment, identity salience, and role behavior: A theory and research example. In: W. Ickes & E. S. Knowles (Eds), *Personality, roles and social behavior* (pp. 199–218). New York: Springer.

Swann, W. B., Jr., & Hill, C. A. (1982). When our identities are mistaken: Reaffirming self-conceptions through social interaction. *Journal of Personality and Social Psychology*, *43*, 59–66.

Thompkins, D., Lucas, J. W., Thye, S. R., & Lovaglia, M. J. (1999). Race and the cost of academic success. Presented to the Annual Meeting of the American Sociological Association, August, Chicago, IL.

MAKING GOOD ON A PROMISE: THE IMPACT OF LARGER SOCIAL STRUCTURES ON COMMITMENTS

Sheldon Stryker, Richard T. Serpe and
Matthew O. Hunt

ABSTRACT

*We present here research on the impact of three levels of social structure –
large-scale, intermediate, and proximate – on commitment to three types
of role-related relationships: family, work, and voluntary associational.
This research is carried out using data from a sample survey of Whites,
Blacks, and Latinos drawn from a five-county area of southern California.
The central problem of this paper is to explicate the social structural
sources of commitment to social network relationships. Our interest in
this problem arises out of earlier work on Identity Theory.*

THEORETICAL AND CONCEPTUAL CONTEXT

Identity Theory and Structural Symbolic Interactionism

Identity theory (Stryker, 1980, 2000) is premised on a conception of self as
comprised of multiple identities tied to interaction in organized networks of

Social Identification in Groups
Advances in Group Processes, Volume 22, 93–123
ISSN: 0882-6145/doi:10.1016/S0882-6145(05)22004-0

social relationships. The theory intends to explain choices made when persons are confronted with alternative action possibilities deriving from role expectations linked to positions in organized social relationships. It sees choice as a function of *identity salience* which in turn is seen as a function of *commitment*.[1] Identity salience is conceptualized as the readiness to enact an identity as a consequence of its properties as a cognitive schema (Stryker & Serpe, 1994), and thereby, the probability of invocation of various identities in or across situations.[2] Commitment is conceptualized as strength of ties to others in networks of social relationships in which persons participate on the basis of positions occupied, roles played and identities assumed (Serpe & Stryker, 1993). The operational referent of commitment is the costs – personal and social – of not fulfilling a role based on a given identity, and so foregoing ties to others premised on that role and identity.

From the standpoint of the structural symbolic interactionist framework (Stryker, 1980) from which identity theory derives, commitments are "lower-level" social structures. They are defined in terms of social relationships – specifically, ties to others in social networks. While commitments are to role relationships, identity salience involves the internalization of meanings in the form of role expectations. The costs which measure commitments are both interactional and affective. The basic identity theory proposition is that variations in commitment lead to variations in identity salience lead to variations in choices among role-related behaviors in situations where multiple possibilities for action exist. This proposition expresses the sociological axiom[3] that social ties are basic to social action. It is a specification of the general symbolic interactionist proposition, drawn from Mead (1934), that society shapes self shapes behavior.

Structural symbolic interactionism accentuates the contribution of sociology to social psychology, asserting the obligation of sociologists researching social psychological processes to further understanding of how social structures impact those processes. The conceptual stress on and causal priority assigned commitment by identity theory reflect the framework by arguing the social rootedness (in networks of relationships) of emergent self-cognitions and the impact of self-cognitions on subsequent behaviors.

Past presentations of identity theory and its underlying framework (see, e.g., Stryker, 1980, 2000) have argued that "larger" social structures represented by such conventional terms as race/ethnicity, gender, SES, and age impact the social psychological process outlined by identity theory. They do so by affecting the probability of persons entering the social relationships to which the concept of commitment ultimately refers (Serpe & Stryker, 1993). Entailed is a sense of larger social structures of whatever kind as boundaries making it more or less likely that persons in particular social locations will enter particular social relationships with particular agendas, symbolic systems (e.g., specifications of the meanings of roles and selves), and resources. Further, the structural symbolic interactionist frame argues that persons' location in larger social structures impacts the identity process through commitment.[4]

Refining the Concept of Social Structure

Evaluation of this structural symbolic interactionist and identity theory argument was a central aim of this research. An auxiliary aim was developing the argument by refining its conceptualization of social structure. Extant discussions do not specify the concept of social structure in a way that enables close depiction of what social structures have what impact on commitments under what circumstances. This paper introduces a set of such refinements. It retains the language of "large" social structure for features of the stratification system of the society as a whole: age, gender, race/ethnicity, gender, socio-economic status (SES). These are generic boundaries which, research has shown, make it more likely that social relationships will form between and among persons sharing a given stratification characteristic than those not sharing the characteristic.[5]

Contrasting with such structures are some more "intermediate" in character relative to the large structures referred above. Some are more intermediate because they are more "localized"; some because they are more "associational".[6] Examples of more local social structures are neighborhoods, schools, and other organized social units which bring sizable sets of persons together in one setting, thus increasing the probability of relationships forming or being maintained. Entities such as neighborhoods and schools bound possibilities for social relationships in the same sense that race/ethnicity, gender, and SES bound such possibilities. By virtue of the propinquity they involve, they are closer to actual arenas of relationships and interaction *per se* than are the generic stratification features of a society. Beyond propinquity, however, local structures systematically involve their participants in interactions and relationships in a way that that persons sharing age, gender, race/ethnic or class "membership" does not.

The present research does not incorporate variables directly reflecting subjects' locations in such "local" structures.[7] However, associational structure is to some degree linked to locality, and is represented in the work reported here. This kind of structure is exemplified by what we call

"Structural Overlap" (SO)[8] and "Ethnic Homogeneity," the referents of which are ways that persons link to smaller, highly distinctive sets of social relationships, That is, associational structures differ from the stratification features of society in an important way: they involve patterned relationship across role areas. SO refers to the degree to which relationships across role areas are to the same persons (i.e., whether persons one relates to through work are the same persons one relates to in the context of voluntary associations, etc.); EH refers to the degree to which relationships across role areas are to persons of the same ethnic background as the respondent. Both SO and EH represent social boundaries, where each makes more or less probable that contacts are limited to particular kinds of persons; and each of these structures makes more or less probable the development of particular relationships and patterns of interaction.[9]

Beyond the levels of large and intermediate social structure in which persons are located, there is a third level we have labeled "proximate" to suggest even greater relative closeness to commitments themselves. The variable in the current research representing the proximate level we call social embeddedness. This variable is based on information we have about subjects' degree of commitment to each of the three networks of relationships – family, work, voluntary association – in which all persons in our restricted sample are implicated (more on this point below). Embeddedness is thus a structure of multiple "other" commitments proximate to the commitment that is of immediate concern. The premise underlying social embeddedness is that the level of commitment to one social network may have an important impact on the level of commitment to another social network of interest.

The focus of our analyses, given the data available, is the impact (if any) of the "larger" levels of social structure on commitment to three role-based relationships. It is also on the impact (again, if any) of the large social structures on the "lower" level structures and through these on commitment. Of course, we are also interested in which social structures have particular impact on which commitments. Finally, we are interested in whether the commitments of Whites, Blacks, and Latinos are impacted in comparable or different ways by any of the social structures under consideration.

We examine the impact of these levels of social structure on relationships having to do with family, work, and voluntary associations. These were selected because both family and work have been the topics of prior identity theory analyses whereas voluntary associations has not, and because we wanted to assure that reasonable proportions of our subjects were involved in the relationships examined. Again, large structures include age, gender, race/ethnicity, and SES. Intermediate structures include EH and SO. The level of proximate structures, social embeddedness, is represented by commitments to other than the particular role-based relationship under scrutiny.

Research Questions and General Expectations

As a precursor to pursuing our interest in relationships between larger social structures and commitment, we first explore whether presence in familial, work, and voluntary associational relationships is affected by location in the larger social structures. On the basis of findings of prior demographic research, we expect some, though not necessarily strong, relationship between persons' location in large-scale social structures and whether they are involved at all in the social relationships under study. The model which the foregoing implies is simple: all of the large-scale social structures are presumed to impact in some degree all three forms of involvement. Specifically, race/ethnicity, gender, age, and SES impact the opportunity to form, and so the probability of forming, stable familial or familial-like relationships, employment-based relationships, and voluntary associational relationships. That family (or family-like) relationships are virtually universal in this society implies that there is no variation in involvement *per se* in such; indeed, only 3% of our full sample have no contact with family. Consequently, for this preliminary analysis (reported in Table 2) we have shifted attention in the analysis of involvement in the family to whether or not persons live with at least one other family member.

There is little or no theory or research justifying strong hypotheses relating particular social structures to one another, or to particular commitments as conceptualized in identity theory. However, the logic of the theory does argue that the impact of the effects of large scale structures (not themselves structures of interaction) will channel through the more directly interactional structures. Thus, we do expect that the effects of gender, age, race/ethnicity, and SES will flow through EH and SO to impact family, work, and voluntary association commitments. Nevertheless, we opt to specify such concerns in models allowing for a more exploratory approach to our data. In particular, we do not have *a priori* predictions of differences among Whites, Blacks, and Latinos in the processes of interest. Recent work on social psychological processes (Jackson, 1997; Hunt, Jackson, Powell, & Steelman, 2000; Schnittker, Freese, & Powell, 2000) emphasizes that such differences may exist and that attentiveness to this fact is important in assessing the generality of research findings and their sociological significance. For this reason, we examine models for the three ethnic categories separately. In general, however, we expect broader (larger) social structures to affect entry into more intermediate structures down through more proximate structures to commitments.

Although we have no theoretical grounds for anticipating that persons' location in large social structures will impact the degree of interactional and affective commitment to all role-based relationships (or particular commitments), we *do* expect to find that large social structures have some impact. This expectation reflects the relative weakening and permeability of some structural boundaries through the geographic and social mobility characterizing American society. It also reflects the homogenization of society as a result of the pervasiveness of the mass media, and an ideology of equality denying the behavioral relevance of structural variation.[10] The last factor implies that, in general, persons in this society will mute to some degree the meanings they attribute to large structural locations with respect to the conduct of their ongoing social relationships, an implication strongly asserted in the metatheoretical underpinnings and logic of network theory (see, e.g., White, Boorman, & Breiger, 1976; Simmel, 1955; Pescosolido & Rubin, 2000).

We expect intermediate social structures to have more substantial impact on degree of commitment, in part simply because this level of structure is closer to the scene of concrete social interactions and social relationships than are stratification features of society. More importantly, if commitment is conceived so as to make costs of relationships foregone an adequate operational index, then high SO will increase commitment to given role relationships because disrupting another (analytically distinct) role relationship is likely to impact negatively those relationships. For example, if one relates to essentially the same persons in family and work, disruption of one of these will threaten the other. Conversely, if relationships across role domains are to different sets of others, disrupting relationships in one role domain will likely have little impact on relationships in the other domains. Comparably with respect to EH: to the degree such homogeneity signals commonality of experience and congruence of role expectations, disruption of relationships in one role area will threaten relationships in other role areas, and commitment to given role relationships will be heightened.

Another line of reasoning supports the supposition that SO and EH will have substantial impact on commitment to role relationships. One implication of high SO is that it increases interaction among members of the sets involved more than among persons whose relationships are less interconnected. As Homans (1950, 1961) argued, and the research has demonstrated (e.g., Byrne, 1971; Berscheid & Walster, 1978; Hill & Stull, 1981), similarity generally leads to greater liking and greater frequency of interaction. This earlier literature on interpersonal attraction suggests that interpersonal trust is implicated in this matrix of variables (Larzale & Huston, 1980). Further, Macy and Skvoretz (1998) demonstrate in a simulation study that high levels of interaction leads to trust;[11] and we can expect trust to underwrite commitment to the role relationships in which trust has developed (see Lawler, 2001 on the role of trust in sustaining enduring exchange relationships).

That expectation is bolstered by recent theorizing and research – both experimental (e.g., Yamagishi, Cook, & Watabe, 1998; Kollack, 1994) and non-experimental (e.g., Burke & Stets, 1999) – on the relation of trust to commitment. Further, other work from Thibaut and Kelley's (1959) pioneering effort on the social psychology of groups to more current work on coalitions and bargaining (Large, 1999; Lawler, Ford, & Large, 1999; Lawler & Yoon, 1993, 1996) implies or provides evidence for that linkage. We will explore, but again have no *a priori* grounds, for anticipating differences in explanatory power of SO as compared with EH on either interactional or affective commitments.

It is particularly unclear what to expect by way of directional impact of our single proximate variable, social embeddedness, on commitments. Given the import sociology generally assigns primary relationships, it seems reasonable to expect that strength of commitments to a set of relationships will strongly impact commitment to another set of relationships. However, on the one hand, a "if you want something done, ask a busy person to do it" principle may operate to make this effect positive, perhaps strongly so. On the other hand, the costs in time, energy and resources of sustaining relationships of one kind may mean that, other things equal, greater social embeddedness will have a negative impact on commitment to relationships of another kind. Alternatively phrased, it may be that commitment to one set of relationships reinforces commitment to another set; or it may be that a price is paid in the form of a negative impact on commitment to one set of relationships of high commitment to another. We do not hazard a guess as to how the proximate level of structure in fact operates on specific commitments, nor will we do so with respect to strength of impact, since competing processes may cancel one another.

The discussion of general expectations to this point has been in terms of the impact of levels of social structure on commitment, without differentiating interactional and affective commitment. However, we do expect, the overall impact of social structure to be greater on affective than on interactional commitment following the reasoning that the latter is more subject to constraints beyond those implied by our structural variables. An example: employment opportunities in communities will constrain the formation of work-related relationships and the character of resulting interactions *per se*, but need not impact the affective quality of relationships formed.

Implied in the foregoing discussion is a provisional model that guides our exploration of the relationships among levels of social structure and social commitments (see Model 2). In this model, all variables except age and gender are unmeasured latent variables whose meanings are given by the items presented in Table 1, reviewed shortly.

RESEARCH DESIGN

The Sample

Our data derive from a computer-assisted telephone-sample survey of our design, executed from January 3 to March 13, 1993 in the five-county region of southern California (Los Angeles, Orange, Riverside, San Bernardino, and San Diego). The sample was developed using the Waksberg Method of Random Digit Dialing. Telephone numbers in census tracts with at least 30% Blacks (according to the 1990 Census) were over sampled. Completed interviews numbered 2854, 1245 with Whites, 646 with Blacks, 737 with Latinos, 148 with Asians, and 62 with"others" (16 persons refused to answer a question calling for self-identification in racial/ethnic terms). Given the purposes of our analyses and the extreme cultural heterogeneity of the Asian category – it includes Japanese, Chinese, Korean, Taiwanese, Vietnamese, Hmong, Cambodian, and Laotian – we use only data for Whites, Blacks, and Latinos. As noted, we over sampled Blacks and under sampled Whites and Latinos when compared with expected numbers based on 1990 Census data for race and gender by county. The sample response rate was 70.2 %.[12] Mean interview time was 23.68 the range from 12–64 minutes. Over half the interviews were completed on a first call; 19.5% required five or more calls. Respondents included in this report were interviewed in English or Spanish, as they preferred. We use this full sample in answering the question of the impact of the large social structures on whether or not subjects occupy positions in family, work, and voluntary association networks. We use a restricted sample of subjects who occupied positions in all three networks and who had scores on all variables in the analyses to answer our questions about the effects of larger social structures on commitments to

Table 1. Descriptive Statistics for all Study Variables by Race/Ethnic Group.

	White		Black		Latino	
	Mean	S.D.	Mean	S.D.	Mean	S.D.
Female	0.55	0.50	0.70	0.46	0.54	0.50
Age	39.13	11.01	39.69	11.86	32.66	11.34
Education	15.75	2.44	15.32	2.41	13.30	3.22
Personal income	6.54	3.37	6.11	2.92	4.39	3.14
How often do things – Family	4.86	1.92	5.16	1.70	5.13	1.68
Hours spent – Family	2.53	1.14	2.57	1.05	2.66	1.04
Money spent – Family	2.18	1.01	2.22	0.99	2.33	1.14
How much miss – Family	3.71	0.61	3.78	0.52	3.71	0.55
How close – Family	3.51	0.70	3.72	0.53	3.56	0.66
How important – Family	3.80	0.48	3.91	0.36	3.92	0.31
Feel unhappy – Family	3.30	0.75	3.43	0.64	3.27	0.78
How often do things – Work	3.36	1.73	2.94	1.68	3.69	1.96
Hours spent – Work	2.27	1.05	2.39	1.12	2.51	1.11
Money spent – Work	1.27	0.52	1.32	0.56	1.33	0.65
How much miss – Work	2.69	0.92	2.51	0.92	2.69	0.89
How close – Work	2.76	0.85	2.64	0.90	2.88	0.91
How important – Work	3.17	0.73	3.07	0.82	3.16	0.81
Feel unhappy – Work	3.31	0.64	3.18	0.65	3.29	0.67
How often do things – Volunteer	4.64	1.45	4.71	1.40	4.85	1.41
Hours spent – Volunteer	2.17	1.16	2.50	1.16	2.45	1.19
Money spent – Volunteer	1.75	0.69	2.01	0.74	1.73	0.78
How much miss – Volunteer	2.87	0.94	3.11	0.85	2.89	0.92
How close – Volunteer	2.79	0.91	3.14	0.79	2.88	0.89
How important – Volunteer	3.11	0.79	3.43	0.65	3.27	0.68
Feel unhappy – Volunteer	3.39	0.65	3.46	0.57	3.38	0.69
Ethnic homogeneity	3.48	0.87	3.22	0.83	2.87	1.06
Structural overlap	1.68	0.63	1.73	0.57	1.84	0.71

family, work, and voluntary association networks; this restricted sample consisted of 398 Whites, 194 Blacks, and 110 Latinos.

The Measures

Entering the analysis of the impact of social structure on whether our respondents live with at least one family member (over a fourth – 27% – do not), work (almost two-thirds do), and are members of a voluntary association (40%) are gender, age, race/ethnicity, education, and personal income. All three outcomes are measured as 0–1 dummy variables, with those not involved assigned the zero. Gender is a dummy variable, coded: Male = 0, Female = 1; females comprise 60% of the total sample. Age is measured in years; the mean age of the total sample is 39 (s.d. = 15.35). Asked what race/ethnicity they considered themselves to be, 47% of our sample said White, 29% Latino, and 25% Black; For the analyses reported in Table 2, race/ethnicity is treated as a dummy variable with White the excluded category. Personal Income was measured using the statement: "I am going to read some income categories. Please stop me when I reach the category that best describes *your* personal income. Do not include income from other members of the household." Response categories ranged from <$9999 = 1, then in $5000 increments to $49,999 = 9, then $50,000−59,999 = 10, $60,000−74,999 = 11 and $75,000 and over = 12. The mean for the sample was 4.21 (s.d. = 3.27), representing an income from $20,000 and $24,999. Education was measured by years of schooling completed, with non-numeric responses of grade school coded "8," high school "12," community college "14," College "16," Master's Degree "18," and Doctorate "20." The mean number of years of schooling for the total sample is 13.5 (s.d. = 3.61).

As our examination of the impact of social structural variables on commitment makes use of the restricted sample and treats the White, Black, and

Table 2. Logistic Estimates of Living with a Relative, Employment Status, and Voluntary Association Membership.

	Lives with a Relative (1 = yes)		Employed (1 = yes)		Voluntary Association Member (1 = yes)	
	b	ex (b)	b	ex (b)	b	ex (b)
Black	0.125 (0.109)	1.134	−0.095 (0.110)	0.907	−0.043.0 (0.103)	0.957
Latino	0.935*** (0.144)	2.547	0.152 (0.128)	1.164	−0.559*** (0.125)	0.571
Female	0.428*** (0.094)	1.534	−0.699*** (0.093)	0.497	0.278** (0.089)	1.320
Education	−0.060*** (0.016)	0.941	0.165*** (0.015)	1.179	0.185*** (0.016)	1.203
Age	−0.009** (0.003)	0.991	−0.035*** (0.003)	0.966	0.014*** (0.003)	1.014
Constant	1.737***		0.157		−3.540***	
−2 Log likelihood	2991.391		3334.085		3487.627	
χ^2	163.320		348.730		356.609	
Pseudo R^2	0.05		0.10		0.10	
N	2595		2543		2593	

$*p<0.05; **p<0.01; ***p<0.001.$
Numbers in parentheses are standard errors.

Latino subsamples separately, we report restricted sub-sample means and standard deviations for items entering these analyses, as well as subsample proportions for categorical variables, in Table 1.

Interactional and affective commitment reflects the items measured in relation to family,[13] work, and voluntary association networks. Family Interactional Commitment (FIC) reflects the responses to three questions: (1) How often do you do things with your family (from never = 1 to daily = 7)? (2) In an average week, how many hours do you spend with your family doing things together, including eating, conversing, talking on the telephone, watching TV, etc.?; (3) Of money you do not need for rent, food, clothing, and other essentials, how much do you spend on family activities? Things like going to the movies and gifts (from almost none = 1, through less than half = 2, about half = 3, more than half = 4, to almost all = 5)?

Family Affective Commitment (FAC) reflects the responses to four questions: (1) How close (in personal and emotional terms) to the members of your family are you (from not close at all = 1 to very close = 4)? (2) How much would you miss your family members if you were not able to spend time or communicate with them (response categories from not at all = 1 to a great deal = 4)? (3) How important are the members of your family to you (from not at all important = 1 to very important = 4)? (4) After I do things with members of my family, I often feel unhappy (from strongly agree = 1 to strongly disagree = 4).

Work and voluntary association commitment were approached analogously (i.e.., replacing "family members" with "co-workers" in questions about work relationships and with "people in voluntary organizations" in questions about voluntary organization relationships). Thus, across all commitment measures, higher scores indicate greater commitment.

The data provided in Table 1 indicate that the Black subsample contained the most "imbalanced" gender distribution (being almost 70% female) with the White and Latino subsamples being very similar in this respect and close to an even split (the White subsample is 55% female, the Latino 54% female). Blacks are on average slightly older (mean age = 39.69) than are Whites (mean age = 39.13), while Latinos are substantially younger (mean age = 32.66). Whites are on average slightly more educated (mean years = 15.75) than are Blacks in the restricted sample (mean years = 15.32), while the Latinos average is roughly 2.5 years less (13.30). The White subsample reported an average personal income level of roughly $32,500, Blacks roughly $30,500, and Latino(as) roughly $22,500.

Sample means and standard deviations for all items that enter into the measurement of our commitment variables are also shown in Table 1. The dependent commitment item scores could range from 1 to 5.3 for the interactive commitment measures, 1 to 4 for the affective commitment measures. There are comparatively few differences of note across the three subsamples in the means of items measuring FIC and FAC.

The two variables indexing the intermediate level of social structure entering our analyses are SO and EH. SO was measured with five items asking respondents to estimate how many of the persons they work with are also relatives, how many of the persons they work with also do things with in voluntary associations, how many of the persons they work with are also friends, how many of the persons they do things with in voluntary associations are also relatives, and how many of the persons they do things with in voluntary associations are friends. The response categories for each item are from almost none = 1 to almost all = 5. The mean score on this scale of the White subsample is 1.68, s.d. = 0.63, the Black subsample's mean is 1.72, s.d. = 0.57, and the Latino subsample mean is 1.84, s.d. = 0.71.

EH was measured with four items asking respondents how many of their co-workers, people at social events they attend, friends, and people in their voluntary associations are of the same ethnic background as themselves. Response categories corresponded to those for SO, almost none = 1 to almost all = 4. Whites Mean score = 3.48, s.d. = 0.87; Blacks Mean score = 3.22, s.d. = 0.83; and Latinos Mean score = 2.87, s.d. = 1.06.[14]

We utilized information on commitment to "other" role relationships to index social embeddedness, since our restricted sample consists only of persons who live with at least one family member, work, and are members of at least one voluntary association. That is, for example, to examine the effect of social embeddedness on commitments to family, we use degree of commitment to work and voluntary association relationships; to examine the effect of social embeddedness on commitments to work, we use degree of commitment to family and voluntary association relationships; and to examine the effect of social embeddedness, we use degree of commitment to family and work relationships.[15]

FINDINGS

Social Structure and Social Ties

Does *having* particular social ties depend on location in large-scale social structure? To answer this question, logically preliminary to our central concern with the relation of social structures to social ties, we regress whether the respondent lives with family member or not, is employed or not, and voluntary association member or not on available large-scale social structural variables except personal income.[16] These results appear in Table 2. The first columns show the effect of large-scale social structural variables on living with a relative. The odds of doing so for Latinos are substantially higher than for Whites, while the odds for Blacks are little different than for Whites. (As this suggests, the odds for Latinos living with a relative are also substantially higher than they are for Blacks.) The odds of females living with a relative are significantly higher than they are for males. As education increases, the odds of living with a relative decrease significantly, and do so marginally with increases in age. The Pseudo R^2 suggests that roughly 5% of the variance in living with a relative is '"explained" by the large-scale structural variables.[17]

The next columns give the results for employment. Education increases the odds of being employed; being female and age significantly decrease those odds, especially the former. Neither being Black nor Latino (relative to White) significantly affects odds of employment. (Blacks are marginally less likely to be employed than Latinos.) Estimated contribution to explained variance of employment by the large-scale structure variables is 10%.

The last columns present results for voluntary association membership. Only being Black (relative to being White) does not affect appreciably the odds of being a member. Being female, educated, and older significantly increases those odds, while being Latino significantly decreases them. (Latinos are significantly less likely to be a member of a voluntary association than Blacks.) This level of structure explains an estimated 10% of the variance in voluntary association membership.

Although there are a few surprises in the findings just reviewed,[18] these results generally confirm conventional wisdom about involvement in particular social relationships and so the role of large social structures in putting persons in positions to establish commitments as identity theory defines that concept.

Social Structures and Commitment to Social Ties

Again, our central concern is with the impact of social structures on commitment. To pursue this concern, we estimate a structural equation model of the impact of three levels of social structures – large-scale, intermediate, and proximate – on commitment to family, work, and voluntary association relationships for each of the racial/ethnic subsamples. The abstract model is

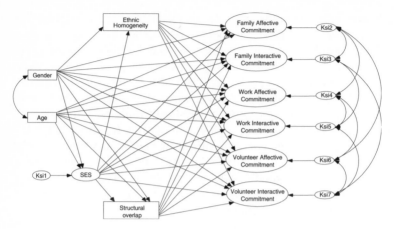

Fig. 1. Theoretical Model

shown in Fig. 1. In order to facilitate seeing whether or not the processes modeled are essentially similar for the three racial/ethnic subsamples, we present the standardized coefficients resulting from these analyses separately.

The White Subsample

The coefficients for the White subsample appear in Table 3. On the level of the large social structures, female subjects, not surprisingly, have significantly lower SES than males, and older subjects have significantly higher SES than younger subjects.

Being female has significant negative effect on the intermediate level structural overlap variable as does SES. None of the large social structures link to EH. Being female directly ties to affective commitment to family and to work, with females showing higher scores on those variables. SES has direct impacts on work interactional and affective commitment and on affective commitment to voluntary associations, with higher status subjects having significantly stronger scores on both work-related commitments and significantly weaker affective commitment to voluntary associations. Gender's link to SES suggests that it has indirect effects through such status on work interactional and affective commitment as well as on voluntary association affective commitment. Age directly and negatively impacts interactional commitment to work, with older subjects exhibiting less

Table 3. Standardized Coefficients for Relation of Social Structural Variables to Commitment, White Subsample.

	Socioeconomic status	Ethnic Homogeneity	Structural Overlap	Family Interactional Commitment	Family Affective Commitment	Work Interactional Commitment	Work Effective Commitment	Volunteer Interactional Commitment	Volunteer Affective Commitment
Female	−0.292***	−0.085	−0.152**	0.085	0.154*	0.096	0.270***	−0.044	0.012
Age	0.406***	−0.008	0.075	−0.012	−0.002	−0.203**	0.040	−0.045	0.087
Socioeconomic status		0.115	−0.194*	0.013	−0.015	0.334**	0.180*	−0.090	−0.213*
Ethnic				0.019	0.064	−0.059	−0.020	0.081	−0.084
Overlap				0.024	0.011	0.381***	0.330***	0.276***	0.289***
R^2	0.253	0.014	0.037	0.007	0.030	0.198	0.161	0.101	0.147

Note:
*$p < 0.05$.
**$p < 0.01$.
***$p < 0.001$.

commitment. Age also has an indirect impact through SES on work interactional and affective commitment.

The most consistent and strongest effects for the White subsample involve the intermediate level variable SO. SO has strong direct effects on both work interactional and affective commitment as well as both voluntary organization interactive commitment. At the same time, SO is linked to gender and SES and serves to tie these large structures to work interactional and affective commitment and to voluntary associational interactional and affective commitment.

It is worth noting that for the White subsample our second intermediate structure variable, EH, is neither affected by the large social structures of gender, age, or SES, nor does it have any impact on commitment to family, work, or voluntary associations. It is also worth noting that for this subsample no large or intermediate structure has any notable consequence for commitments to family. As this last suggests, the variance in the commitment measures explained by the large and intermediate structures for family commitment in minimal, being 1% and 3% for FIC and FAC, respectively. The model does better for the remaining commitments: 20% for Work Interactional Commitment, 16% for Work Affective Commitment, 10% for Voluntary Association Interactive Commitment and 15% for Voluntary Association Affective Commitment.

Thus, in the White subsample SO looms as a strong conduit through which the larger social structures exert their effects on commitment to at least some networks of social relationships and interaction (here, work and voluntary associational), if not to others (here, family). At the same time, some larger structures have direct effects on commitments unexplained by the intermediate structures incorporated into this research; and some intermediate structures (here, EH) have little if any effect on commitments. Commitment to some types of social networks can be better understood here, work and voluntary association by reference to larger social structures than others (here, family).

The Black Subsample

Table 4 contains the standardized coefficients for the Black subsample. Gender and age are related to SES in the same manner and at roughly the same levels as was the case in the White subsample (i.e., Black females have lower SES than do males, and older Blacks have higher SES than do younger). In this subsample, the large social structure gender variable fails

Table 4. Standardized Coefficients for Relation of Social Structural Variables to Commitment, Black Subsample.

	Socioeconomic status	Ethnic Homogeneity	Structural Overlap	Family Interactional Commitment	Family Affective Commitment	Work Interactional Commitment	Work Effective Commitment	Volunteer Interactional Commitment	Volunteer Affective Commitment
Female	−0.215**	0.057	−0.045	0.163*	0.272**	−0.022	0.070	−0.231**	−0.017
Age	0.424***	−0.009	−0.235**	−0.082	−0.180*	0.042	0.152	0.070	0.012
Socioeconomic status		0.209*	−0.245***	0.145	0.109	0.089	0.051	−168	−0.047
Ethnic				0.017	−0.004	−0.267**	−0.232**	0.090	0.128
Overlap				0.038	−0.168*	0.381***	0.233**	0.173*	0.291**
R^2	0.210	0.162	0.053	0.034	0.105	0.197	0.113	0.158	0.118

Note:
$p < 0.05$.
** $p < 0.01$.
*** $p < 0.001$.

to tie directly to either of our intermediate level variables of EH and SO. However, the large social structure socioeconomic variable does relate significantly to both intermediate social structure variables, positively in the case of EH and negatively in the case of SO; thus, gender's tie to SES implies that the former is also tied indirectly to the two intermediate structures. Gender directly affects both FIC and FAC, moreso the latter: females have significantly higher scores than males on the two family commitment variables. And gender also impacts directly and significantly interactive commitment to voluntary associations; in this case the relationship is negative: Black females have lower interactive commitment than do males.

There is a significant negative relationship between age and SO, and age is also negatively related (directly) to FAC (younger Blacks in the subsample are more affectively committed to family than are older Blacks). Age links indirectly through SO to five of the six commitment variables, the exception being FIC. SES also links indirectly to the same five commitment variables; in addition, it links indirectly through its tie to EH to interactive and affective commitment to work.

As suggested in the foregoing, the impact of the two intermediate social structures on commitments in the Black subsample is even more consistent than was true for the White subsample. Not only does SO significantly impact five of the six commitment measures (FAC, Voluntary Association Affective Commitment, Work Affective Commitment, Voluntary Association Interactional Commitment, and Voluntary Association Affective Commitment), it also serves as a channel though which age and SES impact the same set of commitment. Further, not only does EH significantly affect both interactional and affective commitment to work, doing so negatively, it also serves as a channel through which SES affects the two work commitments.

The model explains just 3% of the variance of FIC. It does better for the remaining five commitment variables (11% for FAC; 20% for Work Interactional Commitment; 11% for Work Affective Commitment; 15% for Volunteer Association Interactional Commitment; and 12% for Volunteer Association Commitment.

Results for the Black subsample reinforce the importance of the intermediate structural level of SO in impacting commitments, especially with respect to work and voluntary association relationships, and suggest that EH may be a significant participant in that process at least under some circumstances. The relatively strong role of the large social structural variables, especially gender and SES, in shaping the intermediate level SO is worthy of note, as is the emergence of EH as a variable negatively impacting commitment to work relationships in the Black subsample.

The Latino Sample

Findings for the Latino sample are given in Table 5. The relationships among the large social structural variables that have been noted earlier for the White and Black subsamples once again occur, doing so the same direction and in roughly equivalent size: Latinas have lower SES than do Latin males and older Latinos have higher SES than do younger Latinos. Gender impacts the intermediate structure variables EH and SO, with females having lower scores on both, but gender does not directly impact any of the commitment measures. Gender, however, does have an indirect effect on four of the six commitment measures: FAC, Work Affective Commitment, Voluntary Association Interactive Commitment, and Voluntary Association Affective Commitment. All of these effects occur through SO. Like gender, SES has no direct links to any commitment measure, but it also has the same indirect effects through SO that gender does.

Age directly affects Work Affective Commitment, with older Latinos having higher commitment than do younger, but age does not link indirectly to any of the commitment measures. Higher SES has no direct effects on any commitment variable. It does, however, impact significantly EH and SO, lowering both; and it does have, through SO, indirect impact on the four commitment measures that SO affects. For Latinos, EH has no significant impact on any commitment. The large and intermediate scale variables account for 6% of the variance in FIC, 11% in FAC, 2% in Work Interactional Commitment, 17% in Work Affective Commitment, 11% in Voluntary Association Interactional Commitment and 26% in Voluntary Association Affective Commitment.

In the Latino subsample, once again, the intermediate level structural variable SO exhibits the strongest effects on commitment, both in its own right and through serving as a link between large structures and commitments. Again, two other findings are worthy of note: (1) the absence of any direct effects of gender, SES, and EH on commitments; and (2) the fact that in four of five instances in which commitments are shown to be significantly affected by large or intermediate social structures, it is affective rather than interactive commitment that is involved.

The Impact of Social Embeddedness

Yet to be considered is the impact of social embeddedness, conceptualized as the level of commitment to networks of social relationship other than one

Table 5. Standardized Coefficients for Relation of Social Structural Variables to Commitment, Latino Subsample.

	Socioeconomic status	Ethnic Homogeneity	Structural Overlap	Family Interactional Commitment	Family Affective Commitment	Work Interactional Commitment	Work Effective Commitment	Volunteer Interactional Commitment	Volunteer Affective Commitment
Female	-0.235**	-0.202**	-0.227**	-0.091	0.188	-0.033	0.133	-0.085	-0.078
Age	0.369***	-0.014	0.068	-0.012	0.162	-0.131	0.244**	-0.175	-0.046
Socioeconomic status		-0.375***	-0.368***	0.186	0.146	0.100	-0.007	0.149	-0.105
Ethnic				0.087	0.087	0.054	0.019	0.015	-0.113
Overlap				0.124	0.256*	0.067	0.341***	0.270*	0.458***
R^2	0.198	0.148	0.132	0.057	0.110	0.020	0.169	0.109	0.256

Note:
*$p < 0.05$.
**$p < 0.01$.
***$p < 0.001$.

which is the immediate focus of attention. As noted earlier, we can with the present data get at this variable only inferentially, through examining the intercorrelations of the error terms attached to measures of each of the commitments examined for each of the subsamples. These correlations are given in Table 6. Ten of the 18 correlations are significant; 9 of the significant correlations are positive, only one negative – the correlation of FIC and Work Interactional Commitment for Latinos, suggesting that for this ethnic subsample, higher commitment to one is associated with lower commitment to the other. Three of six possible correlations are significant in the White and Black subsamples, four of six in the Latino(a) subsample. All three of the correlations between FAC and Work Affective Commitment are significant, and at least one of the correlations in each set is significant.

Summary of Empirical Findings

With respect to involvement in the particular networks of social relationships *per se*, it largely suffices to say that the large-scale structural variables of race/ethnicity, age, gender, and education do make a difference in whether persons have the opportunity to become committed to those relationships (Table 2). The difference these variables make is small, less for family relationships than for work or voluntary association membership, and generally in line with the extant literature. Detailed consideration of the data suggests that Blacks do not differ much from Whites in the rates at which they live with a family member, are employed, or are members of a voluntary association. Latinos, on the other hand, do differ from both Blacks and Whites where they are much more likely to live with a relative and much less likely to be a member of a voluntary association and they are more likely to be employed than are Blacks.

With respect to the impact of social structures on commitment:

1. The intermediate level variable SO clearly plays an important role – certainly the most decisive role of all the large and intermediate social structures in this research – in shaping levels of commitment to family, work, and voluntary networks of relationships. It does so in itself, that is, SO exhibits statistically significant effects on commitments in 13 of its 18 "opportunities" to do so, and it does so roughly equally in the White subsample (four of six), the Black subsample (five of six), and Latino subsample (four of six).[19] And it does so by mediating the relationships of the large social structures of gender, age, and SES to SO. SO fails to

Table 6. Correlations of Error Terms on Interactional Commitment and Affective Commitment Within and between Roles.

	Family IC			Family AC			Work IC			Work AC			Volunteer IC			Volunteer AC		
	White	Black	Latino	White	Black	Latino	White	Black	Latino	White	Black	Latino	White	Black	Latino	White	Black	Latino
Family IC																		
Family AC	−0.03	0.09	−0.20*															
Work IC	0.02	0.20**	−0.10															
Work AC							0.14**	0.24**	0.46**									
Volunteer IC							0.15**	−0.10	−0.17									
Volunteer AC										0.04	0.19**	0.21*	0.12**	0.03	0.21*			

$* p < 0.05;\ ** p < 0.01;\ *** p < 0.001.$

affect directly only the two family commitment scores of Whites, the FIC score of Blacks, and the Family Interactive and Work Affective Commitment scores of Latinos. The other intermediate variable EH in itself affects only the two work commitments in the Black subsample, lowering both, and serves only to mediate the relationship of SES to the work commitment scores of Blacks.

2. The majority of large social-structures effects flow through the more interactional and patterned intermediate and proximate variables. SO consistently serves in this way, linking gender and SES to both work commitments and both Voluntary Association Commitments in the White subsample, age and SES to FAC as well as to both work and both Voluntary Association Commitments in the Black subsample, and gender and SES ties to FAC, both Work Commitments and both Voluntary Commitments in the Latino subsample. It is only in the Black subsample that the intermediate structure EH serves in this way. If our interpretation of the implications of the correlations among error terms in the measures of commitment is credible, social embeddedness also serves to mediate the relation of larger (as well as intermediate) structures on commitments.

3. The effects of SO on commitments are positive: in 12 of 13 cases, the higher the SO scores, the higher the level of commitment. The exception is Blacks' affective commitment to family. Again, if our thinking in constructing the social embeddedness variable is reasonable, the evidence says that in general commitment to one social network reinforces commitment to another. The negative correlation of family and work affective commitment provides the only support in our data for the idea that involvement in other sets of relationships carries costs for family relationships.

4. The large scale structures have direct impacts on 11 of the 18 commitment measures they could have affected. No single pattern of direct effects characterizes all three racial/ethnic subgroups.

5. Across the three subsamples, of the 26 cases in which statistically significant links occur between large or intermediate social structures and commitments, a slight majority involve affective commitments (15) rather than interactive commitment (11).

6. The effects of gender on SO are consistently negative, that is, females' relationships across the arenas or family, work, and voluntary associations are lower than males'.

7. SES has a negative impact on SO in all three subsamples. In two of the three subsamples, SES has a significant impact on EH; in one of the these (Latino) that impact is negative, in the other (Black) that impact is positive.

DISCUSSION

For most sociologists concerned with social psychological processes, it is axiomatic that social structure impacts those processes. Identity theory and its parent structural symbolic interactionist frame argue that structural constraints and opportunities shape patterns of social relations. Identity theory then claims patterns of social relations impact the relative salience of identities that are part of self, and that relative salience of identities is an important determinant of choices persons make among available role-related behaviors. Identity theory research to date has focused almost entirely on the latter parts of this set of claims, examining the impact of commitment (patterns of social relations) on identity salience and identity salience on role choice. We initiated the research reported here to specify the broader identity theory argument by asking what types of social structures impact commitment to what kinds of networks of social relationships. Our attempt to answer to this question distinguished three levels of social structure – large-scale, intermediate, and proximate – and related indices of each to interactional and affective commitment to family, work, and voluntary associational relationships.

We first examined the impact of large-scale structural variables on entrance into each kind of network, entrance being a necessary precursor of commitment. We expected the data to show this effect although, not strongly, and they did. We then examined the effect of location in large-scale structures on strength of commitments to the three kinds of networks, also expecting that effect to exist, and – following the logic of identity theory – that generally the impact of large-scale structural variables would channel through smaller structures closer to the actual scene of interaction. However, we had no strong theoretical or research grounds to specify the linkages among our social structural variables beyond that point. We did not expect strong, direct, large-scale structure effects on commitments, given the trends in society that attenuate the power of general stratification variables to set boundaries on social relationships. Rather, we expected a greater impact of social structures on commitment to derive from intermediate structures (closer than the societal level social structures traditionally emphasized by sociology) to where people enter social relationships and interact. In part, we anticipated this finding because we think commitment reflects trust, and trust more readily exists in and through interaction with persons who are, or we assume are, like ourselves. We believed that intermediate social structures would have substantial impact on commitment to networks of social relations. The data strongly support this belief. In particular, SO, whose referent is the degree to which persons interact with the same set of others in multiple networks of social relationships, impacts commitment to voluntary associations and work relationships. Of the two intermediate level variables, SO is consistent in its strong, mostly positive effects on interactive and affective commitment to work and to voluntary association relationships. This finding validates a central thesis of identity theory, since the theory argues that losing a position and related identity in a network of role relationships threatens interactions in another network of role relationships to the degree the sets have common members.

That trust underlies the relationship of SO to commitment is premised on the idea that relating to the same people in multiple arenas of life builds trust. While this idea's plausibility is supported by our findings, the idea cannot be examined directly with our data and must remain conjectural until it is directly researched. The worth of doing that research is evident. Insofar as it is trust that does link SO to commitment, this study joins the chorus of work across the social science disciplines that focuses on trust as a key variable relating persons to one another and to the society of which they are a part (Cook, 2001).

The second of our two intermediate level variables, EH, is not consistently related to commitments, holding only for Blacks and only for work commitments of Blacks and these effects are negative. To conclude that this finding implies the relative impotency of EH in determining commitments to networks of social relationships is certainly premature, as would be the conclusion that this finding negates the import of intermediate social structures for doing so. Such conclusions await research incorporating a wider range of types of social networks, as well as a wider range of types of intermediate structures. However, while an argument linking EH to commitment can be made on the assumption that trust is generated through commonality of experience and congruence of role expectations, it may be that this assumption simply overstates the commonality and congruence resulting from shared ethnicity alone.

The interesting finding that, for the Black subsample, the higher the EH, the lower the interactive and affective commitment to work relationships deserves further study. Would a negative relation be found for other than work were a wide range of relationship arenas be studied is a question worth pursuing, as is the more general question of the conditions under which intermediate social structures affect commitments negatively. The particular finding stimulating these questions may simply reflect the lower status and income of jobs held by Blacks in the sample; it may also reflect selective reinforcements deriving from interaction within a relatively homogeneous social environment.[20] Or, it may be that trust carries over to work when work experiences are as ethnically homogeneous as non-work experiences; perhaps if they are not, a positive relationship between non-work EH and commitment to work ought not to be expected.

That large structures have some, albeit limited, impact on involvement in family, work, and voluntary associations is not a surprising finding from the point of view of identity theory; however, perhaps large structures variables are conceptualized too grossly; e.g., it may be that effects of large-scale structures would be stronger if the research indexed type and institutional context of work rather than simply using an employed-not employed variable. Although, absent studies incorporating a wider array of other, perhaps non-traditional, large structural variables (e.g., how time is organized in various segments of society) and a wider array of types of social networks (e.g., politics or school-based networks), it is premature to conclude that large-scale structures weakly bound networks of relationships of any kind. Still further, given the weakness of the family variable, little should be made of the findings that large structures – or intermediate, for that matter – have relatively little impact on family compared to work or voluntary association commitments.

There are few surprises in how large structures affect living with a relative, employment, or voluntary association membership. However, the findings that chances of employment are enhanced for Latinos relative to either Blacks or Whites,[21] that Blacks and Whites do not differ in their odds of employment, and that Blacks are as likely as Whites to be voluntary association members merit notice. The first may reflect particulars of the southern California labor market as well as long-standing discrimination against Blacks in that market; the second may be due in part to the failure of our sample to include a "proper" proportion of young Black males; and the third may hide differences in the voluntary associations involved, with Blacks more likely to be active in church organizations. That large structures have limited impact on degree of commitment was expected, and confirmed; again, for reasons noted, this finding needs to be viewed with caution.

Interesting for identity theory are findings relating the level of social structure to variation in the nature of commitment to these relationships. Models estimated are somewhat more successful in predicting affective commitment, probably because affect is less subject than interaction to structural constraints. Theoretically important is the finding that (except for family commitment) models including the three levels of social structure account for reasonable proportions of the variance in commitment.

Finally, there are sufficient differences in findings for Whites in relation to Blacks and Latinos and for the latter in relation to one another to make it imperative that research should not generalize across these categories without directly investigating possible differences (Hunt et al, 2000). The same observation holds for gender. For example, Blacks but not Latinos consistently differ from Whites on commitment, having less commitment to work relationships and greater commitment to voluntary association relationships (as well as greater affective commitment to family). With regard to gender, a reasonably consistent finding is that being female rather than male relates to commitment; noteworthy here is that women in the labor force are more affectively committed to their work relationships than are males.[22]

CONCLUSION

We close by asking the question: What meaning do our findings have for the theoretical intuition of a structural symbolic interactionist framework arguing the import of social structural variables for commitment processes? The screening function of large-scale social structural variables in bringing persons together into certain relationships and keeping others out of those relationships is affirmed in these data, at least in degree. While such variables also directly affect the level of commitments to relationships entered, they do so relatively infrequently. Rather, it is social structural variables closer to social relationships *per se*, in particular, here, the degree to which persons' role-sets overlap, that strongly impact commitment, perhaps because of the interpersonal trust engendered by that overlap. This assertion does not deny the relevance and import of societal level stratification variables for most of the problems sociology has traditionally taken as its central concerns. It does assert that with respect to at least some problems of interest to sociology generally as well as to a sociological social psychology, social structural variables at more "local" or "associational" network levels hold more explanatory power.

NOTES

1. The theory neither argues that only commitment structures identity salience, nor that identity salience only organizes behavior.
2. Stryker and Serpe (1994) explicate this conceptualization of identity salience, and differentiate it from other concepts sometimes taken to be equivalent.

3. An axiom that underlies not only symbolic interactionism but various forms of exchange-based theories as well; see, for example, Lawler (2001) and Cook (2001).

4. There are, of course, alternative ways of conceptualizing large social structures. In particular, such structures may be construed as cultural categories carrying meanings that define the content of social life. However, the programmatic point of the structural symbolic interationism argued for by Stryker (1980) is that sociological social psychology is best served by incorporating the structural emphasis of sociology "proper" into the traditional interactionist concerns with meanings, interaction, self, and identity. To see the large structures, whatever the meanings that may be attached to these in society at large, as boundaries functioning to channel or funnel members of the society into the intermediate and proximate structures in which they lead their lives accords with that meta-theoretical program.

5. See, e.g., Burgess and Wallin (1953) and Centers (1949) on marital homogamy; Demerath (1965) on the relative homogamy by class of the various Protestant denominations; Laumann (1973) and Coleman (1961) on friendships among urban men and high school students, respectively.

6. This term was suggested in a conversation with Tom Gieryn.

7. The absence of data on what we called "local" intermediate social structures reflects a decision to focus the questions asked on other variables and limitations on survey time. Data on "associational" structures are more limited than we had hoped as a consequence of foregoing questions interviewers argued were too sensitive to ask given the volatile racial situation in Los Angeles at the time of the survey.

8. In earlier work on identity theory (e.g., Stryker, 1980), SO was said to be an index of commitment. Consideration of the logic of our earlier argument has led to the conclusion that rather than being an index of commitment (costs of relationships foregone), structural overlap represents a state of organized social relationships, a social structure in short, best conceptualized as a potential determinant of commitment.

9. Related to the distinction between "large" and "intermediate" structures is the distinction between "social identities" as conceptualized in social identity theory (Tajfel, 1981; Hogg, 2003; Turner, 1999) and "identity" as it is conceptualized in identity theory (Stryker, 2000).

10. These characterizations of American society admittedly oversimplify very complex situations and issues.

11. See also, in a quite different context, Putnam's (1995) argument relating interaction in voluntary associational contexts to social capital, including trust.

12. The survey was conducted by the Social Science Research Center at California State University Fullerton. The response rate was calculated using guidelines specified by the American Association for Public Opinion Research (1998) and is based on completed interviews divided by the sum of completed interviews, partial interviews, never completed call backs, never completed call backs, refusals, working numbers where answering machines were reached, and working numbers that were never answered.

13. Our measures of commitment to family disadvantage those persons living at a distance from other family members.

14. The zero-order correlations (0.02 for Whites, 0.10 for Blacks, and 0.13 for Latinos between Ethnic Homogeneity and Structural Overlap scores are non-significant.

15. Specifically, we rely on inferences from the intercorrelations among the error terms of measures of commitments to family, work, and voluntary association

relationships for this purpose. We reason that significantly intercorrelated error terms indicate shared variance derived from common unmeasured causes, rendering reasonable the presumption that the level of commitment to one social network potentially affects the level of commitment to another. In earlier analyses, using OLS regression models within a single identity, this relationship is tested by 12 regression coefficients within six equations (one equation for each affective and interactive commitment for each of the three identities). Within the OLS regressions, 10 of the 12 possible tests are significant and demonstrate the same pattern presented in Table 6. Clearly, any findings with regard to Social Embeddedness must be viewed cautiously. However, the analysis presented here is based on theoretically derived relationships. We believe these findings are reasonable and consistent with the theory. As in any modeling of theoretical relationships, the possibility remains that a variable not included in the model could account the pattern that is present within this analysis.

16. Since employment is one of the states being predicted, we omitted income as a predictor. Analyses with and without income in the equations indicate that doing so does not alter findings in any significant way, except that (unsurprisingly) the estimate of explained variance provided by a pseudo-R^2 is substantially higher with income in the equation predicting employment.

17. OLS analyses using the number of family members in subjects' households shows that all of the large-scale structural variables contribute significantly to that variable, another indicator of opportunity for family commitment, with being Latino or Black (compared to White) and being female having the strongest linkages. The large-scale structure variables "explain" 16% of the variance in number of family members in households.

18. See the brief treatment of these in the "Discussion" section of this paper.

19. Structural Overlap has least impact on commitment to family, with statistically significant effects in two of the four opportunities, none in the White subsample. In general, family commitment is less well explained by reference to variables in our model than are work commitment or voluntary association commitment. Why this may be the case is not clear. It does not appear to reflect lesser variation in family commitment measures.

20. Analyses not presented here indicate that this is especially true for Latino males.

21. This comment reflects the belief that models incorporating a wider range of variables on all three levels of social structure, especially if these were well measured, would expand the explanatory power of the models considerably. It would be well to remember, however, that the symbolic interactionist frame from which identity theory derives asserts a principled indeterminacy in social life (see Stryker, 1980, 1994).

22. This finding replicates one appearing in early identity theory research in a general population survey of Indianapolis residents (unpublished); this finding could reflect the greater proportion of females as compared with males for whom paid employment is a relatively voluntary activity.

ACKNOWLEDGMENTS

The comments on an earlier version of this paper by members of the seminar of the Training Program in Social Psychology at Indiana University on identity, self, role and mental health (Grant #2 T32 MH14588) were useful and deeply appreciated, as were the comments received from Brian Powell, Clem Brooks, Michael D. Large, and Michael M. Harrod.

REFERENCES

American Association for Public Opinion Research. (1998). *Standard definitions: Final dispositions of case codes and outcome rates for Rdd telephone surveys and in-person household surveys.* Ann Arbor, MI: American Association for Public Opinion Research.

Berscheid, E., & Walster, E. (Hatfield). (1978). *Interpersonal Attraction* (2nd ed.). Reading, MA: Addison-Wesley.

Burgess, E. W., & Wallin, P. (1953). *Engagement and marriage.* Philadelphia: Lippencott.

Burke, P. J., & Stets, J. E. (1999). Trust and commitment through self-verification. *Social Psychology Quarterly, 62,* 347–366.

Byrne, D. (1971). *The Attraction Paradigm.* New York: Academic Press.

Centers, R. (1949). Marital selection and occupational strata. *American Journal of Sociology, 54,* 530–535.

Coleman, J. S. (1961). *The adolescent society.* New York: Free Press.

Cook, K. S. (2001). Trust in society. In: K. S. Cook (Ed.), *Trust in society* (pp. xi–xxvii). New York: Russell Sage Foundation.

Demerath, N. J., III. (1965). *Social class in American protestantism.* Chicago: Rand-McNally.

Hill, C. T., & Stull, D. E. (1981). Sex differences in effects of social and value similarity in same-sex friendship. *Journal of Personality and Social Psychology, 41,* 488–502.

Hogg, M. A. (2003). Social identity. In: M. R. Leary & J. P. Tangney (Eds), *Handbook of self and identity* (pp. 462–479). New York: Guilford.

Homans, G. C. (1950). *The human group.* New York: Harcourt, Brace and World.

Homans, G. C. (1961). *Social behavior: Its elementary forms.* New York: Harcourt, Brace and World.

Hunt, M. O., Jackson, P. B., Powell, B., & Steelman, L. C. (2000). Color-blind: The treatment of race and ethnicity in social psychology. *Social Psychology Quarterly, 63,* 352–364.

Jackson, P. B. (1997). Role occupancy and minority mental health. *Journal of Health and Social Behavior, 38,* 237–255.

Kollack, P. (1994). The emergence of exchange structures: An experimental study of uncertainty, commitment, and trust. *American Journal of Sociology, 100,* 313–345.

Large, MD. (1999). The effectiveness of gifts as unilateral initiatives in bargaining. *Sociological Perspectives, 42,* 525–542.

Larzale, R. E., & Huston, T. L. (1980). The dyadic trust scale. *Journal of Marriage and the Family, 42,* 595–604.

Laumann, E. O. (1973). *Bonds of pluralism.* New York: Wiley.

Lawler, E. J. (2001). An affect theory of social xchange. *American Journal of Sociology, 107,* 321–352.

Lawler, E. J., Ford, R., & Large, M. D. (1999). Unilateral initiatives as a conflict resolution strategy. *Social Psychology Quarterly, 63,* 240–256.

Lawler, E. J., & Yoon, J. (1993). Power and the emergence of commitment behavior in negotiated exchange. *American Sociological Review, 58,* 465–481.

Lawler, E. J., & Yoon, J. (1996). Commitment in exchange relations: Test of a theory of relational cohesion. *American Sociological Review, 61*, 89–108.

Macy, M. W., & Skvoretz, J. (1998). The evolution of trust and cooperation between strangers: Computational model. *American Sociological Review, 63*, 638–660.

Mead, G. H. (1934). *Mind, self and society*. Chicago: University of Chicago Press.

Pescosolido, B. A., & Rubin, B. (2000). The web of group affiliations revisited: Social life, postmodernism and sociology. *American Sociological Review, 63*, 32–76.

Putnam, R. D. (1995). Bowling alone: America's declining social capital. *Journal of Democracy, 95*, 65–78.

Schnittker, J., Freese, J., & Powell, B. (2000). Nature, nurture, neither, nor? Black–White differences in beliefs about the causes and appropriate treatment of mental illness. *Social Forces, 78*, 1101–1132.

Serpe, R. T., & Stryker, S. (1993). Prior social ties and movement into new social relationships. In: E. T. Lawler, B. Markovsky, J. O'Brien & K. Heimer (Eds), *Advances in group processes*, (Vol. 10, pp. 283–304). Greenwich, CT: JAI Press.

Simmel, G. (1955). *Conflict; the web of group affiliations*. New York: The Free Press.

Stryker, S. (1980). *Symbolic interactionism: A social structural version*. Menlo Park, CA: Benjamin/Cummings.

Stryker, S. (1994). Freedom and constraint in social and personal life: Toward resolving the paradox of self. In: P. Gerald & G. Chad (Eds), *Self, collective behavior and society: Essays honoring the contribution of Ralph H. Turner* (pp. 119–138). Greenwich, CN: JAI Press.

Stryker, S. (2000). Identity theory. In: E. F. Borgatta & R. J. V. Montgomery (Eds), *Encyclopedia of sociology*, (2nd ed., Vol. 2, pp. 1253–1258). New York: Macmillan.

Stryker, S., & Serpe, R. T. (1994). Identity salience and psychological centrality: Equivalent, overlapping, or complementary concepts? *Social Psychology Quarterly*, 16–35.

Tajfel, H. (1981). *Human groups and social categories*. Cambridge, UK: Cambridge University Press.

Thibaut, J. W., & Kelley, H. H. (1959). *The social psychology of groups*. New York: Wiley.

Turner, J. C. (1999). Some current issues in research on social identity and self-categorization theories. In: N. Ellemers, R. Spears & D. DoOosje (Eds), *Social identity* (pp. 6–34). Oxford, UK: Blackwell.

White, H. C., Boorman, S., & Breiger, R. (1976). Social structure from multiple networks I. Blockmodels of roles and positions. *American Journal of Sociology, 81*, 730–780.

Yamagishi, T., Cook, K. S., & Watabe, M. (1998). Uncertainty, trust. and commitment formation in the United States and Japan. *American Journal of Sociology, 104*, 165–194.

THE EFFECTS OF STATUS AND GROUP MEMBERSHIP MODELED IN A GRAPH-THEORETIC SETTING

Christopher Barnum

ABSTRACT

This paper examines social influence in collective task settings using the Berger, Fisek, Norman and Zelditch's graph-theoretic method. The work examines in-group membership in task settings, and models contexts where both status processes and group membership are salient. At the core of these models is a theoretical concept called a group status typification state, defined as an abstract understanding that participants hold of the type of person who would be a good source of information. This paper builds upon recent theory and research and may serve as an initial step toward integration of Status Characteristics Theory and Social Identity Theory.

INTRODUCTION

A significant part of day-to-day social interaction consists of people trying to influence one another. Some attempts at influence are gentle and indirect, such as subtle forms of persuasion, while other forms are stark and

Social Identification in Groups
Advances in Group Processes, Volume 22, 125–153
ISSN: 0882-6145/doi:10.1016/S0882-6145(05)22005-2

intrusive, such as harsh commands and dictates. Although diverse, all forms of influence share a common feature, they are all characterized by a change in behavior or belief resulting from what others say or do (Myers, 2005). Social psychologists have long been interested in this subject matter and social psychological inquiry of this topic subsumes a wide range of issues stemming from the classic investigations of conformity and obedience to more recent work exploring persuasion, status, and in-group bias. This paper examines a limited portion of this assortment, social influence in collective task settings.

A collective task setting is a context in which people attempt to jointly solve a common problem. We encounter many of these settings in our daily lives. Examples are diverse and range from formal work groups such as business or academic committees to informal assemblages such as a group of strangers working to free a stuck car from a snow bank. All these settings share a common feature: the participants have a strong desire to reach a correct solution. Frequently, however, correct answers are complex, puzzling, or difficult to obtain. Social psychologists have long argued that participants in task settings look to each other as sources of information in crafting solutions to their problems (Sherif, 1936; Asch, 1951, 1956; Berger, Cohen, & Zelditch, 1972; Berger, Fisek, Norman, & Zelditch, 1977). Often, people use personal or social characteristics as clues about each other's abilities. For example, a group of strangers working to free a stuck car from a snow bank may use each other's physical size as a clue to solve the problem. If so, the interactants may decide to have the smallest person in the group steer the car, while the larger individuals push it out of the snow bank.

Research has demonstrated that group memberships and status characteristics are two such important social cues that serve as sources of information in collective task settings. To date, two well-developed theoretical research programs have examined the effect that these cues generate in task settings.

Status Characteristics Theory or SCT (Berger et al., 1972; Berger et al., 1977; Berger & Zelditch, 1985; Berger, Norman, & Balkwell, 1992; Webster & Foschi, 1988) investigates the effect that individual properties such as age, gender, and ability have on interaction. The theory asserts that these *status characteristics* are indicative of task ability. In collective task settings, members act as if status characteristics give clues suggesting how capable each individual is of contributing to the successful completion of the group's task (Shelly & Webster, 1997).

Social Identity Theory or SIT (Tajfel, 1974, 1978, 1982; Tajfel & Turner, 1979, 1986; Turner, 1982) looks at the impact that group memberships have on perceptions, thoughts, and behaviors. SIT articulates why phenomena such as in-group favoritism, ethnocentrism, and influence occur in settings where group memberships are salient.

Although SIT and SCT share a common focus, to date, there has been little theoretical overlap between the two theories. Some form of synthesis between the theories would be useful however, because task group members are often differentiated in terms of both status characteristics and group memberships. For example, consider a United States senate committee comprising Republicans and Democrats. Here, SIT and SCT generate potentially conflicting predictions. SCT predicts that the committee members who possess a relatively high state of a status characteristic will be influential, and SIT argues that in-group members will be most influential. But what happens when status and group membership are incongruent? For instance, when an evaluator is assessing the suggestions of a high status out-group actor. Perhaps a context where a junior Democratic member of a senate committee is assessing the suggestions of a senior Republican committee member. In these types of settings, do status and group membership combine in some meaningful way?

Recently, Kalkhoff and Barnum (2000) examined the joint impact of status and group membership in a standardized experimental setting. They reported three important results: (1) the effects of group memberships and diffuse status characteristics were of similar strength, (2) when status and group membership were congruent the effects were additive and (3) when status and group membership were incongruent their effects tended to cancel one another out.[1]

Although Kalkhoff and Barnum's study made strides toward integrating SIT and SCT, their treatment lacked theoretical rigor. Kalkhoff and Barnum demonstrated that status and group membership interacted in predictable ways in task settings, but they did not propose a theory to explain why this should occur. Recently, Barnum (2003) presented a theory that served as an initial step in this direction. This theory is founded on a concept called a "group status typification state" defined as an evaluator's conceptual understanding of in-group members as good sources of information. This paper extends Barnum's formulation by using the Berger et al. (1977) graph-theoretic method to model contexts where both group memberships and status characteristics are salient. This work may prove a first step in explaining contexts where both group memberships and status characteristics affect influence patterns.

The remainder of this paper is organized as follows: first, I summarize SIT and SCT, and then present a discussion of common ground between the two approaches focusing in particular on how graph-theoretic structures containing *behavioral interchange patterns* may serve as a nexus between the two theories. Next, I present the integration theory and examine the distinction between status characteristics and group memberships. Finally, I demonstrate the theory using graph-theoretic structures focusing on settings where status and group membership are salient.

SOCIAL IDENTITY THEORY

SIT seeks to understand the effect that category membership has on thoughts, perceptions, and behaviors. The theory stems from two seminal experiments conducted by Henri Tajfel and colleagues in the late 1950s and early 1960s (Tajfel, 1959; Tajfel & Wilkes, 1963). These experiments investigated the impact that categorization had on subjects' perceptions of physical objects. In these experiments, participants judged the similarity of several lines. In one experimental condition, the lines were divided into two sets and then explicitly presented as groups. In another condition, the lines were separated into sets, but were not explicitly presented as separate groups. Tajfel and colleagues found that when the lines were labeled as groups, the participant's perceptions of the lines were distorted: the participants perceived greater similarity within each set than actually existed and greater dissimilarity between the sets than actually existed. This *accentuation effect* did not occur in conditions where the sets were not explicitly labeled. Tajfel and colleagues reasoned that this biasing effect occurred because people used categorization to bring into focus subjectively meaningful aspects of their context or environment.

From this foundation, Tajfel and his associates developed a cognitive theory of stereotyping (Tajfel, 1969a, b). The investigators reasoned that just as with physical stimuli, the categorization of people into social groups generates an accentuation effect. Specifically, categorization leads people to perceive increased similarity within groups and decreased similarity between groups. According to SIT, this perceptual distortion in conjunction with a self-esteem motive, generates discrimination. People tend to favor others whom they perceive as similar to themselves, but not those whom they perceive as dissimilar. In a series of experiments, Tajfel and his collaborators demonstrated that in conditions marked by uncertainty, categorization per se was sufficient to produce in-group favoritism (Tajfel, 1970; Tajfel, Billig, Bundy, & Flament, 1971; Hogg & Abrams, 1993).

SELF-CATEGORIZATION THEORY

In the late 1970s, John Turner and his associates developed self-categorization theory, which is generally considered to be an extension of SIT, even though the theory places much more emphasis on the cognitive underpinnings of the categorization process than does SIT (Turner, 1985; Turner, Hogg, Oakes, Reicher, & Wetherell, 1987).

Self-categorization theory articulates how the cognitive process of categorization generates certain *intra-group* behaviors. Using SIT's accentuation principle as a starting point, the theory delineates how categorization affects an evaluator's perceptions of self and others. The central idea of the theory is that group behavior is best thought of as a context where individuals are acting more in terms of a *shared* group identity, than in terms of separate personal identities (Turner, 1991, p. 155).

The theory argues that people cognitively represent social groups in terms of "prototypes" (Turner, 1985; Hogg, 1996). A prototype can be thought of as an attribute that embodies the levels of characteristics that an ideal-typical, generalized member of the group would possess. An evaluator perceives a collection of people as a group to the extent that they are similar to her cognitive representation of the group prototype. As articulated by SIT, the process of categorization generates an accentuation effect. When an evaluator categorizes herself and others in terms of group membership she perceives an accentuation of similarity among in-group members and of decreased similarity between in-group members and out-group members. Categorization generates *depersonalization* – the perceived interchangeability of group members in terms of the prototypical features of the group (Turner, 1985; Turner et al., 1987). When categorization occurs then, group members come to see themselves as interchangeable in terms of the prototypical features of the group. They no longer see themselves as unique individuals. In the same way, group members come to perceive out-group members in an interchangeable fashion, rather than as unique individuals.

Self-categorization theory asserts that depersonalization in conjunction with an "uncertainty reduction motivation" are two of the fundamental processes that generate group type behaviors *including influence* (Hogg & Mullin, 1999; Hogg, 2000, 2001). These ideas stem in part from classic social comparison theory (Festinger, 1954; Moscovici, 1976, 1981; Moscovici & Mungy, 1983; Suls & Miller, 1977; Suls & Wills, 1991). Group generated influence is mediated via uncertainty reduction through social comparison. In essence, this argument asserts that the veracity of all social judgements is determined through social comparison. People establish confidence in their beliefs and opinions by comparing them to the beliefs and opinions held by similar others. Often these referents are in-group members. Consensus is important. If all referents agree with an individual's beliefs, then she is confident that she is correct. The evaluator believes that her perceptions are a function of the observable world, not a result of personally distinctive or biased perceptions. However, disagreement generates uncertainty, which is aversive. Lack of consensus with people who are similar implies to an evaluator that her perceptions may be biased. This is because people do not expect to disagree with someone who is similar to themselves. Moreover, in settings where group membership is salient, an evaluator will perceive in-group members as similar to himself in terms of the group prototype (i.e., in-group members are depersonalized). Because uncertainty is aversive, people experience negative affect and feelings of conflict when they disagree with others whom they perceive as similar to themselves (Rink & Ellemers, 2005; Ellemers & Rink, 2005). Disagreement with in-group members then, opens the door to influence because it generates uncertainty and the thought that perceptions may not be a function of the observable world, but rather produced by a personal cognitive distortion.

Uncertainty and group identification may also serve to instigate or strengthen beliefs and values that justify existing social arrangements including who influences whom. Hogg (2000, 2005) argues that these "ideological" belief systems are more likely to occur in contexts where levels of uncertainty are high and groups are cohesive with members who share a common fate. In such contexts, people identify more strongly with their group and influence occurs because groups develop practices and belief systems that are intolerant of internal dissent.

STATUS CHARACTERISTICS THEORY

SCT is a branch of the expectation states research program developed to provide a framework for understanding the emergence of power and prestige structures in group task settings (Berger et al., 1972, 1977; Berger, Rosenholtz, & Zelditch, 1980). SCT explains how certain observable characteristics of task group members generate task ability expectations among group members, and how these expectations in turn, affect participation rates, rewards and influence across group members (Berger et al., 1977). The theory argues that in social contexts such as a task setting, certain characteristics of a person are invested with status value (Berger et al., 1972;

Thye, 2000). This status value generates a status hierarchy among group members and consequently expectations about task competency. Group members act as if they expect the higher status members of the group to be more competent than the lower status members. As such, higher status members rank higher in the *observable power* and *prestige order* of the group. Accordingly, they are given more opportunities to make task suggestions, they do indeed contribute more suggestions, their suggestions are more positively evaluated and they are more influential than other members of the group.

A status characteristic is any property of a person that has two or more levels that are differentially valued, and associated with each level are one or more similarly evaluated expectations for behavior (Berger et al., 1972; Berger, Fisek, & Norman, 1977; Webster & Foschi, 1988). SCT defines two types of status characteristics: specific status characteristics consist of two or more differentially evaluated states and a set of similarly evaluated performance expectations relevant to a specific task. Diffuse status characteristics meet the two parts of the specific status characteristics definition, and further incorporate the idea of a similarly evaluated "generalized expectation state." This means that a diffuse status characteristic carries with it a set of expectations without specific limit. Individuals who possess the high state are thought to be better at a wide variety of tasks than individuals who possess the low state of the characteristic (Webster & Hysom, 1998; Berger et al., 1977).

SCT specifies a well-defined scope of application and five logically connected assumptions that link status characteristics with interaction. The theory applies to settings where interactants are *collectively* oriented to solve an *evaluated* task.[2] Collectively oriented participants believe that it is both necessary and legitimate to consider each other's suggestions in attempting to solve the task. An evaluated task is one that participants believe has a right or wrong answer and one for which there exists an instrumental ability to solve the task (see Appendix B for a more formal presentation of SCT).

COMMON GROUND

As noted, SIT and SCT each generate theoretical arguments that explicate why influence occurs in task settings. SIT's theoretical argument centers on an uncertainty reduction motivation and SCT's centers on ability expectations created by status characteristics. In the search for common ground, it is useful to juxtapose key features of these two approaches.

According to SIT, people experience uncertainty when they disagree with others whom they perceive as similar to themselves. Uncertainty is an aversive state for people because their survival may rest on being able to construct a meaningful and predictable world (Mullen & Hogg, 1999, p. 92). People use social comparison to reduce uncertainty. Group membership plays a significant role in the social comparison process, because when group memberships are salient, depersonalization occurs and people perceive accentuated similarity among group members. Accordingly, when people disagree with in-group members, they experience increased amounts of uncertainty and consequently, are more sensitive to influence.

SCT articulates how status characteristics organize interaction and influence in task groups. The central claim of the theory is that status characteristics serve as potent cues that enable task group members to infer one another's task solving ability. When a status characteristic becomes activated in the task group setting, people act as if they draw on the culturally defined expectations associated with it to guide their interaction with other members of the group. The theory argues that the ordering that results from status characteristics occurs even when the characteristics are not directly relevant to the task.

Ideas developed in the course of investigating *behavioral interaction patterns* (Balkwell, 1991; Fisek, Berger, & Norman, 1991; Skvoretz & Fararo, 1996) may provide a conduit for integrating these disparate explanations. The concept of behavioral interchange pattern was developed in the "evaluation–expectations" branch of the expectation states research program. Expectation states researchers are interested in how interaction patterns in newly formed, freely interacting task groups result in interaction advantages and disadvantages among group members (Fisek et al., 1991, p. 116). Small group researchers have known for some time that influence patterns quickly become stable in both status heterogeneous and status homogeneous task groups. In heterogeneous groups, like the classic jury studies by Strodtbeck and his colleagues (Strodtbeck & Mann, 1956; Strodtbeck, James, & Hawkins, 1957), the cause is well known. Influence patterns are a product of performance expectations associated with status characteristics. In homogeneous groups, for example, Bales research groups of the 1950s, researchers believe that influence patterns result from subtle interaction styles among group members. These interaction styles are the essence of behavioral interchange patterns.

Specifically, in any freely interacting task group, task-oriented behavior can be classified into one of four categories: chances to contribute a task suggestion, an actual task suggestion, a positive reaction, or a negative reaction. As interaction transpires in a task group, these four classifications of behavior serve as the building blocks for "behavior cycles" (Fisek et al., 1991, p. 116). The most fundamental behavior cycle occurs when one actor is offered a chance to contribute a task suggestion, the actor does indeed contribute a suggestion and another actor reacts either positively or negatively to the first actor's suggestion.

If this fundamental behavioral cycle becomes stable during the course of interaction, then it serves to organize the communication, including who influences whom in the group (Fisek et al., 1991, p. 116). A behavioral interchange pattern is simply a context where the interactants accept a repeating fundamental cycle of behavior.

Fisek et al. (1991, p. 117) argue that an established behavioral interchange pattern activates a *status typification state* for actors in the setting. A status typification state is an abstract classification of behaviors into high and low status types. In ordinary terms, it is a conceptual understanding that actors hold of what high and low status behaviors should be like in the setting (Fisek et al., 1991, p. 118). Status typification states are commonly designated by such expressive anchors as "leader–follower," or "initiator–reactor." Salient status typification states are relevant to similarly evaluated abstract task ability states. These in turn are linked to task outcomes. The idea here is that once behavioral interchange patterns become salient they provide paths linking actors in the setting with expectations for task outcomes. These expectations then function to order interaction because they provide cues for actors to use when interacting with one another.

Barnum (2003) used the concept of a status typification state as a nexus for integrating SIT and SCT. Because the idea plays such a key role in extending Barnum's (2003) theory, it is useful to use Berger et al. (1977) graph-theoretic method as a medium for laying out the theoretical integration (see Appendix C for a brief discussion of the graph-theoretic method).

In the completed structure depicted in Fig. 1, actor P possesses the positive position $b(+)$ in the behavioral interchange pattern and actor O possesses the negative position $b(-)$. Consequently, we would expect P to contribute more task suggestions than O, and O to uphold P's contributions with agreement. A stable behavioral interchange pattern activates a similarly evaluated status typification state $B(+)$ or $B(-)$ for actors in the setting. As noted, $B(+)$ and $B(-)$ represent a conceptual understanding that actors hold of what constitutes high and low status behaviors. In this structure, P's frequent task contributions and O's support for them activates in both actors the belief that P's behavior is typical, for example, of a leader represented by $B(+)$, and O's behavior is typical of a follower designated by

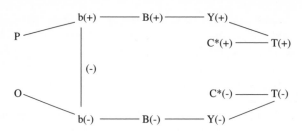

Fig. 1.   Completed Status Typification Structure.

B(−). The salient status typification state induces in both actors a belief that P has more ability (in an abstract sense) than does O, and consequently that P's task contributions are more apt to produce successful task outcomes designated by T(+), than will O's designated by T(−). It should be noted that abstract task ability is an induced element that is brought into existence by the strong task demands of the context, and represented in the graphs by the symbols Y(+) and Y(−). Abstract task ability is an implied element. Actors who possess the positive state are thought to have the ability to do well at many different types of tasks, and actors who possess the negative state are thought to lack this ability. Abstract task ability should not be confused with instrumental task ability, represented by the symbols C*(+) and C*(−). Instrumental task ability is the specific ability or talent necessary to successfully complete the task. For example, mathematical ability is the specific talent necessary to solve a math problem. Instrumental ability C* is always relevant to similarly signed task outcomes T (Berger et al., 1977). However, it is possible for an actor to be linked to abstract ability states, but not instrumental states. For example, an evaluator may not know that another has mathematical ability, but still believe that she will be able to solve a math problem (because the evaluator believes the other has abstract task ability, that is, the ability to do well at many types of tasks). In Fig. 1, neither actor is linked to C*, hence, actor P possesses more abstract ability than does actor O, but not necessarily more instrumental task ability.

GROUP STATUS TYPIFICATION STATE

In task settings, the demands of the context compel people to look for cues to assess who among them may be proficient at solving the task. Group membership serves as one such cue. When group membership information is available, task demands prompt people to regard a fellow in-group member as a "referent" or a "good source of information." As outlined below, support for this thesis comes from traditional arguments found in SIT.

Established accounts of SIT assert two important points: People obtain confidence in their beliefs through social comparison and yet, when making social comparisons, people utilize a limited or restricted range of comparison with others. People tend to focus on comparisons that reflect positively on the groups to which they belong. Motivations for positive self esteem cause people to strive to differentiate the in-group from the out-group on dimensions that favor the in-group (Abrams & Hogg, 1988; Tajfel & Turner, 1979; Turner, 1982; Hogg, Turner, Nascimento-Schulze, & Spriggs, 1986; Oakes & Turner, 1980). Comparisons then, often occur in contexts where people perceive opinions held by in-group members as better or more accurate than those held by out-group members. As people live their lives and evaluate others' suggestions, experience teaches them that in-group members' recommendations are helpful, profitable, and beneficial.

In the uncertainty of a task setting, the in-group provides people with a technique to reduce subjective uncertainty. On some cognitive level, memories of perceiving in-group members in a positive light and recalling past accomplishments becomes linked in the mind of an evaluator with the perception of fellow group members as "advisers," or "good sources of information." This perception is a concept that I call *group status typification state* – an abstract classification of in-group members as good sources of information. It is a conceptual understanding that actors hold of who in the setting is likely to be a reliable source of information. A group status typification state is an implied, unobservable theoretical construct. The idea here is that starting very early in life, people tend to rely on others who are similar, often in-group members (such as family members, schoolmates, etc.) to guide them and help them make decisions. In contexts where group memberships are salient, comparisons often occur in settings where the in-group is seen in a more favorable light than the out-group. Consequently, as people strive to differentiate the positive aspects of the in-group, they often view advice coming from in-group members as better than that coming from out-group members. As life progresses then, people come to understand in an abstract way, that fellow group members are dependable sources of counsel.

Once a status typification state becomes relevant in a task setting, it links actors with outcomes according to standard arguments found in SCT. People act as if they believe group members will be good sources of information and so, afford in-group members interaction advantages in the task group.

Disidentification

During the course of the development of the integration theory, an area of substantial debate has been whether group membership generates out-group disidentification also known as a "boomerang effect." For our purposes, disidentification is defined as a context where an evaluator shows disfavor for out-group members by being predisposed to evaluate them as poor sources of information. In such a context, evaluators act as if out-group members' proposals are more likely to be wrong than to be right. Assuming that people have no preconceived notions about a total stranger's ability, it follows that such evaluators would perceive an out-group member as a worse source of information than a total stranger. The negative evaluations stemming from disidentification are a product of group membership. It seems likely that disidentification is more apt to be present in settings where a group is characterized by high entitativity[3] and strong identification (Hogg, 2004). For example, a setting where there is a long standing history of enmity between groups.

Recent experimental evidence however (Barnum, 2003; Kalkhoff & Barnum, 2000) suggests that, out-group disidentification is not present in settings where identification is less robust.

Barnum (2003) and Kalkhoff and Barnum (2000) each using a modified SCT experimental setting found no evidence of disidentification. In both experiments, subjects were asked to work with partners to complete a task. Barnum's (2003) experiment tested for the existence of disidentification and consisted of three conditions. In the first condition, participants were told that their partner was an in-group member; in a second condition, they were told their partner was an out-group member; and in a third (control) condition participants were given no group membership information (i.e., group membership was not salient).[4]

Barnum tested for the presence of disidentification by predicting that in-group members would be more influential than unknown others, and that unknown others would be more influential than out-group members. The presumption being that if disidentification was present, then participants would perceive out-group members as a poor source of information; in fact, a worse source of information than a total stranger.

Results were contrary to this prediction. Although, in-group members were found to be more influential than unknown others, unknown others were *not* more influential than out-group members. Kalkhoff and Barnum (2000) found corroborative results. Using a slightly different experimental design, they also found that out-group membership did not decrease influence. Contrary to their predictions, participants who were *both* lower status and out-group members were no less influential than participants who were lower status only. Together these studies suggest that in settings marked by low identity, disidentification does not affect interaction.[5]

In settings lacking disidentification, out-group membership has no effect on interaction. Members of the task setting treat it as irrelevant and evaluators do not form negative group status typification states for out-group members. As will be illustrated below, only positive or negative abstract ability expectations become connected to task outcomes. In the integration theory detailed below, I call any actor in the setting linked with task outcomes an *appraised* actor. In settings marked by low identification, only in-group members are appraised actors.

Before using Berger et al. (1977) graph-theoretic method to model contexts where both status characteristics and group memberships are salient, it is useful to explicitly state the integration theory to highlight these ideas.

THE INTEGRATION THEORY

At a minimum, the theory applies to contexts where: (1) A focal actor believes there is a pool of participants each of whom is an in-group member, an out-group member or both. (2) The focal actor believes that she is working with at least one member of the pool as a partner on a collective evaluated task. (3) The focal actor is using group memberships, status characteristics or both as cues for behavior. Any context that satisfies these conditions is called a *task setting*.

Assumption 1. If a group membership differentiates members of a task setting, then it will be *salient*

Assumption 2. If group membership is salient and not explicitly *disassociated*[6] from the task, then the focal actor forms group status typification states for appraised actors.

Assumption 2a. The focal actor forms positive group status typification states for in-group members.

Assumption 3. If the focal actor forms group status typification states for appraised actors, then the focal actor forms similarly evaluated abstract ability expectations for appraised actors.

Assumption 4. If the focal actor forms evaluated abstract ability expectations for appraised actors, then evaluated abstract ability expectations become connected to similarly evaluated task outcome states (see SCT 4 below).

Assumption 5. If evaluated abstract ability expectations become connected to similarly evaluated task outcomes then, the focal actor's levels of uncertainty decrease when he/she agrees with in-group members' suggestions and remain the same when he/she agrees with out-group members' suggestions.

RELEVANT SCT ASSUMPTIONS[7]

SCT 4 (Aggregation): If an actor P is connected to task outcome states in a completed structure, then the P's aggregated expectations e_P may be represented by

$$e_P^+ = [1 - (1 - f(i) \ldots (1 - f(n))]$$

$$e_P^+ = -[1 - (1 - f(i) \ldots (1 - f(n))]$$

$$e_P = e_P^+ - e_P^-$$

where i and n are path lengths and $f(i)$ and $f(n)$ are monotonically decreasing functions of i and n.

Integration Theory Assumption 4a. Aggregated expectations, for non-appraised actors equals zero, $e_O = 0$, where e_O is a non-appraised actor.

SCT 5 (basic expectation assumption): once an actor P has formed aggregated expectation states for self and other, P's power and prestige position relative to other actors O, will be a direct function of P's expectation advantage over $O(e_P - e_O)$ in the situation.

GRAPH-THEORETIC EXTENSION

It is useful to use Berger et al.'s (1977) graph-theoretic method to illustrate the theory. Fig. 2 depicts a three-actor setting where group disidentification is not present. This figure is used as a foundation for the arguments presented below.

First focus on the top portion of this graph. Actors P and O_1 are interactants who perceive each other as belonging to the same group represented

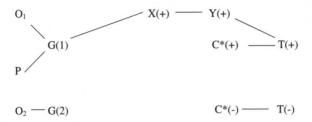

Fig. 2. A Three-Person Structure with No Out-Group Disidentification.

as G(1). The salient group membership activates a positively evaluated group status typification state X(+) for both actors. The symbol X(+) represents a conceptual understanding that actors hold of the type of person who constitutes a good source of information. In this structure, group membership activates in actors P and O_1 the belief that the other is typical of a person that should be used as a source of information. This salient positive group status typification state induces in both actors a belief that the other has abstract ability Y(+) and this in turn is relevant to positive task outcomes T(+).

In the bottom portion of Fig. 2, we see that actor O_2 belongs to a different group, G(2). Hence, actors P and O_1 perceive O_2 as an out-group member. Since out-group disidentification is not present in this structure, out-group membership has no effect on the interaction. That is, actor O_2 does not become linked to task outcomes. In essence, out-group membership impacts behavior to the same degree as no information at all.

In this structure actors P and O_1, are connected to positive task outcomes by a single path of length 4 and as noted, actor O_2 is not connected to a task outcome. Berger et al.'s (1977) function for the calculation of influence, predicts that P and O_1 will be more influential than O_2 and that O_2 would be as influential as a stranger whom the evaluator knew nothing about.[8]

Actors P and O_1 are equally influential in this structure. Although this conclusion may at first appear surprising, the argument is a product of the interdependent nature of group influence. In contexts where group membership is salient, in-group members mutually impact one another. As one group member is influencing a second, the second is contemporaneously influencing the first.

This points to important differences in the essence of status characteristics and group memberships. At the core of this disparity is the potential for consensus in a completed structure. Specifically, the potential for consensus in terms of possession, value and ability. Let us examine each in turn.

Potential for Consensus in Terms of Possession

Although SCT diagrams are constructed from the point of view of a focal actor P, the theory assumes the analysis can be applied to any actor in the structure under the assumption that perceptions are identical (Berger et al., 1977, p. 96; Fisek et al., 1991). In these types of structures, there is consensus among actors regarding who possess specific states of each characteristic. For instance, if one actor possesses the higher state of a diffuse status characteristic, then all actors in the setting agree that this actor possesses that state. Group membership is different. When group membership is salient, there is not consensus among actors concerning who possess distinct states of group membership. Specifically, possession of *in-group* and *out-group membership* is dependent on perspective. Actors in a setting may agree on who belongs to a particular group, but not agree on who is an in-group member and who is an out-group member. For example, in Fig. 2, all actors in the setting would agree that P and O_1 belong to group G(1) and O_2 belongs to group G(2). However, there would not be agreement among the actors concerning in-group membership. Actor P would perceive O_1 as an in-group member, but O_2 would view O_1 as an out-group member. This lack of consensus is notable, because as outlined above, in-group membership generates influence.

Potential for Consensus in Terms of Value

By definition, each state of a status characteristic is differentially evaluated in culture (Webster & Hysom, 1998; Shelley & Webster, 1997). This implies there is consensus among actors in a completed structure concerning which states of a status characteristic are positively or negatively evaluated. Group membership is different. It is not inexorably associated with a consensual value assessment. Rather, group membership can simply be a label used to identify a set of objects as belonging together. Actors in a setting need not agree that association with one label is better than association with the other. For example, SIT researchers frequently use groups consisting of members who are assigned on the basis of a coin flip. These "minimal groups" are arbitrarily labeled using designations such as "Alpha" or "Beta." It seems unlikely that subjects in these settings would reach a consensus that it is, for example, better to be an "Alpha" than a "Beta."[9]

Additionally, traditional accounts of SIT argue that when group membership is salient, the context is often marked by ethnocentrism. In these settings actors value the in-group, but not the out-group, and so there is not a consensus concerning who possess the valued states of group membership. In the preceding example, a context where "Alphas" judge "Alphas" as the best, and "Betas" evaluate "Betas" as best.

Potential for Consensus in Terms of Ability

Under the assumption that perceptions are identical, SCT argues that there is consensus among actors regarding performance expectations. Since the valued states of status characteristics are associated with similarly evaluated expectation states, all interactants in these settings act as if they expect higher status actors to be more capable at solving the task than lower status actors. Again however, group membership is different. When it is salient, actors in a setting do not agree about who is linked with positive task outcomes. Only *in-group membership* generates ability expectations. Applying the illustration above, members of the "Alpha" group would believe that fellow "Alphas" are linked with positive task outcomes because they are good sources of information, but members of the "Betas" would not.

Together, these three sources of incongruity highlight the distinction between group memberships and status characteristics.

TWO-PERSON STRUCTURES

As noted, recent experimental evidence suggests that out-group disidentification does not exist in settings lacking strong identification. In these types of settings out-group membership has no effect on interaction. Consequently, in a two-person setting comprised of interactants who belong to separate groups, the group distinction does not impact interaction patterns in any systematic way. Fig. 3 depicts such a structure.

Neither actor in this setting is linked to task outcomes. The participants act as if they had no information about their partners. Although it seems likely that a behavioral interchange pattern would ultimately develop in

$$P \ \text{---} G(1) \qquad C^*(+) \ \text{------} \ T(+)$$

$$O_2 \ \text{---} G(2) \qquad C^*(-) \ \text{------} \ T(-)$$

Fig. 3. A Two-Person Structure with No Out-Group Disidentification.

this setting (e.g., Fisek et al., 1991; Bales, 1953; Bales, Strodtbeck, & Rosenberg, 1951), they would not be a function of group membership. Instead the patterns would be a product of subtle interaction styles among the interactants.

GROUP AND STATUS CHARACTERISTICS COMBINED

The information presented in Figs. 2 and 3 above provides a means to illustrate settings where both diffuse status characteristics and group memberships are salient. Although there are an infinite number of structures possible, this discussion will be limited to two relatively simple ones that illustrate the potential of this method and the principle claims of this paper.[10]

Fig. 4 depicts a simple two-person structure consisting of interactants who differ in status and group membership. In this structure, group membership does not impact behavior. Actors P and O_1 belong to different groups and there is no out-group disidentification (see Fig. 3). Actor P possesses the relatively higher state of a diffuse status characteristic represented by $D(+)$ and actor O_1 possesses the lower state $D(-)$. In this setting, P is more influential than is O_1 because P is connected to positive task outcomes by paths of length 4 and 5. Actor O_1 is connected to negative task outcomes by paths of length 4 and 5.

Fig. 5 is a little more complex. It illustrates a three-person structure where both status and group membership influence behavior. Actors P and O_1 belong to group G(1) and actor O_2 belongs to group G(2). Actor P possesses

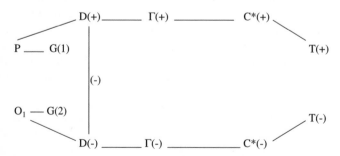

Fig. 4.   A Two-Person Structure Involving Status and Group Membership.

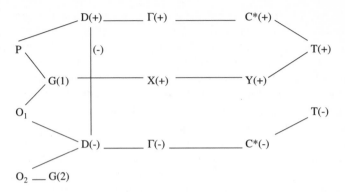

Fig. 5. A Three-Person Structure Involving Status and Group Membership.

the relatively higher state of a diffuse status characteristic $D(+)$ and actors O_1 and O_2 possess the lower state $D(-)$.

The Berger et al. (1977) function for calculation of influence informs that actor P is the most influential in this structure. This follows because P is connected to positive task outcomes by two paths of length 4 and one path of length 5. Actor O_1 is next most influential. O_1 is connected to positive task outcomes by a path of length 4 and to negative task outcomes by a path of length 4 and a path of length 5. Least influential is actor O_2. This actor is connected to negative task outcomes by a path of length 4 and a path of length 5.

Although the preceding two structures are relatively simple, they illustrate the propositions of the integration theory and reveal meaningful aspects of settings characterized by status characteristics and group membership. First, they illustrate how in-group generated influence patterns in task settings are mediated via "group status typification states." This concept refers to an abstract classification of in-group members as a good source of information. From early in life, people rely on advice from in-group members, and as they strive to differentiate the positive aspects of the in-group, they come to view in-group advice as better than out-group advice. When group membership becomes salient in a task setting then, people act as if in-group members are good or reliable sources of information and so are influenced by them.

Second, these structures illustrate how in-group membership affects influence patterns in task settings, while out-group membership does not. These structures model settings where group identification is low. In these settings, people act as if they treat in-group members as good sources of information, but deal with out-group members in much the same way as they would others for whom they had no information at all – as irrelevant.

Third, these structures model the effects of in-group membership and diffuse status characteristics as approximately equal in strength and as joining according to the principles of "organized subsets combing" (Berger et al., 1992). As such, "positive and negative information about each actor is sorted into distinct same valued subsets" (Berger et al., 1992, p. 844). In these sets, each additional piece of group or status information to enter has a decreasing proportional effect. For example, when the effects of a positively evaluated diffuse status characteristic and in-group membership are combined, the effect of the set on performance expectations increases, but it does not double (even though the information in the set has doubled). Each of these claims is theoretical in nature, but readily testable in SCT's standardized experimental setting.

CONCLUSIONS

This paper serves as an initial step toward a theoretical integration of SCT and SIT. Although SCT and SIT have been successful in explaining influence patterns in task group settings, each perspective has approached the problem from a different theoretical orientation. SIT's focus is an uncertainty reduction motivation, and SCT's focus is on performance expectations. This paper presents a graph-theoretic method as an initial step toward a nexus between the two traditions.

At the core of this method is the group status typification state, represented as $X(+)$. A group status typification state is a conceptual understanding that participants hold of the type of person who would be a good source of information. This concept is pivotal in understanding the nature of the relationship between group membership and status and in explaining why in-group membership affects behavior in task settings, but out-group membership does not.

It is important to keep in mind that research on the combined effects of group membership and status is very limited. The available evidence however, suggests that the effects of status and in-group membership unite according to the principle of "organized subsets combining" (Berger et al., 1992). In task settings, people act as if they combine information into like signed sets, where each additional piece of information has a decreasing proportional effect. The evidence also suggests that at least in settings where group identification is not strong, out-group disidentification is not present.

People treat out-group members much the same way as they would total strangers. However, in contexts where identification is stronger, it is possible that disidentification may occur. It may be that in these types of contexts, the increased group salience would cause people to resolve status and group membership inconsistencies (e.g., evaluating information from a low status in-group member or a high status out-group member) using a balancing or canceling strategy,[11] instead of a combining system. These are empirical questions that require further investigation.

Even so, our limited knowledge may prove useful in the development of applied intervention strategies to attenuate the status disadvantages some actors must face. For example, in a classroom setting, this information may prove beneficial in developing strategies that could be used to counteract the status disability (Ridgeway, 1982) that poorer students face. For instance, knowing group membership's strength and how it combines with status could be used to generate locally created minimal groups that would serve to offset the effects of status that poorer students face in the classroom setting. Perhaps the information from this line of research is an initial step in this direction.

NOTES

1. Status and group membership are congruent when in comparison to the person being influenced, the person exerting influence is a high status in-group member or a low status out-group member. Status and group membership are incongruent when the person exerting influence is a high status out-group member or a low status in-group member.

2. In addition, the setting must include at least two actors attempting to success-fully complete the task. (Berger et al., 1977, p. 104) the actors must possess status elements that are related to the task or provide a basis of discrimination between them and the only information that the interactants initially have about one another is their status characteristics (Berger et al., 1977, p. 96).

3. Entitativity is the extent to which a group is a coherent and distinct entity that is homogenous and well structured, has clear boundaries, and whose members share a common fate (Hogg, 2004; Campbell, 1958; Hamilton & Sherman, 1996).

4. The participants believed they would use a computer to communicate with their partners. The partner was actually fictitious. Participants believed that in-group members shared artistic preference, and that out-group members did not. The experiment consisted of 25 binary choice exercises for the subject and his "partner" to solve.

5. See Appendix A for an illustration and further discussion of a structure characterized by out-group disidentification.

6. The terms *salient* and *disassociated* are adapted from SCT (Berger et al., 1977, p. 106). Salient means used as a cue for behavior, and group membership and task outcomes are disassociated when actors believe them to be independent.

7. See Appendix B (Shelley & Webster, 1997).

8. There is no *dimensionality* between group memberships in this structure because Berger et al. (1977) state that dimensionality exists only between two oppositely evaluated states of a characteristic or goal object. As diagrammed above, dimensionality does not exist between in-group membership and out-group membership. Group membership in a minimal group setting is not associated with a shared value assessment, thus no dimensionality exists between the groups in Fig. 2.

9. In addition, a group membership is not a "valued personal characteristic" (Driskell, 1982; Webster & Hysom, 1998). A valued personal characteristic has two or more states that are differentially evaluated in culture, but carries no specific or general performance expectations. Group memberships are excluded from this definition because a particular state is not consensually valued in culture.

10. Refer to Appendix B for an explanation of SCT's graph-theoretic symbols.

11. Balancing occurs when people resolve inconsistencies by ignoring certain pieces of information (such as information that threatens self-esteem). Canceling occurs when people act as if inconsistent information cancels itself out (one piece of positive information cancels out an equal strength piece of negative information).

12. This discussion is adapted from Webster and Hysom (1998), Fisek et al. (1991), Skvoretz and Fararo (1977) and Berger et al. (1977).

13. $f(3) = 0.405556$.

REFERENCES

Abrams, D., & Hogg, M. A. (1988). Comments on the motivational status of self esteem in social identify and intergroup discrimination. *European Journal of Social Psychology, 18*, 317–334.

Asch, S. E. (1951). Effects of group pressure upon the modification and distortion of judgments. In: H. Guetzkow (Ed.), *Groups leadership and men*. Pittsburgh, PA: Carnegie Press.

Asch, S. E. (1956). Studies of independence and conformity: A minority of one against a unanimous majority. *Psychological monographs, 70*, 416.

Bales, R. F. (1953). The equilibrium problem in small groups. In: T. Parsons, R. F. Bales & E. H. Shils (Eds), *Working papers in the theory of action*. New York: Free Press.

Bales, R. F., Strodtbeck, F. L., & Rosenberg, M. (1951). Channels of communication in small groups. *American Sociological Review, 16*, 461–468.

Balkwell, J. W. (1991). From expectations to behavior: An improved postulate for E Expectation States Theory. *American Sociological Review, 56*, 355–369.

Barnum, C.C. (2003). *The effects of group membership and status organizing processes in collective task settings: A step towards theoretical integration*. Unpublished doctoral dissertation, University of Iowa. Iowa City, Iowa.

Berger, J., Cohen, B. P., & Zelditch, M., Jr. (1972). Status characteristics and social interaction. *American Sociological Review, 37*, 241–255.

Berger, J., Fisek, M. H., Norman, R. Z., & Zelditch, M., Jr. (1977). *Status characteristics and social interaction: An expectation states approach*. New York: Elsevier.

Berger, J., Norman, R. Z., & Balkwell, J. (1992). Status inconsistency in task situations: A test of four status processing principles. *American Sociological Review, 57*, 843–855.

Berger, J., Rosenholtz, S. J., & Zelditch, M., Jr. (1980). Status organizing processes. *Annual Review of Sociology, 6*, 479–508.

Berger, J., & Zelditch, M., Jr. (1985). *Status rewards and influence.* San Francisco: Jossey-Bass.

Campbell, D. T. (1958). Common fate, similarity, and other indices of the status of aggregates of persons as social entities. *Behavioral Science, 3*, 14–15.

Driskell, J. E. (1982). Personal characteristics and performance expectations. *Social Psychology Quarterly, 45*, 229–237.

Ellemers, N., & Rink, F. (2005). Identity in work groups: The beneficial and detrimental consequences of multiple identities and group norms for collaboration and group performance. In: E. Lawler & S. Thye (Eds), *Advances in group processes*, Vol. 22. Oxford, England: Elsevier.

Festinger, L. (1954). A theory of social comparison processes. *Human Relations, 7*, 117–140.

Fisek, M., Berger, J., & Norman, R. Z. (1991). Participation in heterogeneous groups: A theoretical integration. *American Journal of Sociology, 97*, 114–142.

Hamilton, D. L., & Sherman, S. J. (1996). Perceiving persons and groups. *Psychological Review, 103*, 336–355.

Hogg, M. A. (1996). Intragroup processes, group structure and social identity. In: W. P. Robinson (Ed.), *Social groups and identities: Developing the legacy of Henri Tajfel.* Oxford: Butterworth-Heinemann.

Hogg, M. A. (2000). Subjective uncertainty reduction through self-categorization: A motivational theory of social identity processes. *European Review of Social Psychology, 11*, 223–255.

Hogg, M. A. (2001). Self categorization and subjective uncertainty resolution: Cognitive and motivational facets of social identity and group membership. In: J. P. Forgas, K. D. Williams & L. Wheeler (Eds), *The social mind: Cognitive and motivational aspects of interpersonal behavior.* New York: Cambridge University Press.

Hogg, M. A. (2005). Uncertainty, social identity and ideology. In: E. Lawler & S. Thye (Eds), *Advances in group processes*, Vol. 22. Oxford, England: Elsevier.

Hogg, M. A., & Abrams, D. (1993). Towards a single process uncertainty reduction model of social motivation in groups. In: M. A. Hogg & D. Abrams (Eds), *Group motivation: Social psychological perspectives.* London: Harvester-Wheatsheaf & Englewood cliffs, NJ, Prentice Hall.

Hogg, M. A., & Mullin, B. A. (1999). Joining groups to reduce uncertainty: Subjective uncertainty reduction and group identification. In: D. Abrams & M. A. Hogg (Eds), *Social identity and social cognition.* Oxford: Blackwell.

Hogg, M. A., Turner, J. C., Nascimento-Schulze, C., & Spriggs, D. (1986). Social categorization, intergroup behavior and self esteem: Two experiments. *Revista De Psicologia Social, 1*, 23–37.

Kalkhoff, W., & Barnum, C. (2000). The effects of status organizing and social identity processes on patterns of social influence. *Social Psychology Quarterly, 63*, 95–116.

Moscovici, S. (1976). *Social influence and social change.* London: Academic Press.

Moscovici, S. (1981). On social representation. In: J. P. Forgas (Ed.), *Social cognition: Perspectives on everyday understanding.* London: Academic Press.

Moscovici, S., & Mungy, G. (1983). Minority influence. In: P. B. Paulis (Ed.), *Basic group processes.* New York: Springer.

Myers, D. G. (2005). *Social psychology* (8th ed.). New York: McGraw-Hill.

Oakes, P. J., & Turner, J. C. (1980). Social categorization and intergroup behavior: Does minimal intergroup discrimination make social identity more positive? *European Journal of Social Psychology, 10*, 295–301.

Ridgeway, C. (1982). Status in groups: The importance of motivation. *American Sociological Review*, *47*, 76–88.

Rink, F. A., & Ellemers, N. (2005). Work value diversity and decision making in dyads: Actual differences or violated expectations. In: E. Lawler & S. Thye (Eds), *Advances in group processes*, Vol. 22. Oxford, England: Elsevier.

Shelly, R., & Webster, M. (1997). How formal status, liking and ability structure interaction: Three theoretical perspectives and a test. *Sociological Perspectives*, *40*, 82–100.

Sherif, M. (1936). *The psychology of social norms*. New York: Harper.

Skvoretz, J., & Fararo, T. J. (1996). Status and participation in task groups: A dynamic network model. *American Journal of Sociology*, *101*, 1366–1414.

Strodtbeck, F. L., & Mann, R. D. (1956). Sex role differentiation in jury deliberations. *Sociometry*, *19*, 3–11.

Strodtbeck, F. L., James, R. M., & Hawkins, C. (1957). Social status in jury deliberations. *American Sociological Review*, *22*, 713–719.

Suls, J. M., & Miller, R. L. (1977). *Social comparison processes*. Washington DC: Hemisphere.

Suls, J. M., & Wills, T. A. (1991). *Social comparison: Contemporary theory and research*. Hillsdale, NJ: Lawrence Erlbaum Associates Inc.

Tajfel, H. (1959). Quantitative judgement in social perception. *British Journal of Psychology*, *50*, 16–29.

Tajfel, H. (1969a). Cognitive aspects of prejudice. *Journal of Social Issues*, *25*, 79–97.

Tajfel, H. (1969b). Social and cultural factors in perception. In: G. Lindzey & E. Aronson (Eds), *Handbook of social psychology*, Vol. 3. Reading, MA: Addison-Wesley.

Tajfel, H. (1970). Experiments in intergroup discrimination. *Scientific American*, *223*, 96–102.

Tajfel, H. (1974). Social identity and inter-group behavior. *Social Science Information*, *13*, 65–93.

Tajfel, H. (1978). *Differentiation between social groups*. London: Academic Press.

Tajfel, H. (1982). *Social identity and inter-group relations*. Cambridge: Cambridge University Press.

Tajfel, H., Billig, M., Bundy, R. P., & Flament, C. (1971). Social categorization and intergroup behavior. *European Journal of Social Psychology*, *1*, 149–177.

Tajfel, H., & Turner, J. C. (1979). An integrative theory of group conflict. In: W. G. Austin & S. Worchel (Eds), *The psychology of intergroup relations*. Monterey, CA: Brooks-Cole.

Tajfel, H., & Turner, J. C. (1986). The social identity theory of inter-group behavior. In: S. Worchel (Ed.), *Psychology of intergroup relations*. Chicago: Nelson-Hall.

Tajfel, H., & Wilkes, A. L. (1963). Classification and quantitative judgement. *British Journal of Psychology*, *54*, 101–114.

Thye, S. R. (2000). A status value theory of power in exchange networks. *American Sociological Review*, *65*(3), 407–432.

Turner, J. C. (1982). Towards a cognitive redefinition of the social group. In: H. Tajfel (Ed.), *Social identity and inter-group relations*. Cambridge: Cambridge University Press.

Turner, J. C. (1985). Social categorization and the self concept: A social cognitive theory of group behavior. In: E. Lawler (Ed.), *Advances in group process: Theory and research*, Vol. 2. Greenwich: JAI Press.

Turner, J. C. (1991). *Social influence*. Milton Keynes: Open Press.

Turner, J. C., Hogg, M. A., Oakes, P. J., Reicher, S. D., & Wetherell, M. (1987). *Rediscovering the social group: A self categorization theory*. Oxford: Blackwell.

Webster, M. J., & Foschi, M. (1988). *Status generalization*. Stanford, CA: Stanford University Press.

Webster, M. J., & Hysom, S. J. (1998). Creating status characteristics. *American Sociological Review, 63*(3), 351–378.

APPENDIX A

Actors in a setting characterized by out-group disidentification show disfavor toward the out-group by evaluating their members' suggestions in a negative fashion. In doing so, they establish an interaction pattern comprised of a positive and negative position between the members of different groups. Fig. A1 depicts such a structure.

In this structure, salient group out-group membership activates a negatively evaluated group status typification state for O_2. The symbol $X(-)$ represents a conceptual understanding that actors hold of the type of person who constitutes a poor source of information. In this context, group membership activates the belief among P and O_1 that O_2 should not be used as a source of information. That is, the presence of $X(-)$ represents a belief among P and O_1 that O_2 would be a worse source of information than a total stranger (i.e., third person for whom they knew nothing about).

Note in this structure, the omni-directional nature of group-generated influence generates ambiguity in interpreting the graphs. Specifically, we see that determining which actors in the setting possess the positive and negative positions is subjective. For example, while we may argue that actors P and

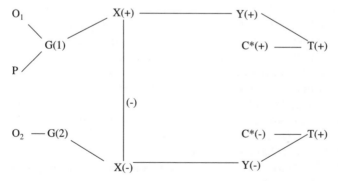

Fig. A1. A Three-Person Structure with Out-Group Disidentification.

O_1 tend to react negatively to O_2's performance outputs, we can equivalently argue that actor O_2 reacts negatively to P and O_1's suggestions. This makes deciding where to place the symbol X($+$) and X($-$) in the graph indeterminate. As a consequence, in structures characterized by out-group disidentification, all signs in the graph must be interpreted from a single actor's perspective. Fortunately, this complication is avoided in models lacking out-group disidentification.

As noted above, Barnum (2003) and Kalkhoff and Barnum (2000) using a modified Status Characteristics standardized experimental setting found support for the claims of the theory characterized by an absence of out-group disidentification (the model depicted in Fig. 2). Specifically, they found that participants were influenced more by in-group members than by out-group members or control subjects (partners for whom no group membership information is known) and no statistically significant evidence for out-group disidentification.

APPENDIX B

The Status Characteristic Theory is given in Table B1.

APPENDIX C

Graph-Theoretic Method

Fig. C1 is a graph-theoretic model of a task setting involving two actors P, the focal actor and O, the other.[12] In this model, the relations between points are depicted as lines. There are three types of relations: A *possession* relation exists between an actor and a status characteristic. It reflects that one actor in the setting possesses a given state of a status characteristic. A *relevance* connection exists between non-actor elements in the graph and reflects that the elements are in some way associated with one another. By convention, possession and relevance connections have a positive sign. The third relation, *dimensionality* holds between two differentially evaluated states of the same characteristic. This connection has a negative sign, showing that if an actor possesses one state the other state is precluded. All elements in the graph have two states, one positive and one negative. The positive sign signifies that the level of the element is the positively evaluated or preferred state and the negative sign signifies that the level of the element

Table B1. Status Characteristic Theory.

Scope Conditions: Individuals are both (1) task oriented and (2) collectively oriented.

Definition 1: A characteristic C is a *specific status characteristic* if:

a. It has ≥ 2 states, differentially evaluated;

b. Associated with each state are specific performance expectations for particular skills

Definition 2: A characteristic D is *diffuse status characteristic* if:

a. It has ≥ 2 states, differentially evaluated;

b. Associated with each state are specific performance expectations for particular skills

c. Associated with each state is a *general expectation state* (ges) for performance at most tasks.

Examples: gender, skin color, age, wealth, beauty

Assumption 1 (Salience)

All D or C characteristics that are already considered by the actor P to be linked to outcome states of T become salient in the situation, and all other C or D characteristics that discriminate between actors also will become salient.

Assumption 2 (Burden of Proof)

If any D or C characteristic is salient, then

a. for each D, the associated general expectation state Γ will also become salient and will become relevant to a similarly evaluated state of C*; and

b. for each C, the relevant the relevant task outcome state τ will become relevant to a similarly evaluated state of abstract ability Y, and Y will become relevant to the similarly evaluated outcome state of T.

Assumption 3 (Sequencing)

A structure of status characteristics and expectation states will become fully connected through the burden of proof process described. If actors leave or enter the situation after become completed, new connections will appear according to the same process, and all parts of the structure previously completed, will remain in subsequent interaction.

Assumption 4 (Aggregation)

If an actor P is connected to task outcome states T+ and T− in a completed structure, then P's aggregated expectations e_p may be represented as

$$e_p^+ = [1 - (1 - f(i)\ldots(1 - f(n))]$$

$$e_p^- = -[1 - (1 - f(i)\ldots(1 - f(n))]$$

$$e_p = e_p^+ - e_p^-$$

where i and n are path lengths and $f(i)$ and $f(n)$ are monotonically decreasing functions of i and n.

Assumption 5 (Behavior)

Once P has formed aggregated expectation states for self and other, P's power and prestige position relative to O will be a direct function of P's expectation advantage over O $(e_p - e_o)$ in the situation.

Adapted from Shelley and Webster (1997).

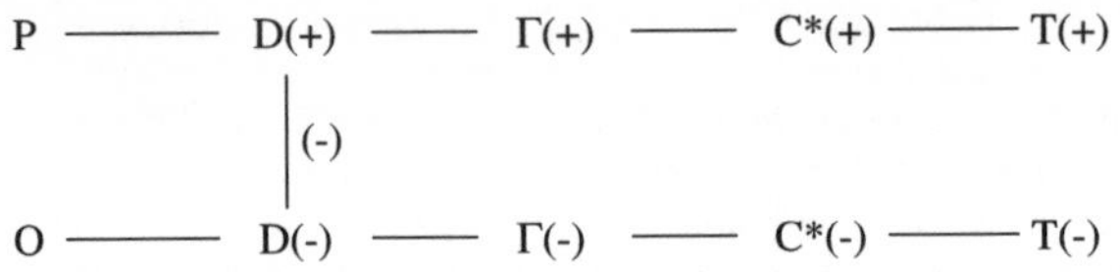

$$P \text{ ------ } D(+) \text{ ------ } \Gamma(+) \text{ ------ } C^*(+) \text{ ------ } T(+)$$

$$\big| (\text{-})$$

$$O \text{ ------ } D(\text{-}) \text{ ------ } \Gamma(\text{-}) \text{ ------ } C^*(\text{-}) \text{ ------ } T(\text{-})$$

Fig. C1.   Graph-Theoretic Structure.

is the negatively evaluated or undesired state. Every situational model contains two elements that represent task outcomes, thus, $T(+)$ denotes a success, and $T(-)$ a failure. D denotes a diffuse status characteristic, with $D(+)$ representing the positively evaluated state and $D(-)$ the negatively evaluated state. Γ represents the respective general expectation states associated with level of D. Finally, the instrumental ability needed to complete the task is represented by C^*.

The length and sign of the paths connecting an actor to a task outcome determine the actor's aggregated expectation state (Berger et al., 1977). The path length is simply the number of lines connecting an actor to a task outcome. The path sign is calculated by multiplying the sign of the path with the sign of the task outcome. For example, in Fig. C1, P is connected to two positive paths, one of length 4, from P to $T(+)$, and one of length 5, from P to $T(-)$.

When calculating each actor's aggregated expectations, denoted e_p, each like signed path is combined according to a decreasing monotonic function, then the negative product is subtracted from the positive product. This can be stated more formally using SCT's 4th assumption (Berger et al., 1977):

If an actor is connected to task outcomes states that are positive and negative in a completed structure, then P's aggregated expectations, e_p, are represented as

$$e_p^+ = [1 - (f(i) \ldots (1 - f(n))]$$

$$e_p^- = [1 - (1 - f(i) \ldots (1 - f(n))]$$

$$e_p = e_p^+ - e_p^-$$

where i and n are path lengths and $f(i)$ and $f(n)$ are monotonically decreasing functions of i and n.

The strength of a path length is denoted as $f(L)$. These values are constrained to fall between 0 and 1 (Berger et al., 1992, p. 853). Estimates of these values differ slightly from source to source. The following example illustrates the calculation of aggregated expectations for both actors in Fig.

C1, using $f(L)$ values found in Berger et al. (1992).[13] As noted above, P is connected to two positive paths, one of length 4 and one of length 5. P is not connected to any negative paths.

$$e_p^+ = \{1 - [1 - f(4)] \ldots [1 - f(5)]\}$$

where $f(4) = 0.150380$ and $f(5) = 0.049779$

$$e_p^+ = 0.19267$$

$$e_p^- = 0$$

$$e_p = 0.19267$$

In Fig. C1, O is connected to two negative paths, one of length 4 and one of length 5. O is not connected to any positive paths.

$$e_o^+ = 0$$

$$e_o^- = -\{1 - [1 - f(4)] \ldots [1 - f(5)]\}$$

where $f(4) = 0.150380$ and $f(5) = 0.049779$

$$e_o = -0.19267$$

Actor P's expectation advantage relative O equals: $e_p - e_o$ or $0.19267 - (-0.19267) = 0.38534$.

POLITICIZED COLLECTIVE IDENTITY: COLLECTIVE IDENTITY AND POLITICAL PROTEST

Bert Klandermans

ABSTRACT

Despite the vast literature on the subject, theory, and empirical evidence regarding the role of collective identity for political protest remains underdeveloped. Some elements of the theory of collective identity and political protest are proposed. Key concepts such as personal and collective identity, identity salience and strength, and politicized collective identity are presented. In addition, some identity processes are conceptualized: politicization of collective identity, the causal relationship between collective identity and protest participation, and the interplay of multiple identities. Illustrative evidence from a study among farmers in Galicia (Spain) and the Netherlands, and among South African citizens is provided.

Some 15 years ago I began to explore the role of identity in political protest. The weakness of the social movement literature on identity and contention at that time was that the discussion was predominantly theoretical. Collective identity was declared to be important, but very little was said about why

Social Identification in Groups
Advances in Group Processes, Volume 22, 155–176
Copyright © 2005 by Elsevier Ltd.
All rights of reproduction in any form reserved
ISSN: 0882-6145/doi:10.1016/S0882-6145(05)22006-4

and how it was important and how it could be assessed. Few seemed to bother about evidence. Indeed, in those days there was not even agreement on what exactly collective identity would be like, let alone how it was formed, and how it declined. Basic questions such as how collective identity is formed, becomes salient, or politicized were phrased nor answered (see Stryker, 2000). Perhaps social movement scholars did not bother too much to question why of the many identities people share precisely the one that was prominent in this instance of protest got to play that role, because they tend to study contention when it takes place and when collective identities are formed and politicised already.

Coming from a social psychological background, I was, of course, familiar with the work of Tajfel and his collaborators on social identity (Tajfel & Turner, 1986). At first sight, I assumed that the two literatures were addressing the same phenomenon, and only employing different labels, namely, collective and social identity, until I figured that they were not. Collective identity in the social movement literature is a group characteristic in the Durkheimian sense. Someone who sets out to study collective identity may look for such phenomena as the group's symbols, its rituals, the beliefs, and the values its members share. Groups differ in terms of their collective identity. The difference may be qualitative, for example, being an ethnic group rather than a gender or occupational group; or quantitative, that is, a difference in the strength of collective identity (Lofland, 1995). Social identity in the social psychological framework refers to a person. It is a characteristic of a person. It is that part of a person's self-image that is derived from the groups he or she is a member of. Social identity supposedly has a cognitive, evaluative, and affective component that is usually measured by means of questionnaires (Ellemers, Spears, & Doosje, 1999; Simon, 1999). Individuals differ in terms of social identity, again both qualitatively (the kind of groups referred to) and quantitatively (the strength of identification with a group).

I use the term collective identity to refer to identity *shared* with other members of a group or category. Collective identity becomes politically relevant when people who share a specific identity take part in political action. In this chapter I will attempt to theorize on the politicization of collective identity by addressing some of the key issues that a theory of identity and protest must account for. The first issue regards the *sequencing* of matters. Must collective identity become salient before protest participation can take place or does collective identity emerge in the course of political protest? Or alternatively, are collective identity and political participation related in a recursive manner so that they reinforce one another?

Furthermore, a theory that accounts for the role of collective identity in political protest must deal with the phenomenon of multiple identities. It must propose dynamics that account for the politicization of a *specific* collective identity rather than any other. Individual citizens occupy numerous places in society and share numerous collective identities with the other occupants. A theory of collective identity and political protest must forward explanations of why some collective identities become the core of a protest movement while others do not (Stryker & Burke, 2000). Finally and social psychologically not the least, theory about collective identity and protest must address the *interplay* of multiple identities. It is very unlikely that collective identities that are *not* the core of political protest are all of a sudden irrelevant altogether. Much more likely is that, various collective identities compete with or reinforce the collective identity that become the core of a protest movement. The rest of this chapter concerns these three issues. I will alternate conceptual pieces with evidence derived from my own empirical work, but first I must elaborate the role of identity in the dynamics of protest participation.

IDENTITY AND THE DYNAMICS OF PROTEST PARTICIPATION

Identity is not the only factor in the dynamics of protest participation. Elsewhere (Klandermans, 2003), I have argued that identity is one out of three fundamental reasons why people participate in political protest. The two others being instrumentality and ideology. People may want to take part in political protest because they want to change their circumstances (instrumentality), to act as members of their group (identity), or to express their views and feelings (ideology). I suggest that together these three motives account for most of the readiness to participate. Social movements may supply the opportunity to fulfil these demands and the better they do, the more movement participation turns into a satisfying experience. The instrumentality–identity–ideology triad is not invented for this field. Indeed, it has a long history in functional theories of attitudes and behavior (see Sears & Funk, 1991), but it provides a useful framework for a discussion of the dynamics of protest participation.

In the rest of this chapter I will concentrate on the role of identity.[1] In the next few pages I will conceptualize the role of identity for the participation in political protest in general. In doing so I will rely on a paper by Bernd

Simon and myself published in the *American Psychologist* (Simon & Klandermans, 2001). Subsequently, I will discuss the issues sequencing and multiple identities that I mentioned in the previous section. In that context, I will, as a matter of illustration, present evidence from my own research.

COLLECTIVE IDENTITY

Simon (1998, 1999) described identity as a place in the society. People occupy many different places. They are student, unemployed, housewife, soccer player, politician, farmer, and so on. Some of those places are exclusive, occupied only by a small number of people. The members of a soccer team are an example. Others are inclusive encompassing large numbers of people such as "Europeans." Some places are mutually exclusive, such as male–female, or employed–unemployed; some are nested, for example, French, Dutch, German versus European; and some are cross-cutting, such as, female and student (Turner, 1999).

Personal and Collective Identity

All these different roles and positions a person occupies form his *personal identity*. At the same time, every place a person occupies is shared with other people. I am not the only professor of social psychology, nor the only Dutch or the only European. We share these identities with other people – a fact that turns them into collective identities. Thus a *collective identity* is a place shared with other people. This implies that personal identity is always collective identities at the same time. However, personal identity is general, referring to a variety of places in the society, whereas collective identity is always specific, referring to a specific place.[2]

Salient Collective Identity

Most of the time collective identities remain latent. Self-categorization theory hypothesizes that, depending on contextual circumstances an individual may act as a unique person, that is, display his personal identity *or* as a member of a specific group, that is, display one of his collective identities (Turner, Hogg, Oakes, Reicher, & Wetherell, 1987; Turner, 1999). Contextual factors may bring personal or collective identity to the fore. Obviously, this is often no matter of free choice. Circumstances may force a collective identity into awareness whether people like it or not, as the Yugoslavian and South African histories have illustrated dramatically. But also in less extreme circumstances, collective identities can become significant. Take, for example, the possible effect of an announcement that a waste incinerator is planned next to a neighborhood. Chances are that within very little time the collective identity of the people living in that neighborhood becomes salient.

Identity Strength

Self-categorization theory proposes that people are more prepared to employ a social category in their self-definition the more they identify with that category. Identification with a group makes people more prepared to act as a member of that group (Turner, 1999). This assertion refers to identity strength. In her review of social identity theory, Huddy (2001) observes that social identity literature tends to neglect that real-world identities vary in strength. But, she argues, identifying more or less strongly with a group may make a real difference especially in political contexts. Moreover, she suggests that strong identities are less affected by context. Following this reasoning, we may expect that strong identities make it more likely that people act on behalf of their group.[3]

Politicized Collective Identity

Salience of a collective identity does not necessarily make that identity politically relevant. Simon and Klandermans (2001) hold that when people become involved in political protest on behalf of a group, the collective identity of that group politicizes. Collective identity politicizes when it becomes the focus of a struggle for power. Social groups are often involved in power struggles in that they try to establish, change, or defend a power structure. Politicized collective identity is not an all-or-nothing or on/off phenomenon. Instead, politicization of collective identity and the underlying power struggle unfold as a sequence of politicizing events that gradually transform the group's relationship to its social environment. Typically, this process begins with the awareness of shared grievances. Next, an external enemy is blamed for the group's predicament and claims for compensation are leveled against this enemy. Unless appropriate compensation is granted, the power struggle continues. If in the course of this struggle the group seeks to win the support of third parties such as more powerful authorities (e.g., the national government) or the general public collective identity fully politicizes. The attempt to involve these parties in the power struggle inevitably turns the issue into a matter of public or general interest. This final step also results in a transformation of the group's relationship to its social environment, because involving a third party implies recognition of society or the larger community (e.g., the city, region, country, or the European Union) as a more inclusive ingroup membership. Politicized collective identity thus implies a cognitive restructuring of the social environment which is no longer defined exclusively in terms of a bipolar ingroup–outgroup confrontation. Instead, the social environment is further differentiated into opponents and (potential) allies, which also involves strategic reformulation of the conflict issue such that it appeals also to potential allies.

So far I have laid out the main elements of a theory of collective identity and political protest. Next I will turn to the two issues that are central to this chapter, causality and multiple identities.

CAUSALITY

The basic assumption regarding identity and participation in collective action is fairly straightforward. The more someone identifies with a group, the higher the chances are that he will take part in collective action on behalf of that group. The available evidence overwhelmingly supports this assumption (Kelly & Kelly, 1992; Kelly, 1993; Kelly & Breinlinger, 1996; Simon et al, 1998; De Weerd, 1999; De Weerd & Klandermans, 1999; Stürmer, 2000; Klandermans, Roefs, & Olivier, 2001). However, most studies are correlational. They demonstrate that high levels of identification go together with high levels of participation, but do not allow any conclusions about causality. The few studies that employed longitudinal or experimental designs and are thus better suited to test causal relations are inconclusive. For instance, whereas data of Simon et al. (1998) and Stürmer (2000) suggest that collective identity stimulates collective action participation, De Weerd and Klandermans (1999) did not find such direct link between identification and participation, but did find that group identification affects action preparedness which in turn affects action participation. Nonetheless, both studies suggest that identification comes first and then participation. Conversely, Reicher and his colleagues (Drury, Reicher, & Scott, 2003; Reicher, 1984, 1996) have demonstrated repeatedly that participation in collective action strengthens identification with the group, but these are studies of participants only, hence it is difficult to decide whether it was action participation that made the difference.

A further complication relates to the fact that action participation presupposes some opportunity to act. In the absence of such opportunities it is difficult for identification to translate into action, but identification might still reflect in high levels of action preparedness. In fact, Fishbein and Azjen (1975) have emphasized that cognitive variables such as beliefs and attitudes influence behavior *intentions,* and that the extent to which such intentions translate into actual behavior depends on contextual factors such as freedom and opportunity to act.

All this suggests a more complicated model than the simple link between identification and collective action participation we began this section with, namely, one that holds that high levels of identification that generate high levels of action preparedness which are translated into high levels of participation if the opportunity to act arise. Following Reicher, 1996 it can be hypothesized that such participation, in its turn, strengthens identification. In a study among farmers in the Netherlands and Spain we employed a panel design, which made it possible to test this model.

FARMER'S IDENTITY AND FARMER'S PROTEST

During winter 1993–1994, 1995, and Fall 1995 we interviewed 167 Dutch farmers and 248 Galician[4] farmers three times.[5] During these 2 years several agricultural measures to be taken by the national governments or the European Union were imminent, varying in impact on the agricultural sector. The study was designed to investigate farmers' responses to these measures. We had chosen the Netherlands and Galicia because they are similar as far as agricultural products are concerned but opposites as far as agricultural development is concerned. In both countries the same kind of farmers were involved, mainly from dairy, arable, and mixed farms, but on modern and large-scale enterprises in the Netherlands and old-fashioned and small-scale farms in Galicia. Agriculture in the Netherlands more than in Spain has been subject of political intervention and regulation. In response, farmers in the Netherlands established early on professional organizations that evolved into a powerful agricultural lobby. Agriculture became one of the best organized sectors of the Dutch economy. The establishment of the European Community has only added to the situation. Dutch and European politics turned farmers in the Netherlands into a group with common interests and opponents. In Spain and certainly Galicia all this got less far. Moreover, Spain entered the European Community more than 20 years later. As a consequence, farmers in Spain are much weaker organized than those in the Netherlands. Therefore, we expect a stronger sense of collective identity among Dutch farmers than among Galician farmers. On the other hand, farmers' organizations in Spain are more politicized than their counterparts in the Netherlands. Spanish farmers' organizations are branches of political parties whereas Dutch farmers' organizations are professional organizations almost any farmer is a member of. Therefore, we expect a stronger effect of membership of farmer's organizations on protest participation in Galicia than in the Netherlands.

Results

The results confirm our expectations. Dutch farmers identify more with other farmers (main effect country: $F = 64.98$, df $= 1$, $p < 0.0001$), and are more often member of a farmers' organization (main effect country: $F = 524.57$, df $= 1$, $p < 0.0001$) than Galician farmers. Altogether, these results suggest that in the Netherlands identification with farmers is stronger than in Galicia. In line with our theoretical reasoning action preparedness (main effect country: $F = 11.21$, df $= 1$, $p = 0.001$) and participation (χ^2 1993–4: 92.04, 1995–(1): 12.44, 1995–(2): 31.25, with df $= 1$ all p's < 0.0001) are higher among Dutch farmers indeed. Overall, this pattern is fairly stable over time (Table 1).

Although in line with our expectations, these results do not necessarily prove that it is identity processes that generate the differences in protest preparedness and participation. In order to solve that matter, we ran a series of regression analyses and ANOVAs, and conducted cross-lagged analyses exploiting our longitudinal design.

As for the results regarding participation, let me just briefly mention that action participation is predicted by action preparedness and nothing else. Group identification does not play a role. However, when it comes to the prediction of action preparedness, collective identity does make a significant difference. Even 2 years later, group identification and participation in identity organizations accounted for differences in action preparedness. Indeed, collective identity seems to foster participation in collective action. Both identification with other farmers and participation in a farmers' organization stimulate action preparedness, which in its turn stimulates action participation. We are not the first to make that observation but there are not that many studies showing that indicators of collective identity are able to predict action preparedness even 2 years later.

Table 1. Action Participation and Action Preparedness.

	Galicia			Netherlands		
	1993–4	1995–(1)	1995–(2)	1993–(4)	1995–(1)	1995–(2)
Action participation	37.3%[a]	2.8%[b]	2.0%[b]	86.8%[a]	11.4%[b]	17.4%[b]
Action preparedness[c]	2.59	2.41	2.50	2.84	2.75	2.80
Identification with farmers[d]	1.77	—	1.66	1.95	—	1.94
Participation in farmers' organization[e]	0.19	0.17	0.19	1.11	1.08	1.04

[a]Participation in the past.
[b]Participation since the previous interview.
[c]On a scale from 1 to 5.
[d]1 = no identification, 2 = identification.
[e]0 = not member, 1 = member, 2 = active member.

As we have longitudinal data, we are also able to further investigate the causal direction of the link between collective identity and action participation. Table 2 provides the results of four regression analyses: the first two of the indicators of collective identity at Time 1 with action preparedness at Time 3, and of the same indicators at Time 3 with action preparedness at Time 1; the second two of the indicators of identity at Time 1 and action participation at Time 3 and identity at Time 3 with action participation at Time 1.

Panel A suggests that the causal link goes from identification with other farmers and participation in farmers' organizations to action preparedness rather than the other way around. The correlations, β's and R^2 of the first equation are higher than that of the second equation, especially that of identification with other farmers. Panel B suggest the opposite for protest participation: participation seems to strengthen collective identity rather than collective identity to stimulate participation.

Discussion

The causal patterns our findings reveal are fascinating. Collective identity appears to foster action preparedness, action preparedness produces action participation, and in its turn, action participation strengthens collective identity. Indeed, collective identity, action preparedness, and action

Table 2.   The Causal Link Between Identity and Collective Action
Participation: Pearson's R and Standardized β's.

	Preparedness at T3			Preparedness at T1	
	r	β		r	β
Identification at T1	0.26	0.20	Identification at T3	0.12	0.06
Identity organization at T1	0.27	0.22	Identity organization at T3	0.20	0.18
R^2		0.11	R^2		0.04

	Participation at T3			Participation at T1	
	r	β		r	β
Identification at T1	0.11	0.03	Identification at T3	0.30	0.17
Identity organization at T1	0.28	0.27	Identity organization at T3	0.45	0.39
R^2		0.08			0.22

participation seem to function as a self-reinforcing mechanism. All this
suggests that strong identities generate the preparedness to participate in
collective action on behalf of the group. If such action is actually staged,
chances are high that preparedness is transformed into action. Participation
in turn reinforces identity strength. This hinges at the possibility that identity strength and movement participation are of a recursive nature. Social
movement literature has forwarded this as a theoretical idea, but so far
provided very little in terms of empirical support.

In fact, our findings suggest a synthesis of the two causal patterns we
encountered in the literature – from identity to participation and conversely
from participation to identity. Note that the transformation of action preparedness into action participation functions as the connection between the
two identity processes. In others words, only if the opportunity to act is
offered, the strengthening of identity occurs. That might explain why we find
evidence of opposite causal direction in the literature. Depending on whether it concerns the link with preparedness or participation, opposite relations
are to be expected if our reasoning hold.

THE INTERPLAY OF MULTIPLE IDENTITIES

The impact of collective identity on political protest is further influenced by
the fact that individuals occupy many different places at the same time. This
raises the question of why a specific identity becomes the focal identity of a

protest movement and how this identity interacts with the other identities. In this Section I will concentrate on the latter question, but before doing so, let me say a few words with regard to the former. At the roots of any protest movements lie shared grievances. The awareness that grievances are shared makes collective identity salient. Attempts to mobilize those who share the same identity in order to redress the grievances further increase the salience of the collective identity. Attempts to make authorities respond to the grievances in addition politicize collective identity. If authorities fail to respond or even repress the movement, the politicization of collective identity speeds up considerably.

Collective identity thus politicized, however, is not the only identity of the individuals involved. It may, for a while, override any other identity, but sooner or later other identities compete for attention. Sometimes the competition is build into the very protest movement. Kurtz (2002) and Fonow (2003), for example, show how gender, race, and class identity compete in workplace-related collective action. Sometimes the competition builds up as the protest campaign evolves, as Goodwin (1997) showed in his study of how kinship ties eventually undermined loyalty to a rebellious movement. Sometimes it is assumed by the surrounding society that identities compete. For example, the opponents of the peace movement in the 1980s, government officials included, seriously questioned the loyalty to the nation of the supporters of that movement (Klandermans, 1991).

In this chapter I will concentrate on one specific conflict: the one between national identity and subgroup identities. Any nation is a conglomerate of many different population groups. The interplay of identification with such subordinated categories and the superordinate national identity is scarcely studied. The political common sense seems to be that subgroup identities and national identity are mutually exclusive. In any event, throughout history governments have tried to foster national identity and to suppress expressions of subgroup identities. For instance, in Franco's Spain, every sign of regional identification was brutally suppressed (Johnston, 1991). In a similar vein, protest groups are easily blamed for being disloyal, unpatriotic, and forsaking the national identity, as the fate of many protest movements on the African continent and the peace movements in the United States and Europe during the cold war showed. However, history has demonstrated time and again that suppression of subgroup identity reinforces rather than weakens identification (Zegeye, Liebenberg & Houston, no date). This suggests that national identity and subgroup identities are not necessarily mutually exclusive but rather made that way if the latter is suppressed in favor of the former.

Political protest presupposes some subgroup identity – as demonstrated in the previous section on causality. Therefore, the interplay of national identity and subgroup identity is an important aspect of a theory of collective identity and political protest. The question I will address in the remainder of this chapter is how national identity and subgroup identity are related to political protest. We know that subgroup identification fosters participation in political protest on behalf of the subgroup, but does that weaken national identification? Or alternatively, does a strong national identity weaken people's willingness to participate in collective action on behalf of some subgroup? In trying to answer these questions I will draw on recent social psychological research on dual identity.

Dual Identity

Recent social psychological research has explored the dynamics of multiple identities (González & Brown, 2003; Brown, 2000; Huo, Smith, Tyler, & Lind, 1996; Klandermans et al., 2001). This research starts from the distinction between subordinate and superordinate identities. The available evidence suggests that subordinate and superordinate identities are not mutually exclusive, but on the contrary, a combination of subgroup and superordinate identity contributes to the stability of an organization or a political system. Indeed, intergroup hostility seems to decline if groups are allowed to nourish both sub- and superordinate identities. González and Brown (2003) and Brown (2000) have shown that a *dual identity*, i.e., a strong superordinate identity in combination with a strong subgroup identity reduces the likelihood of conflicts between subgroups. Huo et al. (1996) demonstrate that a sufficiently high level of superordinate identification makes it possible for authorities to maintain cohesion within an ethnically diverse community. But studies such as those of González and Brown emphasize that superordinate identity only has this effect if people can maintain their subgroup identity as well. These studies show that enforcing people to forsake their subgroup identity (such as class identity, ethnic identity, or gender identity) in favor of a superordinate identity backfires.

It is not always easy to decide what social psychological mechanisms are at work here. We suggest as a possible mechanism that a strong national identity makes it possible for people to look at subgroups in a different way and to accept that subgroups in a society are treated differently. Indeed Americans who identify with *"Americans"* in addition to being *white* take a more positive stand toward affirmative action (Smith & Tyler, 1996). And for East Germans the awareness that "we are all Germans" made it easier to accept the differences between East and West Germany (Mummendey, Klink, Mielke, Wenzel, & Blanz, 1999). Tyler, Boeckmann, Smith, and Huo (1997) argue that this is so because superordinate identity changes the relationship between subgroups and authorities. These authors hold that the absence of superordinate identity makes that relationship solely instrumental – what are authorities doing for *my* group. Superordinate identity makes it possible for people to accept disadvantages done to their subgroup in the interest of the larger community. People trust authorities to make sure that next time their group will benefit. This implies that superordinate identity and trust in authorities are intimately related. But superordinate identity should not undermine subgroup identity, dual identity research seems to warn.

All this suggest that there is no reason to assume that national identity and subgroup identities are mutually exclusive. What is more, dual identities – that is a strong national identity in combination with strong subgroup identities – seems to be beneficial to a political system. A study on patterns of identification in South Africa serves to illustrate the argument.

NATIONAL AND SUBGROUP IDENTITIES IN SOUTH AFRICA

Racial categorization, that is to say registration as black, colored, Indian, or white was the backbone of apartheid for decades. It was, and to a large extent still is, the master frame of the South African society. Whites bonded together in defense of their privileges, blacks, coloreds, and Indians united against their common enemy. But since the dismantling of the apartheid system, the situation changed. Not that the end of apartheid blew the boundaries between the racial categories. Social statistics in the country can and must still be written in terms of black, colored, Indian, and white. But within these racial categories such distinctions as ethnicity,[6] class, gender, and generation are gaining in significance. At the same time, South Africa is attempting to build a rainbow nation, people of all walks of life can identify with. This raises the question whether South Africans are beginning to develop a superordinate national identity as a South African and to what extent emerging subgroup identities compete with national identity? Between these two identities an individual citizen can take three different trajectories: he can develop a strong subgroup identity, but no national identity; a strong national identity and no subgroup identity; or a dual identity. Of course, he can also develop neither identity.

Between 1994 and 2000, we interviewed annually random samples of the South African population.[7] In the last 4 years, in addition to questions about subgroup identity such as ethnicity, class, religion, or gender questions about national identity were included. Thus, from 1997 onwards we were able to assess how many South Africans fitted into any of the four options listed above.

Results

Table 3 reveals the proportion of our respondents who belonged to each of the four categories over the 4 years (1997–2000). People who displayed a strong identification with at least one of the groups included in our study were assigned to the group with a strong subgroup identity.

A few interesting observations can be made. First, national identity and subgroup identity did not exclude each other. In fact, we found a modest positive correlation between the two (approx. 0.20), suggesting that people who identified with a larger variety of groups were also more likely to identify with their nation. Second, the proportion of the population that displayed a dual identity increased over the years and the proportion of those with a subgroup identity only decreased. The two other groups increased as well, but this was after an initial decline. Third, very few people who did not identify with a subgroup displayed a strong national identification. This is especially interesting because it suggests that national identity *presupposes* subgroup identity, rather than that subgroup identity *undermines* national identity. This result confirmed findings from our farmers' protest study (Klandermans, Sabucedo, & Rodriguez, 2004). In this study we also found that identification at a higher level of inclusiveness presupposed identification at a lower level of inclusiveness.[8]

Table 3. National Identity and Subgroup Identity in South Africa: Percentages.

	1997	1998	1999	2000
No strong subgroup identity/no strong national identity	25	22	13	18
Strong subgroup identity/no strong national identity	39	55	51	40
No strong subgroup identity/strong national identity	11	3	3	6
Strong subgroup identity/strong national identity	25	21	33	36

Table 4. Dual Identity and Politics.

Dual Identity	Trust in Government*	Preparedness to Participate in Peaceful Action**
No strong subgroup identity/no strong national identity	2.7	2.4
Strong subgroup identity/no strong national identity	2.7	2.6
No strong subgroup identity/strong national identity	2.8	2.6
Strong subgroup identity/strong national identity	3.2	2.8

*$F/df \ 3 = 79.88$, $p < 0.001$.
**$F/df \ 3 = 39.81$, $p < 0.001$.

But what about political attitudes and behavior? Did subgroup identity and national identity interact in their influence on political attitudes and behavior, and if so, did the two reinforce or undermine one another? In order to answer this question we compared the four groups on two variables regarding people's relation to politics, namely trust in government and people's preparedness to take part in peaceful collective action. The results in Table 4 confirm our expectations.

Trust in government and action preparedness were the highest among those respondents who displayed a dual identity. Interestingly, the figures for trust in government show that only those with a dual identity were different; the remaining three groups did not differ in terms of trust. This suggests that, at least as far as trust in government was concerned, it was the *combination* of subgroup and national identity that made the difference. As for action preparedness, it was the people with no identification at all who differed from the people with either subgroup or national identification. That makes, of course, sense. One needs some level of collective identity to participate in collective action. However, again it is important to note that action preparedness was the highest among those with a dual identity.

Conclusion

National identity and subgroup identity are not mutually exclusive. In fact, we found a moderate positive correlation, which argues against all those who assume that protestors are less loyal to the larger community. Dual identity – a combination of strong national and strong subgroup identity – fostered trust in government and preparedness to take part in peaceful action. This confirms social psychological literature that suggests that the combination of sub- and superordinate identification is beneficial for a political system.

CONCLUSION

In this chapter, I undertook an attempt to develop a theory on the link between collective identity and political protest. Although the basic prediction that collective identity fosters protest participation is fairly straightforward and finds empirical support, there is much more to account for than this simple relationship. Obviously, there is a link, but that link is more complex than that a simple mono-causal model can account for. On the basis of the previous discussion and illustrative evidence, I propose some further conceptualization of the link between collective identity and political protest.

First, the causal link between collective identity and political protest seems to run via action preparedness. A strong collective identity reflects itself in high preparedness to participate in collective action on behalf of the group. If such action is actually staged, action preparedness can be translated into participation. Participation, in its turn, then reinforces collective identity. Depending on the interaction with opponents and allies collective identity further politicizes. Politicization of collective identity, supposedly, intensifies the impact of collective identity on action preparedness.

Second, the fact that individuals have multiple identities further complicates matters. It should not be taken for granted that a collective identity becomes the focal identity in a protest movement. It requires an explanation that out of the many identities individuals have this specific identity acquires that position. Our study on farmers provided an interesting illustration that identification cannot be taken for granted. The second interview wave in Galicia took place in a period when election campaigns were taking place. The election campaign made other identities salient and reduced the number of farmers that indicated that they identified with other farmers. Obviously, contextual factors influence which identity will prevail. As a possible mechanism that explains why a specific identity becomes the focus of a protest movement, I have suggested to look into the factors that politicize collective identity and proposed that shared grievances are at the roots of the politicization of collective identity.

Third, the interplay of the multiple identities of an individual necessitates an even more elaborate framework. Identities may compete with or reinforce each other. I discussed the interplay of (superordinate) national identity and (subordinate) subgroup identities as a special case of the interplay of multiple identities that is particularly interesting in the context of movement participation. I propose that rather than being inversely related – as political common sense tends to assume – the two are independent or even positively related. Moreover, they interact in their influence on political attitudes and behavior. Dual identity – that is, strong national identity and strong subgroup identity – fosters trust in government and the preparedness to take part in collective action. This seems to suggest that subgroup protest presupposes some sort of superordinate identification. Simon and Klandermans (2001) have forwarded an explanation why this is the case. Politicization of collective identity, we argue, implies that the involvement of the wider social and political environment is sought. Such efforts, we hold, require some commitment to or identification with that environment. Why bother to change a nation if one feels no commitment to it, whatsoever.

Fourth and interestingly, superordinate identification seems to presuppose subordinate identification as well. We encountered very few South Africans who had a strong national identity, but no subgroup identity. This is not because people identify always with some group. Substantial numbers of our interviewees had neither a strong national identity nor a strong subgroup identity. This suggests that one will only identify with a highly inclusive group if one identifies with a more exclusive group as well. Brewer's theory of optimal distinctiveness (Brewer & Silver, 2000) might provide the explanation for this finding. Highly inclusive categories such as nations alone do not offer sufficient distinctiveness. In order to acquire optimal distinctiveness, identification with more exclusive categories is needed.

Finally, this is not to say that multiple identities are always reinforcing protest participation. In fact, they do not and this is another complication that a theory on identity and protest must take into account. Let me give two examples: in an interesting paper on the Huk rebellion in Philippines, Goodwin (1997) shows how the ineffective management of loyalty to the movement and loyalty to the family eventually caused the breakdown of the movement. In our own research on the Dutch protests against the deployment of cruise missiles we observed how participants in the protests who at the same time were supporters of the Christian Democratic Party (CDA) came under cross-pressure because the CDA was one of the parties supporting a government coalition that was in favor of deployment (Oegema & Klandermans, 1994).

NOTES

1. In terms of the explanation of protest participation this implies that we are concentrating only on one of the three motives, which necessarily limits the variance that can be accounted for.

2. Burke (2004) and Stryker (2000) distinguish role identity in addition to person and social identity. Person identity refers to the unique characteristics of a person, while role identity and social identity are shared with other people (role occupants and group members).

3. Nation and religious community are typical examples of groups that tend to generate high levels of identification.

4. Galicia is the most northwestern province of Spain.

5. Trained interviewers at the respondents' homes conducted face-to-face, computer-assisted interviews. The interviews lasted on average three-quarters of an hour. The subjects interviewed resulted from samples drawn from selected farming communities. All farmers from the selected communities were asked for their cooperation. This chapter is based on those farmers in the two countries we had complete information of. Obviously, the samples were not random samples of the farmers in Galicia or the Netherlands nor are they necessarily representative. For our panel design this is not a problem as we were interested in changes over time and the group served as its own standard. The mean age of the respondents in the two samples was approximately the same: 46 years in the Netherlands and 49 years in Galicia. Level of education and size of farm illustrate the opposite character of the two areas. In the Netherlands, the vast majority of the respondents (70%) completed secondary or higher agricultural education, whereas most farmers had average to large size farms (70.7%). In Galicia we found the opposite: 90% of our respondents had only primary education, whereas 77% had small farms. *Measures.* The variables relevant for our present discussion have been measured in the following way: *Farmer's identity* was assessed by a measure of group identification (we asked farmers to agree or disagree with the statement "I feel little commitment to other farmers") and by assessing whether our interviewees were member of a farmer's organization. *Action preparedness* was assessed with regard to four forms of collective action which were part of the action repertoire of farmers in those days – demonstrations, blockades, symbolic actions (such as dumping dung on the doorsteps of the ministry of agriculture), and refusal to pay taxes. We asked for each of these action forms whether respondents "would participate if they were to disagree completely with an agricultural measure or with agricultural policy in general." For each action form respondents could indicate on a scale ranging from 1 (not at all prepared) to 5 (very much prepared) to what extent they were prepared to participate. The answers to these questions were taken together into a scale of *action preparedness* ranging from 1 (not at all prepared to take part in any form of collective action) to 5 (very much prepared to take part in all forms selected). Cronbach's alpha of the scale at the three points in time was satisfactory: 0.75, 0.74, and 0.75. In order to register *collective action participation*, we asked in the first interview "whether respondents took part in any collective action directed at agricultural measures or policy in the past." In the second and third interview we asked them "whether they had taken part in

any collective action [directed at agricultural measures or policy] since the previous interview." The answers to these questions were used as a measure of *action participation*.

6. Although the two are related in South Africa ethnicity is not the same as race. Race refers to the four racial groups defined by the apartheid laws. Ethnicity refers to more subtle distinctions within these four groups, such as the Zulus, the Xhosas, the Tswanas, and so on within the black community, or the Afrikaner and the English within the white community, Tamil and Hindu within the Indian community, not to speak of all those finer distinctions we find so many in a society as heterogeneous as the South African.

7. The data in this section stem from seven surveys that were conducted annually between February 1994 and March 2000. The first survey was held in February 1994, just before the first national democratic election in South Africa; the last survey was conducted 6 years later in March 2000, 9 months after the second national election in 1999. The surveys were always held at the same time of year – around February/ March. Face-to-face interviewing was employed as data-collection strategy. *Design.* We employed a separate sample design with new samples drawn every year based on the same sampling frame. The employed sampling procedures required that the data be weighted to make them representative of the population as a whole. Comparisons over time of the four racial groups (blacks, coloreds, Asians, and whites) of the seven samples for age, sex, and education revealed that these groups were similar as far as gender was concerned, but slightly different in terms of age and levels of education. However, ANOVAs with the key variables of our study as dependent variables and with age, education, and time as factors revealed no significant interactions. Hence there was no indication that the observed differences between our samples would distort our conclusions. *Subjects.* The interviews were conducted among representative samples of the South African population. The realized samples totaled 2,286 in 1994, 2,226 in 1995, 2,228 in 1996, 2,220 in 1997, 2,227 in 1998, 2,210 in 1999, and 2,666 in 2000. Data were collected by means of face-to-face interviews in people's homes. The interviews were carried out by trained interviewers and conducted in English or Afrikaans or in the respondent's home language when needed. On average the interviews lasted 30–45 min. *Measures. Subgroup identity* – We asked people how close they felt to those in society they shared an identical place with. This question could be answered on a five-point scale ranging from "not close" to "extremely close." Nine categories were included in the questionnaire: people who spoke the same language, had the same ethnic background, had the same financial situation, had the same kind of job (or were also unemployed), were of the same gender, belonged to the same generation, lived in the same neighborhood, had the same political affiliation, or had the same religion. Language and ethnic background, and financial situation and work were combined into single measures of ethnic and class identification, respectively. People who chose the two highest scale points (very close or extremely close) were assumed to have identified with that category. *National identity* – From 1997 onwards we began to investigate national identity, initially with one question only. We asked people to what extent they agreed with the statement, "Being a South African is an important part of how I see myself." People who chose the highest scale point (strongly agree) were assumed to identify with their nation.

8. In fact, in this study, three levels of identification that with farmers in the community, in the country, and in the European Union, formed an almost perfect Gutmann scale.

REFERENCES

Brewer, M. B., & Silver, M. (2000). Group distinctiveness, social identity and collective mo-bilization. In: S. Stryker, T. J. Owens & R. W. White (Eds), *Self, identity, and social movements* (pp. 153–171). Minneapolis: University of Minnesota Press.

Brown, R. (2000). Social identity theory: Past achievements, current problems and future chal-lenges. *European Journal of Social Psychology, 30*, 745–778.

Burke, P. J. (2004). Identities and social structures: The 2003 Cooley–Mead Award address. *Social Psychology Quarterly, 67*, 5–15.

De Weerd, M. (1999). *Sociaalpsychologische determinanten van boerenprotest: Collectieve actie frames, identiteit en effectiviteit.* Unpublished Dissertation, Vrije Universiteit.

De Weerd, M., & Klandermans, B. (1999). Group identification and social protest: Farmer's protest in the Netherlands. *European Journal of Social Psychology, 29*, 1073–1095.

Drury, J., Reicher, S., & Stott, C. (2003). Transforming the boundaries of collective identity: From the 'local' anti-road campaign to 'global' resistance? *Social Movement Studies, 2*, 191–212.

Ellemers, N., Spears, R., & Doosje, B. (1999). *Social identity.* Oxford: Blackwell.

Fishbein, M., & Ajzen, I. (1975). *Belief, attitude, intention and behaviour.* Reading, MA: Addison-Wesley.

Fonow, M. M. (2003). *Union women. Forging feminism in the United Steelworkers of America.* Minneapolis: University of Minnesota Press.

González, R., & Brown, R. (2003). Generalization of positive attitudes as a function of sub-group and superordinate group identifications in intergroup contact. *European Journal of Social Psychology, 33*, 195–214.

Goodwin, J. (1997). The libidinal constitution of a high-risk social movement: Affectual ties and solidarity in the Huk rebellion. *American Sociological Review, 62*, 53–69.

Huddy, L. (2001). From social to political identity: A critical examination of social identity theory. *Political Psychology, 22*, 127–156.

Huo, Y. J., Smith, H., Tyler, T. R., & Lind, E. A. (1996). Superordinate identification, sub-group identification, and justice concerns: Is separatism the problem; is assimilation the answer? *Psychological Science, 7*, 40–45.

Johnston, H. (1991). *Tales of nationalism. Catalonia. 1939–1979.* New Brunswick: Rutgers University Press.

Kelly, C. (1993). Group identification, intergroup perceptions and collective Action. In: W. Stroebe & M. Hewstone (Eds), *European review of social psychology*, (Vol. 4, pp. 59–83). Chichester: Wiley.

Kelly, C., & Breinlinger, S. (1996). *The social psychology of collective action.* Basingstoke: Taylor & Francis.

Kelly, J., & Kelly, C. (1992). Industrial action. In: J. F. Hartley & G. M. Stephenson (Eds), *Employment relations. The psychology of influence and control at work* (pp. 246–270). Oxford: Blackwell.

Klandermans, B. (Ed.) (1991). *Peace movement in international perspective. International social movement research* 3. Greenwich, CT: JAI-Press.

Klandermans, B. (2003). Collective political action. In: D. O. Sears, L. Huddy & R. Jervis (Eds), *Oxford handbook of political psychology* (pp. 670–709). Oxford: Oxford University Press.

Klandermans, B., Roefs, M., & Olivier, J. (2001). *The state of the people. Citizens, civil society and governance in South Africa, 1994–2000.* Pretoria: Human Science Research Council.

Klandermans, B., Sabucedo, J. M., & Rodriguez, M. (2004). Multiple identities among farmers in the Netherlands and Spain. *European Journal of Social Psychology, 34*, 229–364.

Kurtz, S. (2002). *All kinds of justice: Labor and identity politics.* Minneapolis: University of Minnesota Press.

Lofland, J. M. (1995). Charting degrees of movement culture: Tasks of the cultural cartographer. In: H. Johnston & B. Klandermans (Eds), *Social movement and culture* (pp. 188–216). Minneapolis: University of Minnesota Press.

Mummendey, A., Klink, A., Mielke, R., Wenzel, M., & Blanz, M. (1999). Socio-structural characteristics of intergroup relations and identity management strategies: Results from a field study in East Germany. *European Journal of Social Psychology, 29*, 259–286.

Oegema, D., & Klandermans, B. (1994). Why social movement sympathizers don't participate: Erosion and nonconversion of support. *American Sociological Review, 59*, 703–722.

Reicher, S. D. (1984). The St. Paul's riot: An explanation of the limits of crowd action in terms of a social identity model. *European Journal of Social Psychology, 14*, 1–21.

Reicher, S. D. (1996). The Battle of Westminster: Developing the social identity model of crowd behaviour in order to explain the initiation and development of collective conflict. *European Journal of Social Psychology, 26*, 115–134.

Sears, D. O., & Funk, C. (1991). The role of self-interest in social and political attitudes. *Advances in Experimental Psychology, 24*, 1–91.

Simon, B. (1998). Individuals, groups, and social change: On the relationship between individual and collective self-interpretations and collective action. In: C. Sedikides, J. Schopler & C. Insko (Eds), *Intergroup cognition and intergroup behavior* (pp. 257–282). Mahwah, NJ: Lawrence Erlbaum.

Simon, B. (1999). A place in the world: Self and social categorization. In: T. R. Tyler, R. M. Kramer & O. P. John (Eds), *The psychology of the social self* (pp. 47–69). Mahwah, NJ: Lawrence Erlbaum.

Simon, B., & Klandermans, B. (2001). Towards a social psychological analysis of politicized collective identity: Conceptualization, antecedents, and consequences. *American Psychologist, 56*, 319–331.

Simon, B., Loewy, M., Stürmer, S., Weber, U., Kampmeier, C., Freytag, P., Habig, C., & Spahlinger, P. (1998). Collective identity and social movement participation. *Journal of Personality and Social Psychology, 74*, 646–658.

Smith, H. J., & Tyler, T. R. (1996). Justice and power. *European Journal of Social Psychology, 26*, 171–200.

Stryker, S. (2000). Identity competition: Key to differential social movement participation? In: S. Stryker, T. J. Owens & R. W. White (Eds), *Self, identity, and social movements* (pp. 21–40). Minneapolis: University of Minnesota Press.

Stryker, S., & Burke, P. J. (2000). The past, present, and future of an identity theory. *Social Psychology Quarterly, 63*, 284–297.

Stürmer, S. (2000). *Soziale Bewegungsbeteiligung: Ein psychologisches Zwei-Wege Modell.* Unpublished Doctoral Dissertation. University of Kiel, Germany.

Tajfel, H., & Turner, J. C. (1986). The social identity theory of intergroup behaviour. In: S. Worchel & W. G. Austin (Eds), *The social psychology of intergroup relations* (pp. 7–24). CA: Brooks Cole.

Turner, J. C. (1999). Some current issues in research on social identity and self-categorization theories. In: N. Ellemers, R. Spears & B. Doosje (Eds), *Social identity* (pp. 6–34). Oxford: Blackwell.

Turner, J. C., Hogg, M. A., Oakes, P. J., Reicher, S. D., & Wetherell, M. S. (Eds) (1987). *Rediscovering the social group. A self-categorization theory.* Oxford: Blackwell.

Tyler, T. R., Boeckmann, R. R., Smith, H. J., & Huo, Y. J. (1997). *Social justice in a diverse society.* Boulder: Westview Press.

Zegeye, A., Liebenberg, I., & Houston, G. (no date). *Resisting ethnicity from above: Social identities and the deepening of democracy in South Africa.* Unpublished paper. Human Science Research Council, Pretoria.

RECOGNITION OF GENDER IDENTITY AND TASK PERFORMANCE ☆

Allison K. Wisecup, Miller McPherson and
Lynn Smith-Lovin

ABSTRACT

Gender constitutes one of the fundamental distinctions that organize so-cial interaction. It is a salient social distinction in all societies, is a core personal identity for social actors, and is often used to generate expec-tations for competence in task-focused mixed-sex groups. In this chapter, we explore the effect of androgynous (gender ambiguous) appearance on task performance of observers. We demonstrate that it takes longer for research participants to define the gender identity of such individuals. More importantly, we hypothesize that since androgynous individuals do not fit easily into gender schemas that people use to access information about interaction partners, the presence of an androgynous-looking person will slow performance on a cognitive task. An experimental

☆Part of the data set analyzed here was collected by the first author as an undergraduate honors thesis at the University of Iowa under the direction of Dawn T. Robinson. Additional data collection, analysis and writing was supported by National Science Foundation Grant SES0215369 to the second and third authors.

Social Identification in Groups
Advances in Group Processes, Volume 22, 177–201
ISSN: 0882-6145/doi:10.1016/S0882-6145(05)22007-6

study supports both hypotheses. We conclude with suggestions about how the presence of non-stereotypical interaction partners with ambiguous identities might influence group members' task performance, cognitive inferences about and affective responses to other group members.

Sex category and gender are pervasive, salient parts of the social world (Sanday, 1981). The knowledge structures that are connected to "male" and "female" shape both our own actions and the actions of others toward us (Stets & Burke, 1996). Gender so shapes our expectations for a person that friends and family often find themselves unable to purchase gifts or prepare for a birth without first knowing the sex of the child.

The networks developed by young children in elementary school tend to be dominated by same-sex others (Thorne, 1993; Maccoby, 1998). The sex appropriate behaviors learned through interactions in the home and with peers are reinforced in educational settings. Teachers begin their remarks to classrooms with the phrase "boys and girls" while differential behaviors toward male and female students create self-fulfilling expectations about gender-differentiated interests, competencies, and activities. Peers play a crucial role in sanctioning sex inappropriate behaviors. Moreover, peers influence the types of media consumed by their friends. The messages sent by the many available media sources become an important guide for gender role reinforcement and behavioral expectations. Through these mechanisms, competent members of a social group develop a fairly consensual, richly elaborated understanding of what characteristics are associated with the two dominant sex categories.

Within this consensual context, an individual's expression of gender can manifest itself in a variety of ways. Through clothing choice, mannerisms, and speech styles individuals reveal gender cues to others in their environment. Perceivers then use these gender cues to infer sex. During the infinitesimal time required to access the male or female categories in the memory, perceivers gain access to a great deal of information. This rich information assists perceivers in formulating basic impressions of others. Moreover, this information provides perceivers with the behavioral expectations associated with males and females. Therefore, this process is a fundamental element of the definition of any social situation, guiding interactions, and commonly associated with men and women. Most social actors expect to encounter individuals whose gender expression provides clear cues for inferring sex.

Yet, when this expectation is violated perceivers are likely to experience interesting effects due to the presence of such ambiguous individuals in the social environment. This study is an investigation of the effects of sex category ambiguity on the identification of alters and task performance.

Consider for a moment the following scenario. A young man, Jeff, is walking down a busy sidewalk. Jeff sees an individual sitting on public bench smoking a cigarette. Jeff, a smoker who is out of cigarettes, determines the individual to be a young man approximately his own age and approaches him to ask for a cigarette. As Jeff approaches, he readies himself for the interaction. "Hey bud can I borrow one of those," says Jeff. The individual on the bench looks up, offering a cigarette. Jeff thanks him and sits down. In a slightly high tone, Jeff hears a "you're welcome" from his bench companion. Suddenly Jeff realizes that "he" is really a "she" and he blushes. How does Jeff rectify this situation? Should he? Are there any guidelines for dealing with this type of mistake? These and other questions run through his mind, when he realizes that "she" is asking if he needs a light. Finally, after an uncomfortable pause, Jeff says yes, lights the cigarette, and quickly leaves her alone on the bench. This example illustrates the difficulties of negotiating interactions when we fail to assign the correct sex category to the individuals around us. Sex category classification provides us with the necessary information for orienting the self to others. Incorrect classifications are likely to make individuals uncomfortable because their expectations of others have been violated.

Indeed, the entertainment industry has used this phenomenon to its own purposes. In the late 1980s, the television program *Saturday Night Live* created a popular sketch with Pat, a physically androgynous main character, as the focus. Most of the sketches were set in ordinary places, such as pharmacies, with ordinary people doing commonplace things. The attraction of sketches involved others' attempts to discern Pat's sex. The sketch ingeniously illustrated the importance of sex plays in the basic categorization processes undertaken by perceivers. Pat's novelty and conflicting gender cues caused a significant enough disruption of the categorization process that others were unable to continue with other routine tasks or conversations. Here, we develop an argument using psychological theories of category recognition and impression formation to formulate hypotheses about the effects of gender ambiguity on situation definition and task performance. We then suggest more general implications of our results for social interaction in task groups.

COGNITIVE PROCESSING OF OTHERS' IDENTITIES

A tacit assumption in any model of information processing is that humans have limited cognitive resources. Finite capacity requires individuals to create abstract information structures to increase processing speed and efficiency. These systems allow social actors to quickly process the myriad of stimuli that assail them from their social environment. At the center of such systems, individuals have a variety of knowledge structures including exemplars, schemata, and prototypes. Exemplars are examples used to encode and organize information about new objects. This method often becomes cumbersome when an individual acquires too many examples. Schemas contain bits of information about an object including characteristics and attributes of the object as well as examples. Prototypes portray the representative object at the core of a schema.

Social actors rely on heuristics (cognitive shortcuts) to process and organize incoming information. Heuristics reduce the intricate processing attempts to simpler mental operations, allowing for the efficient processing of information. The most often used is the representative heuristic. When relying on this, individuals compare the salient aspects of a new object to the prototype at the center of a category or schema. Reliance on this heuristic is often associated with stereotyping (Howard, 1995). Although sometimes faulty, heuristics provide actors with a means through which they can categorize and understand their surroundings and the individuals in them. In their dependence on heuristics, actors ultimately sacrifice accuracy in the interest of speed.

Categorization permits perceivers to conserve limited cognitive resources while increasing efficiency. Moreover, this process provides perceivers with a set of beliefs and expectations about others and an initial interactional orientation. The categorization process not only allows perceivers to make denotative inferences about others' characteristics, it also activates affective responses that guide future expectations, actions, and emotional responses (MacKinnon, 1994).

Models of memory assume schemata to be a complex organization of interconnected sets of nodes operating on the principle of diffusion (Andersen & Klatzky, 1987; Pavelchak, 1989). Upon retrieval of a schema, other nodes, including affective evaluations and behavioral expectations, are also activated. Schemata are conceptualized as hierarchical structures with general or category labels at the upper levels; category labels become increasingly exclusive and specific at the lower levels (Pavelchak, 1989). Cohen (1981b, p. 49) defines schema as "a hypothetical cognitive structure that represents association among lower level units of information, resulting in a functional higher-level cohesive meaningful unit." Schemata provide a translation of the continuous stream of others' behaviors and allow perceivers to understand and make sense of their social environment.

People possess an assortment of features, any of which can be used by others as the impetus for categorization. These factors can be roughly organized into three broad, but by no means exhaustive, categories: novelty/ salience, relative accessibility of categories in a perceiver's cognitive constructs, and the physical appearance of the target.

Individuals who, as social objects, are novel relative to their surroundings tend to be categorized in terms of the trait that differentiates them from the environment (Taylor, 1981). Bargh and colleagues (Bargh & Pratto, 1986; Bargh, 1989) indicate that categories with frequent and repetitive activation in the past are likely to become chronically active and used in the future categorization of others. Particular categories may be perpetually activated and used as the initial basis for the categorization of all individuals encountered. Features such as occupation or religion may not be as readily discernable as other physical characteristics; thus individuals are likely to rely on visual cues when commencing the categorization process of defining a social situation. Moreover, if an individual's physical characteristics make him or her novel and if this dimension is one that is chronically activated and used by others, it is highly likely that the physical characteristic will become the primary basis for categorization (Madson, 1996).

Research on person perception indicates that in the initial stages of person perception, perceivers use rudimentary categories such as age, sex, and race (Bruner, 1957; Brewer & Lui, 1989; Fiske & Neuberg, 1990). Furthermore, the first stages of categorization are unconscious and nearly automatic. Although perceivers may use multiple dimensions in forming impressions of others, Brewer and Lui (1989) claim the dimensions of age and sex are the primary categories and other information processing attempts fall along these dimension (i.e. young woman, older man).[1]

Stangor, Lynch, Duan, and Glass (1992) conducted a battery of experiments to determine which social features perceivers use to categorize individuals. In the first experiment, Stangor et al. presented subjects with 24 statements made by two Black women, two Black men, two White men, and two White women in a group discussion. Subjects were then given a surprise recall test, wherein they were asked to match each statement with the appropriate speaker. Subjects made more within-sex errors than between-sex errors. Similarly, there were more within-race than between-race errors.

The researchers replicated Experiment 1 using 10 times as many target stimuli, to eliminate potential categorization based on clothing color, style, or posture. The results refined their conclusions, indicating that sex, not race, was most often used as an independent category for organizing information about the targets and their comments. Following participation in the study, subjects were asked to rate, on a 9-point scale, how much certain social information would give them insight to a individual's personality. The results indicate subjects felt sex, not race, was the most informative piece of information they could receive about another person (Stangor et al., 1992). The results of five experiments support models of person perception that suggest perceivers generally use broad social categories as a starting point for the impression formation process (Brewer & Lui, 1989; Fiske & Neuberg, 1990). The results of these studies indicate that perceivers are extremely likely to use sex a primary classification, before race or age.

Schemas are constructed over the life course and contain a large amount of information. When perceivers access a particular node in the memory, it is highly likely that other nodes will also be implicated. The information nodes associated with the male and female schemas provide individuals with a means for orienting the self toward the other. This process occurs very quickly and usually without incident. If a physically androgynous individual disrupts this process, perceivers are likely to experience a great deal of difficulty proceeding with the person perception processes. This investigation is an attempt to discover the effects of such disruptions.

Impression Formation

Much of the person perception process occurs at an unconscious level. Perceivers generally do not take notice of the process unless they do not have a schema for understanding or encoding an individual in their social environment. Mead's view of the person perception process suggests social actors actively select stimuli from their social environment (Mead, 1934). This process involves extracting a particular stimulus from the environment, holding it apart from the others and giving it meaning. Actors then proceed to the manipulation phase, wherein they hypothesize about the nature of the indicated object. Finally, actors enter the consummation stage of the perception process. In this final stage, perceivers make decisions about the object and determine which course of action they should take. In the Meadian view of the perception process, perceivers may take note of and classify a multitude of the information in their surroundings; social actors ultimately decide which objects come to the fore of consciousness. So, which people do actors extract from their environments and give conscious attention to and which people are classified in an almost unconscious and automatic manner? Cohen (1981a) comments that it is only when perceivers are confronted with individuals for whom there are no schemata that they consciously attend to the process of person perception.

According to models of impression formation, the time required to formulate an impression of an object depends on the fit between prior knowledge and the stimulus (Bruner, 1957; Brewer & Lui, 1989; Fiske & Neuberg, 1990). If a perceiver encounters an object or person that is relatively congruent with prior knowledge, the process of impression formation may take little or no time. Moreover, this process may occur at a preconscious level and require few if any of the available cognitive resources. Conversely, if a perceiver encounters an object or person whose traits are highly inconsistent with prior knowledge or experience, the time and resources required to formulate an impression should increase dramatically (Burnstein & Schul, 1983).

The Fiske and Neuberg (1990) Impression Formation Continuum Model brings together previously competing notions of impression formation. One end of the model contains category-based processes, while the other includes attribute-based processes. According to this model, perceivers may use category-based processes to the exclusion of attribute-based processes or vice versa. Moreover, perceivers may use both types of processes in their attempts to formulate an impression of another individual. Fiske and Neuberg (1990) define categories as a broad social feature used by perceivers to organize and comprehend other features of a particular target. Categories often operate as cognitive structures that are very rich in information. Attributes, on the other hand, are likely to be a single feature of a target. Fiske and Neuberg (1990) argue that upon initial exposure to an individual, perceivers are likely to rely on category-based processes to make initial inferences.

The model contains five basic premises. The first premise holds that attribute-based processes are secondary to category-based processes in the process of impression formation. Secondly, movement along the continuum is contingent upon the ease with which perceivers can find a good fit between the target and some pre-existing category. Should a perceiver encounter an individual whose features are not readily compatible with a category, Fiske and Neuberg predict a movement away from category-based processes toward the specific attributes of the individual. The third premise states that initial attention by perceivers to attribute information arbitrates the use of the continuum. The fourth premise asserts that motivation influences impression formation outcomes. Moreover, according to this premise, perceivers can be manipulated toward either end of the continuum. The last premise claims that motivational influences are mediated by attentional and interpretive responses to specific attributes of an individual.

The Impression Formation Continuum model (Fiske & Neuberg, 1990) includes six steps in the formulation of an impression. During initial categorization, perceivers utilize the physical attributes of a target or verbal or written category labels to cue a label in memory. Once a category is activated, perceivers also access information regarding affective orientation toward, evaluations of, and behavioral expectations for a target. Nearly every target possesses at least four basic types of categories accessible to perceivers: age, sex, ethnicity, and social class. This process occurs very rapidly and is almost imperceptible provided that a target possesses category consistent characteristics.

After initial categorization occurs, perceivers quickly determine if the target is at least minimally or personally relevant. If the target does not meet either of the above criteria, the perceiver dispenses with the impression formation processes and moves on to other information in their social environment. If the target satisfies one of the criteria, the perceiver then attends to other conspicuous information required to form a clearer impression of the target. The perceiver then focuses on other information to determine whether stereotypic or individuating processes will be utilized.

Fiske and Neuberg (1990) incorporate theoretical work by Bruner (1957) indicating that perceivers will attempt to confirm the initial categorization of a target. If confirmation is possible, perceivers will likely utilize the stereotypic process relying on the affective and evaluative orientations and behavioral expectations activated by the accession of the category label. The inability to confirm the initial categorization will result in recategorization. This involves the search for a different category. This process may involve accessing a subcategory, which ultimately allows the perceiver to retain many of the characteristics of the initial category label while simultaneously attending to the exceptional features of the target. Additionally, perceivers may access exemplars or self-categories, all of which have similar consequences for the impression formation process. If recategorization fails, perceivers then shift to individuating processes involving an attribute-by-attribute formulation of an impression.

Impression Formation and Gender Ambiguity

An application of the Fiske and Neuberg (1990) continuum model of impression formation to the central research question of this study provides some interesting predictions. The presence of a physically androgynous individual in a perceiver's social environment should disrupt the impression formation process. As individuals move through their social environment, they take a rough survey of those around them. This survey, according to the Fiske and Neuberg model, should fall along the dimensions of sex, age, or race. Most targets in the environment will not propel perceivers to undertake any further steps in the impression formation process. Yet, if a target is novel, or attracts the attention of a perceiver based on one of the above rudimentary categories, perceivers are likely to spend more time formulating an impression of the person. Thus, the presence of a physically androgynous individual in a perceiver's environment should force toward attribute-based processing strategies, ultimately requiring the perceiver to spend an increased amount of time in impression formation process.

Madson (1996) built upon this impression formation literature to argue that physically androgynous individuals who do not convey clear cues regarding sex would likely divert a participant's attention away from a cognitively demanding task. She speculated that this distraction would increase response times and decrease accuracy on those tasks. Madson (1996) created an experimental task with a picture of an androgynous person on the right side of a split screen while a Stroop task[2] appeared 2 sec later on the left half. The experiment had two conditions. In one condition, the androgynous person had a name label which made his or her sex unambiguous. In the other condition, the picture had a gender-neutral word like "water" under it. In this experiment, participants' response times and accuracy did not vary with the ambiguity of the sex of the pictured person on the right side of the screen.

Other studies, however, found that androgynous pictures led to attributions about non-gender stereotypical traits and about sexuality[3] (Madson, 2000). In addition, participants showed negative affective reactions to sex-ambiguous individuals. These results give us reason to think that the hypotheses about task performance and accuracy might have been rejected because of the experimental format rather than because of theoretical inadequacy. In Madson's (1996) study, the pictures of individuals were all androgynous; whether or not they were sex-ambiguous was manipulated by the label under the picture either a gendered name or a neutral word. We find two problems with this experimental format. First, since all research participants were exposed to a highly atypical gender presentation, it may be that all were required to do additional processing to encode attributes more consciously. The assumption that supplying a clearly gendered name label would simplify categorization to a stereotypical, schematic level (or at least one that is significantly less complicated than the unlabeled person) may not be justified. The fact that Madson (2000) showed androgynous appearance leads to numerous attributions about non-gender-stereotypical traits, suggests that such appearance may lead to more complex processing even when sex category is established by a name label. Secondly, while the pictures were in the environment of the task, the participants were not actively engaged in the process of categorizing the pictured individuals. Research suggests that if they expected a social interaction to occur, they would have been engaged in a categorization process. But it is possible that if the sex was ambiguous and classification had not occurred by the time that the Stroop task appeared on the other half of the screen, participants might have abandoned their (unmotivated) attention to the picture in favor of the prescribed task at hand (the Stroop task). Therefore, we elaborate the Madson hypotheses to include more restrictive scope conditions that reflect more active engagement by defining the situation with regard to the individual's sex category.

HYPOTHESES

This study was designed to test four primary hypotheses:

1. Exposure to physically androgynous individuals will require an increased amount of time for categorizing the individual as either male or female, relative to gender-stereotypical individuals.
2. More errors of classification as male or female will result from androgynous appearance than from gender stereotypic appearance.
3. Exposure to physically androgynous individuals will cause cognitive interference in other areas, resulting in increased response times on tasks following exposure (relative to exposure to gender-stereotypical individuals).
4. Exposure to physically androgynous individuals will result in lower accuracy in task performance than exposure to gender-stereotypical individuals.

We expect these hypotheses to hold when research subjects actively engage in the task of categorizing the individuals to which they are exposed (as they would if they expected to actually interact with these individuals in a social situation) in close temporal proximity to the task to be performed. Some level of motivation to complete the task accurately is also necessary, so that cognitive processing will be engaged to a substantial degree. Therefore, we expect these hypotheses, previously rejected by Madson (1996), to hold when (1) physically androgynous stimuli alters are compared with gender-stereotypical alters, (2) the research subjects are actively engaged in the task of defining the situation (categorizing the alters to whom they are exposed), and (3) the research participants are actively engaged in the cognitively challenging task. We design a study to test the four hypotheses within these scope conditions.

METHODS

Constructing Gender-ambiguous Stimuli

A survey was distributed to 36 undergraduate students enrolled in an upper-level sociology course at the University of Iowa. The survey consisted of 30 pictures that had been downloaded from online dating services – 10 males, 10 females, and 10 individuals determined to be physically androgynous by the first author. Participants indicated the sex category of the individuals in the photographs by checking a male or female box. Participants then rated the confidence of their decision for each photograph on a 7-point Likert scale, with 1 being not at all confident and 7 indicating complete confidence. The six pictures with the lowest level of agreement and lowest mean confidence ratings were used as the physically androgynous stimulus photographs in the program. Conversely, the 15 photographs yielding high levels of agreement and mean levels of confidence were used as the stereotypical male and female individuals.

Participants for the Study

Participants for the study were recruited from classes offered at the University of Iowa in the Spring semester of 2002 and at Duke University in the summer of 2004. Procedures and stimulus programs were identical at the two locations; institution is entered into the analysis as a control variable but in no case does it interact with the hypothesized relationships.

Students interested in participating in a sociological study completed a recruiting form and were then called and scheduled to participate in the study reported here. During the scheduling telephone call, participants were told that the study would take less than an hour and compensation would be approximately $10. A total of 123 students participated in the study, 67 females and 56 males. The average age of participants was 19.9, based on data reported by 120 participants. Participants were randomly assigned to condition within sex.

Experimental Procedures

We designed an experimental study[4] using a 2×2 factorial design which presented participants with a computer-based task similar to that used by Madson (1996). Upon arriving at the laboratory, participants were instructed to read and sign an informed consent document. After addressing any questions raised by the informed consent, they were given a brief overview of the study. Participants were told that they were participating in a study titled Cognitive Processing. They were told that we were interested in how quickly and accurately they could answer the questions and that their payment would be based on the number of correctly answered questions.

The participants were then left alone in a small room with a computer screen, keyboard, and mouse. They were instructed to complete the tutorial and then place a card calling the experimenter under the door of their cubicle room. The experimenter answered any questions that they had about the procedures and then instructed the participants to complete the rest of the tasks, sliding the card under the door when they had finished.

The program used in this investigation presents participants with a number of stimuli; participants select their answers by using a mouse. The stimuli are grouped into three categories: words, pictures, and letter sequencing tasks. Participants are instructed to classify the words as either masculine or feminine, pictures as either male or female and select the correct answer from five choices in the letter sequencing task.

The program consists of 12 rounds of stimuli; each round contains word stimuli, followed by picture stimuli and letter sequencing tasks.[5] Stimuli are presented on a screen that is divided in half horizontally by a bold red line. A stimulus and the corresponding answer options appear in the bottom portion of the screen. After making a choice among the possible answers, the stimulus (but not the chosen answer) moves to the top portion of the screen and a new stimulus and set of potential responses appears in the bottom half of the screen. For example, the word "clerk" would appear in the bottom portion of the screen along with buttons labeled masculine and feminine. After the experimental participant decided whether the word "clerk" was masculine or feminine with a mouse click, the word "clerk" would appear in the top half of the screen and a new word, such as "aggressive", would appear in the bottom half of the screen along with masculine and feminine buttons.

The first two rounds of stimuli are contained in the tutorial segment of the program and consist of two words, two pictures, and two tasks. While not differing from the rest of the program in presentation, the tutorial was designed to provide participants with a chance to practice the type of tasks they would be asked to complete and allow them to become acquainted with the program presentation style.

The remaining 10 rounds are identical in format for both conditions, gender ambiguous (androgynous) and non-ambiguous. The only difference between the two conditions is the presentation of six androgynous pictures in the gender ambiguous condition. In six of the ten rounds, the third picture differed in the gender ambiguous (androgynous) and non-ambiguous conditions.[6] The third picture presented in the manipulation rounds in the gender ambiguous condition was an androgynous individual (as rated in the stimuli development study). Participants in the non-ambiguous condition were presented with pictures that were all stereotypically male or female (again, as rated in the stimulus development study). Other than the six androgynous pictures in the gender ambiguous condition, participants in both conditions saw the same stimuli in the same order.

After the participants had completed the computer task, they slipped a card under the door of their cubicle indicating to the experimenter that they had finished. The study participants then filled out a short questionnaire that consisted of a short form of the Personal Attributes Questionnaire (Spence & Helmreich, 1978) and socio-demographic questions (age, sex, race, major ACT or SAT scores, and GPA). The participants were then de-briefed.

Methods and Measures

Our dependent variables take two forms. Because our dependent variable for Hypotheses 1 and 3 will be time elapsed between exposure to a stimulus and the time of response, we measure the duration of this interval in seconds (to the 14th decimal place). We use multivariate event–history techniques to model the timing of the response. The hazard of a response at time t is the probability that the participant responds with an answer at that time, given that s/he has not responded prior to time t. The general form of the hazard model is:

$$h(t|x) = h_0(t)\exp(xNb)$$

where $h(t|x)$ is the hazard at time t, $h_0 t$ the baseline hazard at time t, x the covariation matrix of the independent variables, and b the vector of coefficients to be estimated. Since we do not want to make any strong assumptions about the functional form of the hazard distribution, we use the discrete approximation of the continuous time model described above (Allison, 1984; Yamaguchi, 1991). Here, we construct a data set where the time of response is divided into discrete units (in this case, of 1/100th of a second). Using logistic regression to analyze these time periods in a discrete time approximation of the hazard model has the advantage that it makes no assumptions about the functional form of the underlying hazard distribution, as well as controlling for the possible confounding effects of other variables.

For Hypotheses 2 and 4, the dependent variable is simply the accuracy of the participant's judgment about the stimulus person's sex category or the pattern recognition task that immediately follows the experimental manipulation (the androgynous pictures in the gender ambiguous condition in rounds 3, 5–7, 9, and 10 or the stereotypical pictures in those same rounds for the non-ambiguous condition). Since logistic regressions modeling the relationship between the probability of being correct and the independent variables showed effects only for the experimental manipulation, we present frequency tables and t-tests for these hypotheses.

The most important independent variable is, of course, the experimental condition, *gender ambiguity*. Participants who were exposed to the androgynous pictures as part of their programmed task were coded 1, while participants who saw only stereotypically male or female pictures were coded 0. *Sex* was coded as 1 if the participant was male, female otherwise. *Institution* was coded 0 if the participant was from the first data collection at the University of Iowa, 1 if the participant came from Duke University. To control for heterogeneity of individual response times in performing the tasks, an *individual average response time* variable was constructed for both pictures and tasks.[7] The average picture response time was constructed by summing each participant's response times for the eight pictures that appeared in the program *before* the manipulation occurred under the androgynous condition. This total time was then divided by eight to produce an average picture response time for each individual. The task variable was constructed in a similar fashion, using the eight tasks that appeared before the first androgynous picture in the experimental procedure.

RESULTS

The survival functions for the responses to the gender stereotypical and the physically androgynous picture stimuli are presented in Fig. 1. While

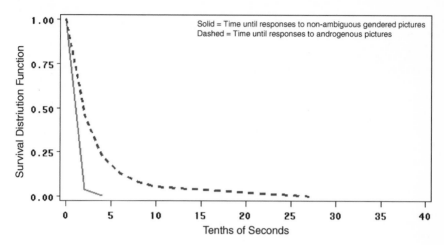

Fig. 1. Survival Plot of Picture Responses by Gender Ambiguity.

virtually all of the gender schematic pictures had been classified as male or female within three of the 0.01time periods, participants had classified only half of the androgynous pictures within that time frame. More dramatically, virtually none of the participants took more than four time periods to classify the picture, while a quarter of the participants in the androgynous condition took longer.

The mean response time of participants in the non-ambiguous condition to the gender-stereotypical photographs was 1.198 sec, while the average response time to stimulus pictures in the gender ambiguous condition was 3.007 sec. The mean difference between response times to pictures between the conditions is nearly 2 sec. This large difference provides tentative support for Hypothesis 1 and illustrates how the cognitive processing undertaken by perceivers differs when a category target match is not initially possible.

More complete support is offered for Hypothesis 1 in Table 1, which reports the discrete-time approximation hazard analysis, including the effects of time dependence (without making any assumptions about functional form) and the effects of covariates. Gender ambiguity condition (androgynous vs. non-ambiguous) is highly significant. The individual average response time is a significant determinant of the time needed to classify the stimulus pictures as male or female: some people simply respond more quickly to the mouse-click task than others. Sex of participant and institution have neither main nor interaction effects, and so we omit them

Table 1. Accuracy of Picture Recognition by Gender Ambiguity.

Number of Pictures Classified Correctly as Male or Female	Androgynous		Non-ambiguous	
	Frequency	Proportion	Frequency	Proportion
0	17	0.27	0	0.00
1	8	0.13	0	0.00
2	15	0.23	0	0.00
3	15	0.23	0	0.00
4	8	0.13	0	0.00
5	1	0.02	2	0.03
6	0	0.00	57	0.97
Total	64	1.01[a]	59	1.00

Notes: $T = 21.53$ with 121 df, $p < 0.001$.
[a]Proportions do not sum to 1.00 because of rounding.

from this analysis. There is time dependence in our reaction time data; dummy variables representing time periods are significant when taken as a group.

The accuracy of sex-category judgments (Hypothesis 2) was strongly associated with gender ambiguity condition (androgynous vs. non-ambiguous) condition, which we would expect since we selected the picture stimuli based on a pretest of this variable. Only two of the 59 participants in the control (gender-stereotypical) condition made even one mistake about the gender classification of the stimulus pictures; all of the others got all classifications correct (see Table 2).[8] In the gender ambiguous condition, however, more of the judgments were incorrect than correct (i.e., matching the pictured person's own sex category designation and gender identity). None of the participants in the gender ambiguous (androgynous) condition got all of the classifications correct, and only nine got more than half of them correct.[9] Indeed, one of the first indications that our predictions about ambiguity of sex classification interfering with task performance were supported from the fact that participants in the gender ambiguous condition often moved closer to the computer screen, squinted, or glanced back up at the androgynous pictures even when the classification task was finished and the picture stimulus has moved to the top of the screen. A multivariate logistic regression analysis of classification accuracy confirms the strong pattern shown in Table 2; condition (androgynous vs. gender-stereotypical picture) has a strong, statistically significant effect. The only other variable that has a marginal effect is participant's sex: men were slightly more accurate than women in classifying the androgynous pictures as male or female.

Table 2. Time Until Picture Classification by Gender Ambiguity.

Independent Variable	Parameter Estimate	Standard Error
Intercept	−2.00***	0.13
Gender ambiguity (1 = androgynous)	1.08***	0.09
Average response time[a]	−0.27***	0.07

Notes: (1) The model also includes five dummy variables representing time dependence in the hazard of responding, not reported here because they are not substantively interesting. (2) N of response events = 749; N of time periods = 16,065. (3) Likelihood ratio χ^2 = 213.40 with 7 df, $p < 0.001$.
[a]The average duration of the responses to tasks *before* the first manipulation of gender ambiguity occurred in the androgynous condition.

Our more interesting hypotheses, of course, involve the letter sequencing task that followed the stimulus pictures (and while the pictures were still present on the top of the computer screen above the task). Hypothesis 3 suggests that the presence of an ambigiously categorized others will interfere cognitively with the task performance, resulting in slower response times. Fig. 2 shows the survival curves for both the androgynous and stereotypical conditions. While not as dramatic as the time difference required to categorize the pictured person, these descriptive data show a clear pattern of longer response times in the androgynous condition. The mean response time to the letter sequencing task following gender-stereotypical pictures was 12.034 sec, while the average response time for the treatment condition was 14.142 sec. The resulting mean difference is over 2 sec. We present a multivariate test of Hypothesis 3, using the discrete approximation model, in Table 3. Gender ambiguity condition (androgynous vs. stereotypical) has a significant effect ($p = 0.008$). The average response speed (computed from stimuli that occurred before the first manipulation) has a strong impact as well. Finally, the Duke students responded somewhat more quickly than the University of Iowa students to the tasks following the experimental manipulation. There was no effect of participant sex, and the two- and three-way interactions among sex, institution, and condition were not significant; therefore, we dropped these variables from the analysis presented in Table 3. There is significant time dependence in our task response data; dummy variables representing timer periods were significant, taken as a group.

Our final hypothesis suggests that accuracy at the problem-solving task will decline as a result of the distraction and cognitive load of exposure to non-schematic alters. Accuracy on the task was fairly high, with the great

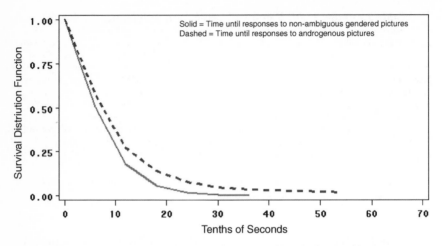

Fig. 2. Survival Plot of Picture Responses by Gender Ambiguity.

Table 3. Task Accuracy by Gender Ambiguity.

Number of Tasks Answered Correctly	Androgynous		Non-ambiguous	
	Frequency	Proportion	Frequency	Proportion
0	0	0.00	0	0.00
1	0	0.00	0	0.00
2	0	0.00	0	0.00
3	2	0.03	0	0.00
4	2	0.03	0	0.00
5	11	0.17	6	0.10
6	49	0.77	53	0.90
Total	64	1.00	59	1.00

Note: T-value for difference in means $= 2.32$ with 121 df, $p = 0.022$.

majority of the participants deliberating until they had the correct answer. Still, Table 4 shows a marked difference in task performance between the gender ambiguous condition and the non-ambiguous condition. Six percent of the participants who were distracted by a sex-ambiguous person in the top half of the screen missed more than two of the task questions, more than any of the control participants. More than twice as many participants in the experimental condition got at least one task solution incorrect (14 vs. 6). The difference in task accuracy is statistically significant, ($p < 0.022$). As with

Table 4. Time Until Task Completion by Gender Ambiguity.

Independent Variable	Parameter Estimate	Standard Error
Intercept	-5.96^{***}	0.18
Gender ambiguity (1 = androgynous)	0.20^{**}	0.08
Average response time[a]	-0.09^{***}	0.01
Institution (0 = Duke)	0.26^{**}	0.08

Notes: (1) The model also includes seven dummy variables representing time dependence in the hazard of responding, not reported here because they are not substantively interesting. (2) N of response events = 748; N of time periods = 97,848. (3) Likelihood ratio χ^2 = 644.00 with 10 df, $p < 0.001$.
$^{***}p < 0.001$.
$^{**}p < 0.01$.
[a]The average duration of the responses to tasks *before* the first manipulation of gender ambiguity occurred in the androgynous condition.

accuracy of sex classification, a multivariate analysis of task accuracy confirms the strong pattern shown in Table 4; the experimental condition (androgynous vs. stereoetypical) has a statistically significant effect. Participant's sex, institution, and average response time did not have significant effects on task accuracy.

DISCUSSION

We find support for all four of our hypotheses. It was more difficult for research participants to identify the sex category for physically androgynous people who were pictured – both in terms of the amount of time that it took them to process the identification and the accuracy with which they matched the alters' own gender identification. The mean response times for the photographs indicate that individuals in the androgynous condition required more than twice as long to categorize the alters as either male or female. Furthermore, the participants *misidentified* the sex category of the alter over half of the time, an error that would have had serious interactional consequences in a real social situation.[10] The support of our first two hypotheses indicates that definitions of situations in terms of the key personal identities of social actors may sometimes be problematic. When things are confusing, when they do not fit our prototypes for social identities, when our schemata fail and when we have to resort to more detailed processing of characteristics, things take longer and we make more mistakes.

But in a sense, our first two hypotheses are self-evident. We think that Hypotheses 3 and 4 have more interesting, complex implications for group processes. Here, we predicted that participants would experience cognitive interference after exposure to a physically androgynous alters and would require longer processing times and make more mistakes on subsequent cognitive tasks. The data support these less obvious predictions as well.

Our findings suggest support for the Fiske and Neuberg (1990) model of impression formation. Without pre-existing schemas for the categorization of physically androgynous individuals, perceivers were required to proceed through more phases of the impression formation process, resulting in longer response times. The data also support the cognitive miser perspective of information processing and expand the boundaries of the Fiske and Neuberg (1990) model of impression formation. Despite accounting for the presence of a physically androgynous individual in their social environment, participants in the treatment condition experienced cognitive interference when they proceeded to the letter sequencing tasks. The longer response times on the tasks appearing directly after the stimuli indicate that the impression formation process may not conclude once the situation is "defined" and identities labeled. Although the physically androgynous alters were of little social significance to participants in the experimental condition, participants clearly continued to devote some of their cognitive resources to those alters, despite having other tasks at hand.

It might be useful to draw out how we think the phenomena that we have studied here might be important for group interaction. It is these extrapolations that will guide our future research agenda. First, group members that are atypical and hard to classify into basic, ubiquitous categories are likely to create a number of challenges for the initial definition of the situation in the group. If members are initially unsure of the definition, they may engage in cognitive work and interactive probes in order to classify alters correctly. The status structure of the group may not initially be clear. Such status structures are determined partially by classifications on basic status characteristics like sex, age, and race/ethnicity – if these identities are not clear, there may be some period of interaction (either momentary or in the case of age or race, quite extended) where private and public definitions may differ. Non-prototypical instances of male, female, old, young, minority, or majority may also lead to inferences about other non-typical traits or characteristics that the individuals possess. Madson (2000), for example, found that experimental participants assumed that physically androgynous stimulus people were homosexual; and Webster, Hysom, and Fullmer (1998) found that the homosexual/heterosexual distinction has status value. In

Affect Control Theory (Smith-Lovin & Heise, 1988), atypical instances of an identity are labeled with modifiers that describe their difference from the prototypical identity occupant. These modifiers have affective meanings that combine with the fundamental sentiments associated with the identity to create a new fundamental sentiment for the person (Averett & Heise, 1987). Maintaining a differing fundamental sentiment, of course, changes the intended actions toward the person by other group members, the expected actions from that individual, and the emotional responses that are predicted by other group members for that person.

We are even more intrigued by the implications of our findings for task performance. Even though our experimental situation was very minimally social in nature, the presence of someone who did not fit cultural schemas associated with gender and sex category was disruptive. One suspects that this effect might be much stronger if any one of a number of additional features were present. First, just knowing that they had classified the other person into the wrong sex category might increase the effect on cognitive processing.[11] Certainly, in an actual social interaction, the embarrassment and negative effect that the situation would arouse would be expected to have substantial effects on later actions.[12] Even more interesting is the potential impact of collaborating with a person whose identity is unclear on a task. This interaction would presumably increase the salience of the ambiguous, problematic identity classification, and heighten its negative impact on task performance. There is also an interesting potential for status dynamics. Are non-schematic individuals who are far from our prototypical identity occupants evaluated more negatively in general, and therefore accorded lower status in the power and prestige orders that develop in task-focused groups? Or does this derogation only occur when and if the individual's appearance leads to inferences about status characteristics that are already negatively evaluated? For example, would the status effect be reversed if ambiguity of identity led to a positive inference (e.g., a racial minority who look almost White/Anglo)?

Finally, lest our results lead to a conclusion that non-traditional looking people are a potentially negative influence on group interactions and task performances, we want to point out some potentially positive effects of non-prototypical group members. Charlen Nemeth has developed a research program that argues for the positive effects of a strongly voiced minority opinion, *regardless* of that opinion's correctness or content (Nemeth, 1986; Nemeth, Connell, Rogers, & Brown, 2001). She argues that a minority opinion helps to break up the rapid convergence on a majority framing of a task or issue, preventing premature closure and allowing more creative solutions to problems. Here, we suggest a broadening of this proposition. While non-schematic individuals may be harder to classify, harder to predict, and somewhat distracting, their presence may lead to more complex processing and cognitive connections to a wider array of nodes in impression formation. While the affect associated with this extra effort and ambiguity might be negative, there might be payoffs in creativity. Nemeth's research participants ended up disliking the minority and rejecting its influence, but eventually ended up with better performances because of its presence. Perhaps on tasks where creative thought and non-paradigmatic framing are valuable, difficulties in determining the identities of others might have similar positive effects on performance.[13]

The speculations above lead to several directions for further research. First, we would like to see whether sex category is unique in its fundamental importance to the definition of a situation. Will stimulus pictures that are ambiguous in terms of their age, race/ethnicity, or other more role-based identities have the same impact on cognitive processing? Second, will information about the accuracy of the research participant's initial definition of the situation (i.e., the extent to which it agrees with the alter's own self-identity) influence processing? Will this impact be mediated by affective reactions, or will it be cognitive in nature? Third, will making the situation more social make a difference? If the research participants anticipate interacting with the pictured person in the future, will their attempts to define the alter's identity be more important? If they "interact" with the pictured alter in a standard expectation state experimental task, how will the ambiguity of identity (on gender or on other status characteristics) affect the power and prestige order? Finally, are there positive effects on creativity or other group decision-making processes when we encounter group members whose basic identities are unclear or problematic?

NOTES

1. This perceptual literature fits well with anthropological observations that sex and age divisions are present in all known human societies, and form the basis for more elaborated systems of differentiation and stratification (Sanday, 1981).

2. A Stroop task involves the presentation of a color word in which the color of the letters either matches the color named by the word or is incongruent with the named color. The task requires that the participant answers a question with the color of the letters. Not surprisingly, participants respond more quickly and more accurately when the color word and the text color are congruent than when they are not.

3. Subjects were more likely to assume that androgynous looking individuals were homosexual.

4. The study design was developed by the first author for her undergraduate honors thesis under the direction of Dawn T. Robinson at the University of Iowa. Additional data and the current analyses were conducted at Duke University.

5. The trait and occupation words included in the program are taken from Freedman and Lips (1996). The pattern-completion problem-solving tasks are taken from a cognitive abilities measure developed by Schaie (1985).

6. The manipulation occurred in the third, fifth, sixth, seventh, ninth, and tenth trials.

7. This control variable is conceptually similar to a covariate in a MANOVA.

8. These two mistakes were almost certainly accidental clicks of the mouse used to answer the question.

9. The participants were not informed that their classification was incorrect, as they almost certainly would have been in a social interaction situation. We discuss the implications of this fact in our suggestions for future research.

10. We acknowledge that in many situations other cues might be available to disambiguate the alter's identity. However, physically androgynous individuals often embrace that characteristic and dress, act and otherwise indicate a lack of gender schematic cultural traits. The fact that one of the authors has heard several reports of sex category misidentification from student diaries in sociology of gender classes means that this phenomenon is not unheard of in actual social interactions.

11. Alternatively, having a definitive answer to the question of sex classification could lead to a firm definition of the situation and reduce the impact of the physically androgynous person on task performance. Recall that Madson (1996) used labeled vs. non-labeled pictures to manipulate sex ambiguity in her experimental studies of androgyny and its effects.

12. Wharton and Baron (1987) have shown that workers in mixed sex work groups have lower satisfaction with their jobs (but also see Fields & Blum, 1997). Here, we are suggesting that this effect might be much broader than just a straightforward negative effect of heterogeneity. It could be that task interactions with people who we do not understand and can not predict as well are problematic in general. Other-sex people might fit this description to some degree. People whose basic identities are unclear to us initially, and who do not fit our schemas for occupants of those identities might be problematic in similar, perhaps even stronger ways.

13. Clearly, the pattern recognition task that we used in this study does not meet these criteria. There was a single correct answer, which most of the college students were able to discover in a fairly short time frame. Nemeth typically uses tasks where there is an easily accessible but flawed solution, and a better solution that requires "thinking outside the box".

REFERENCES

Allison, P. D. (1984). *Event history analysis: Regression for longitudinal event data*. Beverly Hills, CA: Sage Publications.

Andersen, S. M., & Klatzky, R. L. (1987). Traits and social stereotypes: Levels of categorization in person perception. *Journal of Personality and Social Psychology, 53*, 235–246.

Averett, C., & Heise, D. R. (1987). Modified social identities: Amalgamations, attributions, and emotions. *Journal of Mathematical Sociology, 13*, 103–132.

Bargh, J. A. (1989). Conditional automaticity: Varieties of automatic influence in social perception and cognition. In: J. S. Uleman & J. A. Bargh (Eds), *Unintended thought* (pp. 3–51). New York: Guilford Press.

Bargh, J. A., & Pratto, F. (1986). Individual construct accessibility and perceptual selection. *Journal of Experimental Social Psychology, 22*, 293–311.

Brewer, M. B., & Lui, L. N. (1989). The primacy of age and sex in the structure of person categories. *Social Cognition, 7*, 262–274.

Bruner, J. S. (1957). On perceptual readiness. *Psychological Review, 64*, 123–152.

Burnstein, E., & Schul, Y. (1983). The informational basis of social judgements:Operations in forming and impression of another person. *Journal of Experimental Social Psychology, 19*, 49–57.

Cohen, C. E. (1981a). Person categories and social perception: Testing some boundaries of the processing effect of prior knowledge. *Journal of Personality and Social Psychology, 40*, 441–452.

Cohen, C. E. (1981b). Goals and schemata in person perception: Making sense from the stream of behavior. In: N. Cantor & J. F. Kihlstrom (Eds), *Personality, cognition, andsocial interaction* (pp. 45–68). Hillsdale, NJ: Lawrence Erlbaum Associates.

Fields, D. L., & Blum, T. C. (1997). Employee satisfaction in work groups with different gender composition. *Journal of Organizational Behavior, 18*, 181–196.

Fiske, S. T., & Neuberg, S. L. (1990). A continuum of impression formation, from category-based to individuating processes: Influences of information and motivation on attention and interpretation. *Advances in Social Cognition, 23*, 1–74.

Freedman, S. A., & Lips, H. M. (1996). A response latency investigation of the gender schema. *Journal of Social Behavior and Personality, 11*, 41–53.

Howard, J. A. (1995). Social cognition. In: K. S. Cook & J. S. House (Eds), *Sociological perspectives onsocial psychology* (pp. 90–117). Boston: Allyn and Bacon.

Maccoby, E. E. (1998). *The two sexes: Growing up apart, coming together*. Cambridge, MA: Belknap Press of Harvard University Press.

MacKinnon, N. J. (1994). *Symbolic interaction as affect control*. Albany: State University of New York Press.

Madson, L. (1996). *The 'pat' effect: Perceiving (and misperceiving) physically androgynous individuals*. Unpublished dissertaion. Department of Psychology, Iowa State University, Ames, IA.

Madson, L. (2000). Inferences regarding the personality traits and sexual orientation of phys-ically androgynous targets. *Psychology of Women Quarterly, 24*, 148–160.

Mead, G. H. (1934). *Mind, self & society from the standpoint of a social behaviorist*. Chicago, IL: The University of Chicago Press.

Nemeth, C. J. (1986). The differential contributions of majority and minority influence. *Psychological Review, 93*, 23–32.

Nemeth, C., Connell, J., Rogers, J., & Brown, K. (2001). Improving decision making by means of dissent. *Journal of Applied Social Psychology, 31*, 48–58.

Pavelchak, M. A. (1989). Piecemeal and category based evaluation. *An idiographic analysis. Journal of Personality and Social Psychology, 56*, 354–363.

Sanday, P. R. (1981). *Female power and male dominance: On the origins of sexual inequality*. Cambridge, New York: Cambridge University Press.

Schaie, K. W. (1985). *Manual for the Schaie-Thurstone Adult Mental Abilities Test (STAMAT)*. Palo Alto, CA: Consulting Psychologists Press.

Smith-Lovin, L., & Heise, D. R. (1988). *Analyzing social interaction: Advances in affect control theory*. New York: Gordon and Breach Science Publishers.

Spence, J. T., & Helmreich, R. L. (1978). *Masculinity and femininity: Their psychological dimensions, correlates, and antecedents*. Austin: University of Texas Press.

Stangor, C., Lynch, L., Duan, C., & Glass, B. (1992). Categorization of individuals on the basis of multiple social features. *Journal of Personality and Social Psychology, 62,* 207–218.

Stets, J. E., & Burke, P. J. (1996). Gender, control, and interaction. *Social Psychology Quarterly, 59,* 193–220.

Taylor, S. E. (1981). A categorization approach to stereotyping. In: D. L. Hamilton (Ed.), *Cognitive processes in stereotyping and intergroup behavior* (pp. 83–114). Hillsdale, NJ: Lawrence Erlbaum Associates.

Thorne, B. (1993). *Gender play: Girls and boys in school*. New Brunswick, NJ: Rutgers University Press.

Webster, M., Jr., Hysom, S. J., & Fullmer, E. M. (1998). Sexual orientation and occupation as status. In: J. Skvoretz & J. Szmatka (Eds), *Advances in group processes*, (Vol. 15, pp. 1–21). New York: JAI Press.

Wharton, A. S., & Baron, J. N. (1987). So happy together? The impact of gender segregation on men at work. *American Sociological Review, 52,* 574–587.

Yamaguchi, K. (1991). *Event history analysis*. Beverly Hills, CA: Sage Publications.

UNCERTAINTY, SOCIAL IDENTITY, AND IDEOLOGY

Michael A. Hogg

ABSTRACT

A social identity analysis, based on Hogg's (2000) uncertainty reduction theory, of the emergence and maintenance of ideological belief systems is presented. Uncertainty, particularly self-uncertainty, motivates identification with high-entitativity groups and behaviors that promote entitativity. Under more extreme uncertainty, identification is more pronounced and entitativity can be associated with orthodoxy, hierarchy and extremism, and with ideological belief systems. I develop and describe a social identity and uncertainty reduction analysis of ideology, and contextualize this in a brief discussion of the concept of ideology and in coverage of other contemporary social psychological treatments of ideology, such as social dominance theory, system justification theory, right-wing authoritarianism, belief in a just world, and the protestant work ethic.

Karl Marx, in *Das Kapital*, famously wrote about the end of ideology. He proposed that once people were made aware of the contradictions and inconsistencies inherent to most large-scale explanatory belief systems, he had religion (the "opium of the people") and capitalism in his sights, people

Social Identification in Groups
Advances in Group Processes, Volume 22, 203–229
Copyright © 2005 by Elsevier Ltd.
All rights of reproduction in any form reserved
ISSN: 0882-6145/doi:10.1016/S0882-6145(05)22008-8

would be free from their oppressive mantle. They would see the world for what it really was, and therefore finally be truly in control of their destiny. But, such freedom rested on a radical change in the structure of society.

Ideology is one of the most written-about and fiercely contested concepts in political theory, political praxis, political science, and sociology (e.g., Larrain, 1979; Thompson, 1990). Most of the world's most appalling human atrocities have been and continue to be fueled, framed, or justified by ideology – genocides, pogroms, persecutions, and wars can almost always be laid at the feet of ideology, examples of which are too numerous to mention. Ideology clearly has not ended – it is still with us. Indeed, some have argued that there is a postmodern paradox that makes the certainties and absolutes offered by ideologies particularly attractive in a postmodern world of moral and behavioral relativities (e.g., Dunn, 1998).

From a social psychological point of view, it would seem plausible that ideology persists because it serves a vital adaptive function for human beings – a point echoed by the Marxist Althusser's (1965) claim that "ideology (as a system of mass representations) is indispensable in any society if men are to be formed, transformed, and equipped to respond to the demands of their conditions of existence" (Althusser, 1965, p. 235). We, as human beings, need ideology – it is part of the human condition. Many years ago Randy Newman wrote a wonderfully perceptive song called *God's Song (That's why I love mankind)*, at the end of which, God, as an ideology, speaks:

> I burn down your cities – how blind you must be
>
> I take from you your children and you say how blessed are we
>
> You all must be crazy to put your faith in me
>
> That's why I love mankind
>
> You really *need* me
>
> That's why I love mankind

From the perspective of the individual human being, an ideology is an integrated system of apparently congruent beliefs and values that explain and justify the world, our place within it, our relationship with others, and our own and others' actions. Furthermore, it is a belief system that is shared within a group or community, in which case, again from the perspective of the individual, we can ask how do we acquire ideologies, what impact do we have on their formation, how do they influence our behavior, and so forth?

These are social psychological questions – and yet, social psychology has had surprisingly little to say about ideology. One reason for this silence is that ideology is a politically loaded term – which some people may avoid engaging with because they believe that as social psychologists they should not be doing politics. Another is that, as social psychologists, we feel that ideology is a murky abyss cruised by the huge and fearsome shadows of political science and sociology – few of us dare venture into this alien environment.

A third reason is that for most of its life, since Floyd Allport's notorious dictum that "There is no psychology of groups which is not essentially and entirely a psychology of individuals" (Allport, 1924, p. 4), social psychology has primarily focused on the individual, or on individuals in interaction in close interpersonal relationships or in small task-oriented face-to-face interactive groups (Farr, 1996; Jones, 1998). The study of large-scale intergroup relations has been a marginal enterprise, often translated into the study of stereotypes as individual cognitive structures in person perception (e.g., Hamilton, 1981). Since ideology is not only about individual belief systems but also about the intergroup relations that form, sustain, structure, and change them, this agenda for social psychology makes the study of ideology difficult.

However, it is not the case that social psychologists have never studied ideology or constructs closely related to ideology. Pre-experimental social psychology focused on collective phenomena. For example, Wundt studied religion, customs, and myth, because he believed that social psychology was the study of "those mental products which are created by a community of human life and are, therefore, inexplicable in terms merely of individual consciousness since they presuppose the reciprocal action of many" (Wundt, 1916, p. 3). Durkheim (1898), influenced by Wundt, went on to appropriate the study of collective representations and public knowledge for the new discipline of sociology, which he sometimes called "collective psychology" – individual psychology was left with the study of private beliefs. Nevertheless, the legacy of Wundt and Durkheim is very evident in early social psychology's study of collective phenomena, in particular crowd behavior (e.g., LeBon, 1908; McDougall, 1921; Tarde, 1901; Trotter, 1919).

The post-World War II reconstruction of social psychology in Europe crystallized in the 1960s around a research agenda that prioritized the study of large-scale intergroup relations in societal context (e.g., Billig, 1976; Hogg & Abrams, 1988; Moscovici, 1976; Tajfel, 1984). For the purposes of this chapter, some of the most significant influences of European social psychology are social identity theory (Tajfel & Turner, 1979), the focus of this chapter, and social representations theory (e.g., Farr & Moscovici, 1984), and research by Billig on ideology (e.g., Billig, 1982, 1991), and by Deconchy on orthodoxy (Deconchy, 1984).

In recent years there has been renewed interest in ideology and related constructs. Generally, social psychologists studying ideology or constructs closely related to ideology use different words and a different language. This may not be such a bad thing, because they often conceptualize and approach ideology in terms that are somewhat different to those used in political science and sociology. The concepts and literatures I am referring to here include research on social dominance orientation (e.g., Sidanius & Pratto, 1999), right-wing authoritarianism (e.g., Altemeyer, 1998), system justification theory (e.g., Jost, Banaji, & Nosek, in press; Jost & Hunyady, 2002), the protestant work ethic (e.g., Furnham, 1990; Quinn & Crocker, 1999), belief in a just world (e.g., Furnham, 2003; Furnham & Procter, 1989; Rohan, 2000), religious fundamentalism (e.g., Altemeyer, 2003; Rowatt & Franklin, 2004), cultural divides (see Prentice & Miller, 1999), and essentialism (e.g., Haslam, Rothschild, & Ernst, 1998). There is also a more general, recent social psychology literature on ideology-related constructs (e.g., Crocker & Major, 1994; Duckitt, 2001; Greenberg, Koole, & Pyszczynski, 2004; Jost, Glaser, Kruglanski, & Sulloway, 2003; Jost & Major, 2001; Major, Quinton, & McCoy, 2002). I return to these literatures later in the chapter, after having described a social identity analysis of ideology.

In this article, I focus specifically on how subjective uncertainty may instantiate or strengthen ideological belief systems via the mediating process of group identification. Building on previous research on subjective uncertainty and group identification (e.g., Hogg, 2000) and on the role of entitativity (i.e., the property of a group that makes it appear a coherent, distinctive, and clearly structured entity) in this relationship (Hogg, 2004), I argue that people strive to reduce feelings of uncertainty about themselves, the world around them, and their place within it. Such uncertainty is reduced by group identification, because of the social-cognitive effects of the social categorization and depersonalization processes associated with identification. High-entitativity groups (e.g., ones that are distinctive, internally homogeneous, clearly defined, purposeful, and well structured) are best suited to identification-mediated uncertainty reduction, and when uncertainty is particularly high, these groups are characterized by ideological belief systems.

I briefly overview key aspects of the social identity approach in order to summarize in detail uncertainty reduction theory and the role of entitativity in the reduction of subjective uncertainty, especially self-uncertainty. Implications of this process for the emergence of orthodox, hierarchical, and totalist groups are discussed, and the argument extended to show how this underpins and is related to ideological belief systems. Finally, the social identity analysis of ideology is contextualized in a critical discussion of some of the other contemporary social psychological analyses of ideology cited above. The uncertainty reduction perspective on ideology is summarized at the end of the article in the form of five premises.

SOCIAL IDENTITY AND INTERGROUP RELATIONS

The social identity approach (Tajfel & Turner, 1979; Turner, Hogg, Oakes, Reicher, & Wetherell, 1987) is an integrated analysis of the role of self-conception in group membership, group processes, and intergroup relations. It embraces a number of interrelated concepts and sub-theories that focus on social-cognitive (e.g., social categorization), motivational (e.g., self-enhancement), social interactive (e.g., social influence), and macro-social (e.g., intergroup beliefs) facets of group life (see Hogg, 2003, in press a, b).

One important distinction that can be made within the social identity approach is between "the social identity theory of the group … (and) … the social identity theory of intergroup behavior" (Turner et al., 1987, p. 42, parentheses added). The former, self-categorization theory, specifies how the process of social categorization transforms self-conception to conform to and express group-defining attributes, and the latter, social identity theory, focuses on the course of intergroup behavior as a function of intergroup beliefs and the pursuit of evaluatively positive social identity.

Categorization, Self-Evaluation, and Group Behavior

People cognitively represent social groups as prototypes, which are fuzzy sets of features that define and evaluate one group and clearly differentiate it from other groups. Prototypes are cognitively constructed according to the metacontrast principle – their configuration, in terms of what attributes are represented, maximizes the ratio of intergroup differences to intragroup differences. As such, our cognitive representation of a group is tied to both intra- and intergroup comparisons, and is responsive to changes in the social comparative field. Group prototypes strive to maximize entitativity – the extent to which a group is a coherent and distinct entity that is homogeneous and well structured, has clear boundaries, and whose members share a common fate (Campbell, 1958; Hamilton & Sherman, 1996).

When a particular social categorization is psychologically salient, people categorize themselves and others and thus automatically assign prototypical attributes to self and others – a process called *depersonalization* (Turner et al., 1987). From the perspective of *self*-definition, depersonalization represents a contextual redefinition of self in group terms. We view ourselves as and feel like group members, and we experience ourselves and perceive, think, feel, and behave in terms of the attributes that define the group and its relations to other groups.

Because depersonalization affixes evaluative group attributes to self, groups and their members work hard to ensure that group evaluations are as favorable as possible – favorable group attributes imply positive self-attributes and possibly positive self-esteem (see Abrams & Hogg, 1988; Rubin & Hewstone, 1998). Groups struggle with one another to maintain or achieve relative evaluative superiority – there is competition over status, positive intergroup distinctiveness, and positive social identity. One consequence of this process is ethnocentrism – a belief that all things ingroup are superior to all things outgroup (Brewer & Campbell, 1976; Sumner, 1906).

Social Beliefs and Social Stereotypes

Social categorization, depersonalization, and self-evaluation give group and intergroup behavior a distinctive form. However, the actual content of group behavior, what people actually think and do as members of a group, is shaped by a more (macro-)social dimension of social identity processes. Specifically, Tajfel argued that the stereotypes (shared prototypes) we hold of our own and other groups are not merely descriptive but are also functional (e.g., Tajfel, 1981). For example, our stereotype of an outgroup we plan to exploit, or have exploited in the past, might emphasize their incompetence, backwardness, and inability to manage their own affairs – a constellation of beliefs that clearly serves to justify and legitimize our actions and maintain a self-serving status quo.

Likewise, one of the most familiar aspects of the social identity analysis of intergroup behavior is that people have beliefs about group status differentials, about the stability and legitimacy of these differentials, about the permeability of intergroup boundaries, and about the possibility and prob-ability of achieving a different more favorable status quo (e.g., Ellemers, 1993; Hogg & Abrams, 1988; Tajfel & Turner, 1979). These "social beliefs," which strongly influence the actual behaviors that people engage in to pro-tect or promote positive social identity, are social constructs – they are rarely an accurate reflection of the true nature of intergroup relations, and more often than not they have been developed and promulgated by groups in a position of power, for their own ends. For example, it can be advan-tageous for dominant groups to make members of subordinate groups be-lieve that it is easy to pass into the dominant group because the boundary is permeable. This discourages collective action on the part of the subordinate group and, because the boundary is in reality impermeable, it fragments the subordinate group into an aggregate of powerless individuals with marginal identities (e.g., Breakwell, 1986).

These macro-social aspects of social identity processes clearly relate to ideological belief systems – in our 1988 social identity theory book, Abrams and I actually had a chapter entitled "From stereotyping to ideology" (Hogg & Abrams, 1988, pp. 64–91). Stereotypes and social beliefs are gen-erally embedded in and part of relatively coherent ideological belief systems that explain and justify our place in the world and our relations to other people and groups, and prescribe particular forms of individual and group-based conduct and social action.

UNCERTAINTY REDUCTION AND GROUP IDENTIFICATION

Social identity processes are not motivated only by group and self-enhance-ment concerns. They are, according to uncertainty reduction theory (Hogg, 2000, 2001a), also motivated by subjective uncertainty reduction, particu-larly self-conceptual uncertainty reduction. This is an epistemic motive that is directly associated with the social categorization process. People strive to reduce feelings of uncertainty, particularly uncertainty about and related to themselves, and about their social world and their place within it – they like to know who they are and how to behave and what to think, and who others are and how they might behave and what they might think. Some uncer-tainty is exciting, making us feel edgy and alive, but for most of us most of the time acute uncertainty, enduring uncertainty, and uncertainty about and related to self in social context is aversive.

Social categorization is a particularly effective way to reduce subjective uncertainty because it furnishes group prototypes that describe how people (include self) will and ought to behave and interact with one another. Such prototypes are relatively consensual ("we" agree that "we" are like this and "they" are like that) – thus, one's world view and self-concept are validated. Social categorization renders one's own and others' behavior predictable and thus allows one to avoid harm and plan effective action. It also allows one to know how one should feel and behave. Having achieved a stable and validated sense of self, people are invested in maintaining and protecting this self-view, and are likely to pursue a range of strategies to confirm and verify their self-concept (e.g., Swann, Polzer, Seyle, & Ko, 2004; Swann, Rentfrow, & Guinn, 2003).

The most basic uncertainty reduction hypothesis, that people are more likely to identify, or identify more strongly with groups when they are feeling uncertain, has been supported by a series of studies (for overview see Hogg, 2000). The general paradigm uses minimal groups in which (a) contextual subjective uncertainty and/or type of uncertainty is manipulated, (b) participants are explicitly categorized or not (or category salience is manipulated), and/or (c) prototypical properties of the category are manipulated. The key-dependent measures are self-report measures of group identification and behavioral measures of resource allocations.

A number of experiments have shown that ingroup identification and intergroup discrimination only occur, and occur significantly more when people are categorized under uncertainty than not categorized or categorized under conditions of reduced uncertainty (e.g., Grieve & Hogg, 1999). Other similar experiments have shown that the effect occurs irrespective of how uncertainty is caused (simply feeling uncertain seems to be sufficient), but that it is strongest when the dimension of subjective uncertainty is important to self and when the social category is relevant to the dimension of uncertainty (e.g., Mullin & Hogg, 1998). Self-uncertainty is the most potent motive for identification.

Perhaps uncertainty has its effect on identification because it is associated with lowered self-esteem, and self-enhancement is the real motivation. This possibility has been ruled out in two experiments by Hogg and Svensson (2004) in which the predicted effects of uncertainty on identification remained after effects of uncertainty on self-esteem were partialed out, and after participants had self-affirmed to elevate lowered self-esteem. In addition, Reid and Hogg (2005) conducted two experiments showing that identification with a low-status group, one that does not satisfy self-enhancement motives, was predicted by elevated uncertainty.

ENTITATIVITY AND UNCERTAINTY REDUCTION

Given that uncertainty motivates identification, the obvious next question is what kinds of groups are best equipped to reduce uncertainty? The answer is high-entitativity groups (Hogg, 2004). Entitativity is the property of a group, resting on clear boundaries, internal homogeneity, clear internal structure, and common fate, which makes a group "groupy" (Campbell, 1958; Hamilton & Sherman, 1996). Groups vary widely in entitativity, from a loose collection of unrelated people (e.g., people waiting in line at the movies) to a tight, coherent, and distinctive entity (e.g., a fraternity) (e.g., Lickel et al., 2000; Hamilton, Sherman, & Rodgers, 2004). Although entitativity can be measured objectively, it is primarily measured in terms of people's perceptions of how coherent, distinctive, and so forth a particular group is. Perceived entitativity has more immediate effects on people's entitativity-related behavior.

As uncertainty increases people gravitate toward high-entitativity groups, they identify more strongly with them, and they transform existing ingroups to have greater entitativity. High-entitativity groups are better at resolving self-uncertainty than low-entitativity groups, because they typically have the very concrete kinds of prototypes that best resolve uncertainty. Recall that identification via self-categorization reduces uncertainty because self is governed by a prototype that prescribes cognition, affect, and behavior. Prototypes that are simple, clear, unambiguous, prescriptive, focused, and consensual are much more effective than those that are vague, ambiguous, unfocused, and dissensual. High-entitativity groups are much more likely to have the former prototype, and low-entitativity groups the latter – indeed, prototype clarity can be included as an important property of high-entitativity groups (e.g., Hamilton et al., 2004; Rothbart & Park, 2004). It is important to remember that it is the prototype that resolves uncertainty – if there was a high-entitativity group with a fuzzy prototype, it would be less effective in reducing self-uncertainty than an equally unlikely low-entitativity group with a clear prototype.

The uncertainty reduction prediction can now be qualified. Uncertainty and entitativity interact such that people identify most strongly when they are uncertain about themselves, self-uncertain, and the group has high entitativity. There is some indirect support for this hypothesis. Yzerbyt, Castano, Leyens, and Paladino (2000) summarized four studies finding that Europeans with moderate rather than strong attitudes toward the European Union identified more with a high- than low-entitativity characterization of the European Union – uncertainty was not manipulated or measured, but was inferred to be higher among those with moderate attitudes.

Jetten, Hogg, and Mullin (2000) manipulated general perceptual uncertainty and ingroup homogeneity, and found that people who were uncertain showed greater interest in the ingroup (Study 2) and greater ingroup–outgroup stereotype differentiation (Study 1) when the ingroup was more than less homogeneous – however, group identification was not measured, and homogeneity is only one aspect of entitativity, and not a central one, according to Hamilton et al. (2004).

Sherman, Hogg, Maitner, and Moffitt (2004) investigated the interactive effect of uncertainty (in Study 1 it was measured in terms of general life uncertainty, in Study 2 it was primed in terms of feelings of self-uncertainty) and entitativity (measured in terms of perceptions of groupiness) on perceptions of intergroup attitude polarization. They found that polarization (which can be assumed to be associated with ingroup identification) was highest where uncertainty and entitativity was highest – but, like Jetten et al. (2000), group identification was not measured, only inferred.

Direct support comes from two studies by Hogg, Sherman, Dierselhuis, Maitner, and Moffitt (2004) in which self-uncertainty was manipulated via a priming procedure and group identification was measured with a reliable multi-item scale. Study 1 ($N = 114$) was a field experiment and the ingroup was the political party that participants supported (the Australian Labor Party or the Australian Liberal Party) – ingroup entitativity was a measured variable (participants were asked how much of a group they felt their party was). Study 2 ($N = 89$) was a computer-mediated minimal group lab experiment in which ingroup entitativity was manipulated via controlled information, concerning group distinctiveness and ingroup similarity, allegedly based on responses to a questionnaire administered at the start of the study. In both studies, group identification was significantly stronger among uncertain participants in the high-entitativity condition.

MANAGING PROTOTYPES AND ENTITATIVITY

Thus far, we have seen that uncertainty enhances identification with high-entitativity groups. However, it is important to recognize that entitativity and prototype clarity are not static properties of a group. Group members can perceptually or actually change the entitativity of their group and the nature of the group's prototype in order to further reduce uncertainty. This requires a degree of identity management that is only likely to occur in groups that people feel invested in, because there are no other viable identity solutions such as leaving the group.

We saw above that social identity theory considers social beliefs and the motivation for evaluatively positive social identity to interact to determine the kinds of group and intergroup behaviors that people pursue (e.g., Tajfel & Turner, 1979). What I propose here is that social beliefs also interact with the uncertainty reduction motive to influence social identity-related behaviors. Where self-uncertainty is high and people believe group boundaries are permeable, they are more likely to dis-identify and try to identify with alternative higher-entitativity groups to resolve uncertainty.

However, where mobility and dis-identification are not viable, people will remain identified with their group and will try to raise its entitativity and focus its prototype in a number of ways. For example, they can focus attention on less entitative outgroups that make the ingroup seem relatively more highly entitative, or they can work on ingroup norms to remodel the ingroup prototype to be more highly focused, more prescriptive, more consensual, and more distinct from relevant outgroups. Where a group feels particularly uncertain about its norms, prototypes, and identity, it may develop structures, practices, and belief systems that are markedly orthodox and ideological, and which are associated with hierarchical leadership and power structures, and fierce intolerance of internal dissent.

There is abundant evidence that groups do engage in prototype and entitativity management – and that language and communication are central to this and the broader management of identity (e.g., Fiol, 2002; Hogg & Tindale, 2005; Reid & Ng, 2000). Group leaders play a critical role here and more broadly in identity management. From the social identity theory of leadership (Hogg, 2001b; Hogg & van Knippenberg, 2003; van Knippenberg & Hogg, 2003; also see van Knippenberg, van Knippenberg, De Cremer, & Hogg, 2004) we know that leaders of groups whom people identify strongly with are more effective if they are seen to be highly prototypical, and that highly prototypical leaders tend to be trusted more, are more influential, and are allowed extensive latitude to be normatively innovative.

So, for example, under conditions where there is some uncertainty about what the group stands for and what its identity really is, leaders can offer a simplified orthodox definition of the group, which hinges on pillorying ingroup deviants as traitors and "revisionists" and focusing attention on hated outgroups that stand for everything that "we" do not stand for, and so forth. Coincidentally, this behavior can make the leader seem more prototypical and more charismatic, and can strengthen his or her hand substantially. These kinds of processes have been documented, social psychologically, in studies of political and national leadership rhetoric (e.g., Reicher & Hopkins, 1996, 2001), the dynamics of ideological schisms in religious organizations (e.g., Sani & Reicher, 2000), and the way that deviants and dissenters are often treated in groups (e.g., Hogg, 2005).

Moving away from the role of leaders, and returning to the lab, there is some evidence that when people identify with high-entitativity groups under uncertainty they proceed further to accentuate their group's entitativity. In the first study by Hogg et al. (2004), described above, we found that not only did self-uncertainty and ingroup entitativity interact to produce strongest identification when both were high, but these participants also accentuated their perception of the political outgroup as being homogeneous. It was argued that this reflected an attempt to further differentiate ingroup from outgroup, on one of the only dimensions available in the study, and thus consolidate or increase ingroup entitativity and distinctiveness. The studies by Sherman et al. (2004), also described above, explicitly tested the idea that uncertainty and entitativity would interact to produce a perception of ingroup–outgroup attitude polarization – again with the consequence of enhanced intergroup distinctiveness and entitativity.

The ideas of accentuated entitativity and prototype clarity relate to two other phenomena – but also show the interplay of self-uncertainty, ingroup entitativity, and group identification. The first is Tajfel's (1959; see Eiser & Stroebe, 1972) accentuation effect, in which people perceptually accentuate ingroup similarities and intergroup differences on dimensions stereotypically associated with the intergroup distinction. The second is the metacontrast principle, discussed above (Turner et al., 1987), in which people in groups configure and structure ingroup prototypes to optimize the ratio of intergroup differences to intragroup differences.

THE STORY SO FAR: AN INTERIM SUMMARY

Let us summarize the argument presented so far, in terms of five premises.

Premise 1: People strive to reduce feelings of uncertainty about themselves and about perceptions, judgments, attitudes, and behaviors that relate to self and to their interactions with other people.

Premise 2: Group identification can reduce uncertainty because, via social categorization and depersonalization, it assimilates self to a prototype, grounded in substantial ingroup consensus, which defines self and prescribes perceptions, attitudes, feeling, and behaviors, and specifies and regulates the course of interaction with ingroup and outgroup members.

Premise 3: Prototypes are better at resolving uncertainty to the extent that they are simple, clear, unambiguous, prescriptive, focused, and consensual, and this matters more to the extent that uncertainty is higher.

Premise 4: High-entitativity groups typically have such prototypes, and therefore under high uncertainty, people prefer to identify with high-entitativity groups.

Premise 5: People can and do perceptually, and actually, accentuate entitativity and prototype concreteness in order to further enhance entitativity.

ORTHODOXY AND EXTREMISM AS CONSEQUENCES OF UNCERTAINTY

Self-uncertainty motivates identification with groups that are distinct, clearly structured, internally homogeneous, and so forth, and behaviors that consolidate or enhance the entitativity of such groups. However, there are other identification-related effects of pronounced or extreme uncertainty, which have important ramifications for high-entitativity groups in terms of the nature of the general belief systems that characterize them.

There is a constellation of effects produced by group identification under conditions of acute and chronic uncertainty (Hogg, 2004). These extreme effects might include the following: (a) strong and uncompromising identification and loyalty; (b) a simple, highly focused and internally coherent belief system that prescribes normative group membership-contingent behaviors and provides a cogent ideology to explain and justify the totality of group life; (c) intolerance of normative disagreement, dissent, and deviance within the group; (d) a single uncomplicated version of the "truth"; (e) an "us versus them" silo mentality that is highly ethnocentric, and views outgroups as fundamentally wrong, perhaps evil and immoral; and (f) a hierarchical internal structure that vests authority and power in leaders who are completely trusted to determine the groups destiny and what the group and its identity stand for.

What is being described here is, of course, the orthodoxy and extremism of what Baron, Crawley, and Paulina (2003) refer to as "totalist" groups – groups such as cults, terrorist cells, extremist political groups, and fundamentalist religious, and lifestyle groups. One thing that these groups share is possession of a powerful all-embracing ideology that delivers up one version of reality that explains and justifies all things without confusing the mind with subtlety and contradiction.

That these kinds of groups may be spawned by uncertainty and maintained by fear of uncertainty comes as no surprise. For example, Staub (1989) describes how genocides through history seem to be sponsored by groups (e.g., the Nazis) that furnish people with a sense of certainty in times of great uncertainty, and many writers see similar circumstances producing extremist cults (e.g., Curtis & Curtis, 1993; Galanter, 1989; Singer, 1995) and ultra-nationalist groups (e.g., Billig, 1978, 1982). More broadly, religious fundamentalism may become entrenched in a similar environment (e.g., Altemeyer, 2003; Batson, Schoenrade, & Ventis, 1993; Rowatt & Franklin, 2004).

Some forms of nationalism and patriotism are similarly ideological and may be reactions to uncertainty. Adorno and colleagues differentiate between pseudo and genuine patriotism and define the former as "blind attachment to certain cultural values, uncritical conformity with the prevailing group ways, and rejection of other nations as outgroups" (Adorno, Frenkel-Brunswik, Levinson, & Sanford, 1950, p. 107). Kosterman and Feshback (1989) describe nationalism as a view that one's nation is superior and should be dominant, and Staub (1997) describes "blind patriotism" as a rigid and inflexible attachment to country, characterized by unquestioning positive evaluation, staunch allegiance, and intolerance of criticism (also see Duckitt, 1989).

Marris (1996) places uncertainty reduction at the motivational core of intergroup relations. Groups struggle against one another over "certainty" as a scarce resource, each group trying to make the other feel uncertain – certainty is power, and ideological combat serves to bolster or undermine ideologies and the identity-related certainties they deliver. He argues that intergroup relations are a struggle to transfer uncertainty to other groups and to thus construct a hierarchy of uncertainty with desirable high-status groups characterized by low uncertainty.

Recent analyses of terrorist groups hint at the role of uncertainty, group identification, entitativity, and prototype clarity, in the formation and maintenance of orthodox totalist groups with strong ideologies (e.g., Moghaddam, 2004; Taylor & Louis, 2004). Particularly appropriate is Hoffer's (1951) notion of the "true believer," or fanatic, characterized as follows:

> To live without an ardent dedication is to be adrift and abandoned. He sees in tolerance a sign of weakness, frivolity, and ignorance … He hungers for the deep assurance which comes with total surrender – with the wholehearted clinging to a creed and cause. What matters is not the contents of the cause but the total dedication and communion with a congregation (Hoffer, 1951, p. 90).

Marsella (2004) summarizes, in his discussion of terrorism, that "Belief provides meaning and purpose – it reduces uncertainty and facilitates adaptation and adjustment" (Marsella, 2004, p. 41), and goes on to write about the "discomfort of doubt":

> For the terrorist and other "true believers", blind commitment to political, economic, religious, or philosophical beliefs comforts the mind by eliminating or reducing the uncertainty (Marsella, 2004, p. 42).

Marsella believes that terrorist groups attract and retain people who he describes in the following terms:

> the minds of people who willingly embrace violence and seek to coerce others for political and social ends may have certain shared characteristics, including a commitment to a set of beliefs that offers certainty and a psychological immunity to reason, negotiation, and empathy (Marsella, 2004, p. 14).

Although the terrorist acts of groups such as al-Qaeda, Shining Path, Hamas, Hizballah, Abu Nidal, Abu Sayyaf, and Jamaiah Islamiah stand out and are given media prominence, one should not forget that many groups try to get their way by terrorizing ordinary people and communities – for example, ethnicity-based urban gangs in large American cities, neo-Fascist Skinhead groups in British and German cities, and some right-to-life and animal rights groups in the UK and the United States.

More broadly, there is a general socio-historical analysis that may link uncertainty, via group identification, to totalism and ideological fundamentalism in the modern era. Contemporary Western society is often characterized as postmodern – in the sense that there is no absolute morality and few limitations on the sorts of people we can subjectively be or become – a world in which "reality" is what we construct it to be, and each person's reality is as authentic as each other person's reality. In the postmodern world, one's self-concept is largely individual and personal – it is a portable and infinitely malleable construction that can be reconfigured as we wish. Subjectively, there are few limits to self-conception and few absolutes that can guide us in the type of person we ought to be.

This state of affairs is the consequence of a process of secularization, enlightenment, and industrialization that has been underway since the 17th century. In the medieval world, social relations were fixed and stable, and legitimized in religious terms. People's lives and identity were clearly mapped out according to position in the social order – by ascribed attributes such as family membership, social rank, birth order, and place of birth. People were locked into a matrix of prescribed group memberships and social relations. Nowadays, in western culture, people are units of production that are expected to reorganize their lives, their relationships, and their self-concept around mobility, change, and transient relationships.

Independence, separateness, and uniqueness have become more important than connectedness and the maintenance of enduring relationships.

Sociologically oriented commentators have observed that this has produced a "postmodern paradox" – people with today's less-structured self actually yearn for community and the collective affiliations of former times (e.g., Dunn, 1998; Gergen, 1991), a yearning which may be reflected in contemporary religious fundamentalism, ethnic and racial revival, and the re-emergence of nationalism and "new" racism. People are striving to construct a more certain sense of self in an uncertain world.

UNCERTAINTY AND IDEOLOGY

Our discussion has taken us from social identity through uncertainty and entitativity to orthodoxy, extremism, and ideology. The key claims of uncertainty reduction theory are that ideological belief systems arise under uncertainty and are kept in place by fear of uncertainty, and that people internalize, preserve, and promote such belief systems because they identify, via self-categorization and depersonalization, with the group defined by possession of the ideology.

But, what is an ideology? In the introduction to this chapter, I acknowledged the long and tempestuous history of research on ideology and the fact that the field is marked by disagreement. From the perspective of the present chapter I would like to characterize an ideology as an integrated and coherent system of beliefs, attitudes, and values, which are internally consistent and serve to explain one's world, and one's place and experiences within it. Ideologies are widely shared within groups and differ from group to group – they map the contours of social categories, often starkly differentiating groups, and thus have a powerful identity-defining function. Because ideologies are tied to group membership, they often serve to explain one's own group's treatment of and by another group, and are associated with intergroup power differentials, and associated beliefs that can legitimize and justify oppression or social change.

Ideologies are typically relatively simplistic and consensual world views that paper-over contradictions and circumscribe thought, so that the problematic (for example, why are we exploited by group-X?) is defined in such a way that only the ideology can provide sensible answers. Ideologies are intricately tied to group membership, and they certainly reduce uncertainty.

Belief systems associated with group membership can vary in the degree to which they have the properties of an ideology. For example, a set of relatively un-integrated stereotypes about an outgroup coupled with fairly non-prescriptive and laissez-faire norms for ingroup behavior are not very ideological, but nevertheless define group membership and are cognitively represented as a prototype. Under high (threat of) uncertainty, this kind of prototype would be less attractive than a more ideological prototype – because the latter would address uncertainty concerns more powerfully.

As outlined at the start of this chapter, there are a number of recent discussions in the social psychology literature that invoke or connect with ideology. Let us briefly examine some of these, and their relationship to the uncertainty reduction perspective on ideology. I conclude this section by recapping on the uncertainty reduction analysis of ideology and reflecting it back onto notions of hierarchy, dominance, system justification, and social change.

Right-Wing Authoritarianism

Right-wing authoritarianism (RWA) is a socialization-based personality constellation, described by Altemeyer (1988, 1998). It has three components: (1) adherence to social standards endorsed by authority (conventionalism), (2) support for aggression against deviants (authoritarian aggression), and (3) submission to society's established authorities (authoritarian submission). In the West, right-wingers score high on RWA, but in former Soviet bloc countries left-wingers score high (McFarland, Agayev, & Djintcharadze, 1996). Typically, authoritarianism is associated with religious fundamentalism (Altemeyer & Hunsberger, 1992).

RWA is likely to develop under uncertainty. For example, people who see the world as dangerous tend to subscribe to an authoritarian ideology (e.g., Lambert, Burroughs, & Nguyen, 1999), and widespread social threat and uncertainty are associated with endorsement of authoritarian ideologies (e.g., Doty, Peterson, & Winter, 1991). RWA reduces uncertainty because it imposes authority and rules that closely structure one's life.

Social Dominance Theory

According to social dominance theory (SDT: Sidanius & Pratto, 1999) group-based hierarchies in society are maintained ideologically by legitimizing myths, defined as "any set of beliefs, attitudes, values or group stereotypes which provide moral or intellectual support for group based inequality" (Sidanius, Levin, Federico, & Pratto, 2001, p. 310). People differ in the extent to which they endorse hierarchy-enhancing myths such as this, with some people endorsing hierarchy-attenuating myths instead. This preference reflects people's enduring social dominance orientation (SDO). Sidanius and Pratto (1999) have suggested an evolutionary correlate – men are always more hierarchy enhancing than women because of sex differences in reproductive roles. SDO, like RWA, is strongly correlated with prejudice. According to Altemeyer, prejudice is "largely a matter of personality, and two kinds of personality are basically involved: the social dominator and the right-wing authoritarian" (1998, p. 60).

In contrast, Duckitt (2001) believes that SDO and RWA are ideological belief systems, not personality constellations. This view is consistent with research showing that local group norms can overrule SDO preferences (e.g., Foels & Pappas, 2004; Guimond, Dambrun, Michinov, & Duarte, 2003; Schmitt, Branscombe, & Kappen, 2003; Wilson & Liu, 2003), and is also consistent with the uncertainty reduction and social identity analyses presented in this chapter (also see Turner & Reynolds, 2003). People may well have an enduring preference for high or low SDO, but this will be a reflection of their location in the social structure and thus the group norms that define their social identity. Furthermore, conditions of acute or chronic uncertainty may incline people, if possible, to locate and define themselves in terms of groups with high SDO or RWA norms – such ideological belief systems may be attractive and effective ways to reduce uncertainty.

Belief in a Just World, and the Protestant Work Ethic

Belief in a just world (BJW) and the Protestant work ethic (PWE) are related belief systems or ideologies (Furnham & Rajamanickam, 1992). BJW is the belief that good things happen to good people, and bad things to bad people (e.g., Lerner & Miller, 1978). It is a very broad belief system that brings order and a sense of justice to a complicated and uncertain world (Furnham, 2003; Furnham & Procter, 1989; Rohan, 2000). Groups that build BJW into their world view and ideology in some form or other (many religions do this) will have a very effective uncertainty-reducing ideology.

The PWE originally associated Protestantism with asceticism, disdain for leisure, and reverence for hard work (Furnham, 1990). However, more generally it is a belief system that values diligence and hard work, and associates this with successful outcomes, and attributes failure to lack of effort, weakness of character, and so forth. The PWE is an ideology that justifies social inequality (Quinn & Crocker, 1999). Its link to uncertainty reduction is less clear, except that PWE does provide a controllable and stable world view (which may arise in response to uncertainty).

System Justification Theory

System justification theory (SJT) postulates the existence of a "system justification motive, whereby people justify and rationalize the way things are, so that existing social arrangements are perceived as fair and legitimate, perhaps even natural and inevitable" (Jost & Hunyady, 2002, p. 119; also see Jost et al., in press, 2003). This need causes dominant and subordinate group members alike to construct ideologies to justify why things are as they are. SJT explains why, despite omnipresent disadvantage, social change is the exception not the rule.

According to Jost and Hunyady, "system-justifying ideologies serve a palliative function in that they reduce anxiety, guilt, dissonance, discomfort, and uncertainty for those who are advantaged *and* disadvantaged" (Jost & Hunyady, 2002, p. 111, italics in original). However, although SJT cites reduction of uncertainty as one function of system-justifying ideologies, it conceptualizes this in terms of individual differences in intolerance of ambiguity and uncertainty, integrative complexity, and needs for order, structure, and closure (Jost et al., 2003). SJT does not theorize contextual variability in self-uncertainty as a primary motive that may generate ideologies, nor does it tie ideologies to specific groups and the process of identifying with such groups. However, if contextual uncertainty were built into SJT, then SJT would presumably predict that uncertainty always leads to endorsement of system-justifying ideologies.

Subjective Uncertainty, Social Identity, and Ideology

Uncertainty reduction theory argues that subjective uncertainty (which may or may not reflect reality) motivates people to identify with groups that can resolve uncertainty. Such groups have high entitativity and possess consensual prototypes that clearly define self and tightly regulate thought, feelings, actions, and social interaction. More broadly, these prototypes are part of a representational system that can be considered ideological, because it is internally consistent and coherent and serves a key explanatory and justificatory function that renders the world meaningful.

From this perspective, uncertainty is just as likely to produce system-justifying or hierarchy-enhancing ideologies as system-challenging or hierarchy-attenuating ideologies. As long as the ideologies are tight and coherent and grounded in a high-entitativity consensual group that furnishes an all-embracing identity. In this way, uncertainty can lead to social stasis or social change. Take the 1920s and 1930s in Germany as an example – the entire spectrum of radical and conservative ideologies emerged as a reaction to overwhelming uncertainty and fear of uncertainty. The United States in the 1960s is another example – in the face of uncertainty, radical ideologies of social change confronted ultra-conservative ideologies of the right. Iran in the late 1970s – political uncertainty spawned revolutionary ideologies and Islamic fundamentalism.

However, it is probably true that, in the uncertainty reduction stakes, system-challenging and hierarchy-attenuating ideologies may have more of an uphill struggle than system-justifying and hierarchy-enhancing ideologies. The latter leave the status quo unchanged, whereas the former need to be especially tight and coherent in order to defuse uncertainty over the prospect of social change.

SUMMARY AND CONCLUSIONS

My aim in this chapter has been to show how ideology may be sustained by subjective uncertainty. Adopting a social identity perspective on the relationship between self-conception and collective behaviors and representations, the core of the argument is that subjective uncertainty motivates people to identify with high-entitativity groups that have ideological belief systems.

In full recognition of the controversial nature of the concept of ideology in the social sciences, I suggested that an ideology is an integrated, coherent, and internally consistent system of beliefs, attitudes, and values (e.g., stereotypes) that serve to explain one's world and one's place and experiences within it. Ideologies are shared within groups and differ, often starkly, between groups – they serve as critical defining attributes of group membership and social identity. Ideologies tend to be simplistic and consensual world views that obscure contradictions, and circumscribe thought so that the problematic (set of questions you can ask) is defined in such a way that only the ideology can provide sensible answers. Ideologies are often associated with intergroup power differentials – they can legitimize and justify oppression or social change, and explain one's own group's treatment of and by other groups. The more ideological a group membership-based belief system is, the better the job it does at reducing feelings of uncertainty, particularly uncertainty about oneself in society.

Drawing on uncertainty reduction theory (e.g., Hogg, 2000) and its analysis of the role of entitativity (e.g., Hogg, 2004), I proposed five premises linking uncertainty, identification, prototypes, and entitativity. Let us now add ideology into the mix – bearing in mind that a prototype is one's cognitive representation of the features of a social group, and so an ideology can be part of one's prototype of a group (e.g., a prototypical Christian fundamentalist is someone who subscribes to a particular religious ideology). The five premises that capture the essence of the uncertainty reduction perspective on ideology presented in this chapter are as follows.

Premise 1: People are motivated to reduce their feelings of uncertainty about themselves, and about their perceptions, judgments, attitudes, and behaviors that relate to themselves and to their interactions with other people.

Premise 2: Group identification reduces uncertainty, because through the processes of social categorization and depersonalization, it assimilates self to a group prototype, grounded in substantial ingroup consensus – a prototype which defines self and prescribes perceptions, attitudes, feeling, and behaviors, and specifies and regulates the course of interaction with ingroup and outgroup members.

Premise 3: Prototypes are better at resolving uncertainty to the extent that they are ideological – they are simple, clear, unambiguous, prescriptive, focused, and consensual, as well as coherently integrative, self-contained, and explanatory. The greater the subjective uncertainty, the greater the attractiveness of an ideological belief system/prototype.

Premise 4: High-entitativity groups typically have such prototypes, and thus more ideological belief systems – therefore under high uncertainty people prefer to identify with high-entitativity groups.

Premise 5: Because entitativity and ideological belief systems are so effective at reducing self-uncertainty through identification, people strive, both cognitively and behaviorally, to accentuate the entitativity, prototypical clarity, and ideological quality of their group.

On the surface, this analysis may seem to imply that conservative ideologies and preservation of the status quo are inevitable – a gloomy prognosis that sees basic social psychological processes "driving" people and society toward conservative fundamentalism and resistance to social innovation and change. While system-justifying and hierarchy-enhancing ideologies are appealing solutions to extreme uncertainty, the uncertainty reduction analysis provided here hinges on the argument that *any* ideological belief system, including those that are system-challenging and hierarchy-attenuating, can reduce acute uncertainty – the key factor is that the belief system is ideological and is grounded in a distinctive identity that people can use to define themselves and regulate cognition, affect, behavior, and interaction.

ACKNOWLEDGMENT

The writing of this chapter was made possible by generous grant support from the Australian Research Council that has helped fund my research program on uncertainty and social identity. I also wish to acknowledge discussions with Brenda Major and her lab group at the University of California, Santa Barbara, and with Fiona Barlow, Louise Burgess, and Graham Moffitt at the University of Queensland.

REFERENCES

Abrams, D., & Hogg, M. A. (1988). Comments on the motivational status of self-esteem in social identity and intergroup discrimination. *European Journal of Social Psychology, 18,* 317–334.

Adorno, T. W., Frenkel-Brunswik, E., Levinson, D. J., & Sanford, R. M. (1950). *The authoritarian personality.* New York: Harper.

Allport, F. H. (1924). *Social psychology.* Boston: Houghton-Mifflin.

Altemeyer, B. (1988). *Enemies of freedom: Understanding right-wing authoritarianism.* San Francisco, CA: Jossey-Bass.

Altemeyer, B. (1998). The other "authoritarian personality". In: M. P. Zanna (Ed.), *Advances in experimental social psychology,* (Vol. 30, pp. 47–92). Orlando, FL: Academic Press.

Altemeyer, B. (2003). Why do religious fundamentalists tend to be prejudiced. *International Journal for the Psychology of Religion, 13,* 17–28.

Altemeyer, B., & Hunsberger, B. (1992). Authoritarianism, religious fundamentalism, quest, and prejudice. *The International Journal for the Study of Religion, 2,* 113–133.

Althusser, L. (1965). *For Marx.* London: Penguin.

Baron, R. S., Crawley, K., & Paulina, D. (2003). Aberrations of power: Leadership in totalist groups. In: D. van Knippenberg & M. A. Hogg (Eds), *Leadership and power: Identity processes in groups and organizations* (pp. 169–183). London: Sage.

Batson, C. D., Schoenrade, P., & Ventis, W. L. (1993). *Religion and the individual: A social-psychological perspective.* New York: Oxford University Press.

Billig, M. (1976). *Social psychology and intergroup relations.* London: Academic Press.

Billig, M. (1978). *Fascists: A social psychological view of the National Front.* London: Harcourt Brace Jovanovich.

Billig, M. (1982). *Ideology and social psychology: Extremism, moderation and contradiction.* London: Sage.

Billig, M. (1991). *Ideology and opinions: Studies in rhetorical psychology.* London: Sage.

Breakwell, G. (1986). *Coping with threatened identities.* London: Methuen.

Brewer, M. B., & Campbell, D. T. (1976). *Ethnocentrism and intergroup attitudes: East African evidence.* New York: Sage.

Campbell, D. T. (1958). Common fate, similarity, and other indices of the status of aggregates of persons as social entities. *Behavioral Science, 3,* 14–25.

Crocker, J., & Major, B. (1994). Reactions to stigma: The moderating role of justifications. In: M. P. Zanna & J. M. Olson (Eds), *The psychology of prejudice: The Ontario symposium,* (Vol. 7, pp. 289–314). Hillsdale, NJ: Erlbaum.

Curtis, J. M., & Curtis, M. J. (1993). Factors related to susceptibility and recruitment by cults. *Psychological Reports, 73,* 451–460.

Deconchy, J.-P. (1984). Rationality and social control in orthodox systems. In: H. Tajfel (Ed.), *The social dimension: European developments in social psychology,* (Vol. 2, pp. 425–445). Cambridge, UK: Cambridge University Press.

Doty, R. M., Peterson, B. E., & Winter, D. G. (1991). Threat and authoritarianism in the United States, 1978–1987. *Journal of Personality and Social Psychology, 61,* 629–640.

Duckitt, J. (1989). Authoritarianism and group identification: A new view of an old construct. *Political Psychology, 10,* 63–84.

Duckitt, J. (2001). A dual-process cognitive-motivational theory of ideology and prejudice. *Advances in Experimental Social Psychology, 33,* 41–113.

Dunn, R. G. (1998). *Identity crises: A social critique of postmodernity.* Minneapolis, MN: University of Minnesota Press.

Durkheim, E. (1898). Représentations individuelles et représentations collectives. *Revue de Metaphysique et de Morale, 6,* 273–302.

Eiser, J. R., & Stroebe, W. (1972). *Categorization and social judgement.* London: Academic Press.

Ellemers, N. (1993). The influence of socio-structural variables on identity management strategies. *European Review of Social Psychology, 4,* 27–57.

Farr, R. M. (1996). *The roots of modern social psychology: 1872–1954.* Oxford, UK: Blackwell.

Farr, R. M., & Moscovici, S. (Eds) (1984). *Social representations.* Cambridge, UK: Cambridge University Press.

Fiol, C. M. (2002). Capitalizing on paradox: The role of language in transforming organizational identities. *Organization Science, 13,* 653–666.

Foels, R., & Pappas, C. J. (2004). Learning and unlearning the myths we are taught: Gender and social dominance orientation. *Sex Roles, 50,* 743–757.

Furnham, A. (1990). *The Protestant work ethic: The psychology of work-related beliefs and behaviors.* New York: Routledge.

Furnham, A. (2003). Belief in a just world: Research progress over the past decade. *Personality and Individual Differences, 34,* 795–817.

Furnham, A., & Procter, E. (1989). Belief in a just world: Review and critique of the individual difference literature. *British Journal of Social Psychology, 28,* 365–384.

Furnham, A., & Rajamanickam, R. (1992). The Protestant work ethic and just world beliefs in Great Britain and India. *International Journal of Psychology, 27,* 401–416.

Galanter, M. (Ed.) (1989). *Cults and new religious movements.* Washington, DC: American Psychiatric Association.

Gergen, K. J. (1991). *The saturated self: Dilemmas of identity in contemporary life.* New York: Basic Books.

Greenberg, J., Koole, S. L., & Pyszczynski, T. (Eds) (2004). *Handbook of experimental existential psychology.* New York: Guilford.

Grieve, P., & Hogg, M. A. (1999). Subjective uncertainty and intergroup discrimination in the minimal group situation. *Personality and Social Psychology Bulletin, 25,* 926–940.

Guimond, S., Dambrun, M., Michinov, N., & Duarte, S. (2003). Does social dominance generate prejudice? Integrating individual and contextual determinants of intergroup cognitions. *Journal of Personality and Social Psychology, 84,* 697–721.

Hamilton, D. L. (Ed.) (1981). *Cognitive processes in stereotyping and intergroup behavior.* Hillsdale, NJ: Erlbaum.

Hamilton, D. L., & Sherman, S. J. (1996). Perceiving persons and groups. *Psychological Review, 103,* 336–355.

Hamilton, D. L., Sherman, S. J., & Rodgers, J. S. (2004). Perceiving the groupness of groups: Entitativity, homogeneity, essentialism, and stereotypes. In: V. Yzerbyt, C. M. Judd & O. Corneille (Eds), *The psychology of group perception: Perceived variability, entitativity, and essentialism* (pp. 39–60). New York: Psychology Press.

Haslam, N., Rothschild, L., & Ernst, D. (1998). Essentialist beliefs about social categories. *British Journal of Social Psychology, 39,* 113–127.

Hoffer, E. (1951). *The true believer.* New York: Time.

Hogg, M. A. (2000). Subjective uncertainty reduction through self-categorization: A motivational theory of social identity processes. *European Review of Social Psychology, 11,* 223–255.

Hogg, M. A. (2001a). Self-categorization and subjective uncertainty resolution: Cognitive and motivational facets of social identity and group membership. In: J. P. Forgas, K. D. Williams & L. Wheeler (Eds), *The social mind: Cognitive and motivational aspects of interpersonal behavior* (pp. 323–349). New York: Cambridge University Press.

Hogg, M. A. (2001b). A social identity theory of leadership. *Personality and Social Psychology Review, 5,* 184–200.

Hogg, M. A. (2003). Social identity. In: M. R. Leary & J. P. Tangney (Eds), *Handbook of self and identity* (pp. 462–479). New York: Guilford.

Hogg, M. A. (2004). Uncertainty and extremism: Identification with high entitativity groups under conditions of uncertainty. In: V. Yzerbyt, C. M. Judd & O. Corneille (Eds), *The psychology of group perception: Perceived variability, entitativity, and essentialism* (pp. 401–418). New York: Psychology Press.

Hogg, M. A. (in press a) The social identity approach. In: S. A. Wheelan (Ed.), *The handbook of group research and practice.* Thousand Oaks, CA: Sage.

Hogg, M. A. (in press b). Social identity theory. In: P. J. Burke (Ed.), *Contemporary social psychological theories.* Palo Alto, CA: Stanford University Press.

Hogg, M. A. (2005). All animals are equal but some animals are more equal than others: Social identity and marginal membership. In: K. D. Williams, J. P. Forgas & W. von Hippel (Eds), *The social outcast: Ostracism, social exclusion, rejection and bullying* (pp. 243–261). New York: Psychology Press.

Hogg, M. A., & Abrams, D. (1988). *Social identifications: A social psychology of intergroup relations and group processes.* London and New York: Routledge.

Hogg, M. A., Sherman, D. K., Dierselhuis, J., Maitner, A. T., & Moffitt, G. (2004). *Uncertainty, entitativity and group identification.* Manuscript submitted for publication, University of Queensland.

Hogg, M. A., & Svensson, A. (2004). *Uncertainty reduction, self-esteem and group identification.* Manuscript submitted for publication , University of Queensland.

Hogg, M. A., & Tindale, R. S. (2005). Social identity, influence, and communication in small groups. In: J. Harwood & H. Giles (Eds), *Intergroup communication: Multiple perspectives* (pp. 141–164). New York: Peter Lang.

Hogg, M. A., & van Knippenberg, D. (2003). Social identity and leadership processes in groups. In: M. P. Zanna (Ed.), *Advances in experimental social psychology*, (Vol. 35, pp. 1–52). San Diego, CA: Academic Press.

Jetten, J., Hogg, M. A., & Mullin, B.-A. (2000). Ingroup variability and motivation to reduce subjective uncertainty. *Group Dynamics: Theory, Research, and Practice, 4,* 184–198.

Jones, E. E. (1998). Major developments in five decades of social psychology. In: D. T. Gilbert, S. T. Fiske & G. Lindzey (Eds), *The handbook of social psychology*, (Vol. 1, pp. 3–57). New York: McGraw-Hill.

Jost, J. T., Banaji, M. R., & Nosek, B. A. (in press). A decade of system justification theory: Accumulated evidence of conscious and unconscious bolstering of the status quo. *Political Psychology.*

Jost, J. T., Glaser, J., Kruglanski, A. W., & Sulloway, F. J. (2003). Political conservatism as motivated social cognition. *Psychological Bulletin, 129,* 339–375.

Jost, J. T., & Hunyady, O. (2002). The psychology of system justification and the palliative function of ideology. *European Review of Social Psychology, 13,* 111–153.

Jost, J. T., & Major, B. (Eds) (2001). *The psychology of legitimacy: Emerging perspectives on ideology, justice, and intergroup relations.* New York: Cambridge University Press.

Kosterman, R., & Feshbach, S. (1989). Towards a measure of patriotic and nationalistic attitudes. *Political Psychology, 10,* 257–274.

Lambert, A. J., Burroughs, T., & Nguyen, T. (1999). Perceptions of risk and the buffering hypothesis: The role of just world beliefs and right-wing authoritarianism. *Personality and Social Psychology Bulletin, 25,* 643–656.

Larrain, J. (1979). *The concept of ideology.* London: Hutchinson.

LeBon, G. (1908). *The crowd: A study of the popular mind.* London: Unwin (French original 1896).

Lerner, M. J., & Miller, D. T. (1978). Just-world research and the attribution process: Looking back and ahead. *Psychological Bulletin, 85,* 1030–1051.

Lickel, B., Hamilton, D. L., Wieczorkowska, G., Lewis, A., Sherman, S. J., & Uhles, A. N. (2000). Varieties of groups and the perception of group entitativity. *Journal of Personality and Social Psychology, 78,* 223–246.

Major, B., Quinton, W. J., & McCoy, S. (2002). Antecedents and consequences of attributions to discrimination: Theoretical and empirical advances. In: M. P. Zanna (Ed.), *Advances in experimental social psychology*, (Vol. 34, pp. 251–330). San Diego, CA: Academic Press.

Marris, P. (1996). *The politics of uncertainty: Attachment in private and public life.* London: Routledge.

Marsella, A. J. (2004). Reflections on international terrorism: Issues, concepts, and directions. In: F. M. Moghaddam & A. J. Marsella (Eds), *Understanding terrorism: Psychosocial roots, consequences, and interventions* (pp. 11–47). Washington, DC: American Psychological Association.

McDougall, W. (1921). *The group mind.* London: Cambridge University Press.

McFarland, S. G., Agayev, V. S., & Djintcharadze, N. (1996). Russian authoritarianism two years after communism. *Personality and Social Psychology Bulletin, 22,* 210–217.

Moghaddam, F. M. (2004). Cultural preconditions for potential terrorist groups: Terrorism and societal change. In: F. M. Moghaddam & A. J. Marsella (Eds), *Understanding terrorism: Psychosocial roots, consequences, and interventions* (pp. 103–117). Washington, DC: American Psychological Association.

Moscovici, S. (1976). *Social influence and social change*. London: Academic Press.

Mullin, B.-A., & Hogg, M. A. (1998). Dimensions of subjective uncertainty in social identification and minimal intergroup discrimination. *British Journal of Social Psychology, 37*, 345–365.

Prentice, D. A., & Miller, D. T. (Eds) (1999). *Cultural divides: Understanding and overcoming group conflict*. New York: Russell Sage Foundation.

Quinn, D. M., & Crocker, J. (1999). When ideology hurts: Effects of belief in the Protestant work ethic and feeling overweight on the psychological well-being of women. *Journal of Personality and Social Psychology, 77*, 402–414.

Reicher, S. D., & Hopkins, N. (1996). Seeking influence through characterising self-categories: An analysis of anti-abortionist rhetoric. *British Journal of Social Psychology, 35*, 297–311.

Reicher, S. D., & Hopkins, N. (2001). *Self and nation*. London: Sage.

Reid, S. A., & Hogg, M. A. (2005). Uncertainty reduction, self-enhancement, and ingroup identification. *Personality and Social Psychology Bulletin, 31*, 1–14.

Reid, S. A., & Ng, S. H. (2000). Conversation as a resource for influence: Evidence for prototypical arguments and social identification processes. *European Journal of Social Psychology, 30*, 83–100.

Rohan, M. J. (2000). A rose by any name? The values construct. *Personality and Social Psychology Review, 4*, 255–277.

Rothbart, M., & Park, B. (2004). The mental representation of social categories: Category boundaries, entitativity, and stereotype change. In: V. Yzerbyt, C. M. Judd & O. Corneille (Eds), *The psychology of group perception: Perceived variability, entitativity, and essentialism* (pp. 79–100). New York: Psychology Press.

Rowatt, W. C., & Franklin, L. M. (2004). Christian orthodoxy, religious fundamentalism, and right-wing authoritarianism as predictors of implicit racial prejudice. *International Journal for the Psychology of Religion, 14*, 125–138.

Rubin, M., & Hewstone, M. (1998). Social identity theory's self-esteem hypothesis: A review and some suggestions for clarification. *Personality and Social Psychology Review, 2*, 40–62.

Sani, F., & Reicher, S. D. (2000). Contested identities and schisms in groups: Opposing the ordination of women as priests in the Church of England. *British Journal of Social Psychology, 39*, 95–112.

Schmitt, M. T., Branscombe, N. R., & Kappen, D. M. (2003). Attitudes toward group-based inequality: Social dominance or social identity. *British Journal of Social Psychology, 42*, 161–186.

Sherman, D. K., Hogg, M. A., Maitner, A. T., & Moffitt, G. (2004). *Polarization under uncertainty*. Manuscript submitted for publication, University of California, Santa Barbara.

Sidanius, J., Levin, S., Federico, C. M., & Pratto, F. (2001). Legitimizing ideologies: The social dominance approach. In: J. T. Jost & B. Major (Eds), *The psychology of legitimacy: Emerging perspectives on ideology, justice, and intergroup relations* (pp. 307–331). New York: Cambridge University Press.

Sidanius, J., & Pratto, F. (1999). *Social dominance: An intergroup theory of social hierarchy and oppression.* New York: Cambridge University Press.

Singer, M. (1995). *Cults in our midst.* San Francisco, CA: Jossey-Bass.

Staub, E. (1989). *The roots of evil: The psychological and cultural origins of genocide and other forms of group violence.* New York: Cambridge University Press.

Staub, E. (1997). Blind versus constructive patriotism: Moving from embeddedness in the group to critical loyalty and action. In: D. Bar-Tal & E. Staub (Eds), *Patriotism: In the lives of individuals and nations* (pp. 213–228). Chicago: Nelson-Hall.

Sumner, W. G. (1906). *Folkways.* Boston, MA: Ginn.

Swann, W. B., Jr., Polzer, J. T., Seyle, C., & Ko, S. (2004). Finding value in diversity: Verification of personal and social self-views in diverse groups. *Academy of Management Review, 29,* 9–27.

Swann, W. B., Jr., Rentfrow, P. J., & Guinn, J. S. (2003). Self-verification: The search for coherence. In: M. R. Leary & J. P. Tangney (Eds), *Handbook of self and identity* (pp. 367–383). New York: Guilford.

Tajfel, H. (1959). Quantitative judgement in social perception. *British Journal of Psychology, 50,* 16–29.

Tajfel, H. (1981). Social stereotypes and social groups. In: J. C. Turner & H. Giles (Eds), *Intergroup behaviour* (pp. 144–167). Oxford, UK: Blackwell.

Tajfel, H. (Ed.) (1984). *The social dimension: European developments in social psychology.* Cambridge, UK: Cambridge University Press.

Tajfel, H., & Turner, J. C. (1979). An integrative theory of intergroup conflict. In: W. G. Austin & S. Worchel (Eds), *The social psychology of intergroup relations* (pp. 33–47). Monterey, CA: Brooks/Cole.

Tarde, G. (1901). *L'opinion et al foule.* Paris: Libraire Felix Alcan.

Taylor, D. M., & Louis, W. (2004). Terrorism and the quest for identity. In: F. M. Moghaddam & A. J. Marsella (Eds), *Understanding terrorism: Psychosocial roots, consequences, and interventions* (pp. 169–185). Washington, DC: American Psychological Association.

Thompson, J. B. (1990). *Ideology and modern culture: Critical social theory in the era of mass communication.* Stanford, CA: Stanford University Press.

Trotter, W. (1919). *Instincts of the herd in peace and war.* London: Oxford University Press.

Turner, J. C., Hogg, M. A., Oakes, P. J., Reicher, S. D., & Wetherell, M. S. (1987). *Rediscovering the social group: A self-categorization theory.* Oxford, UK: Blackwell.

Turner, J. C., & Reynolds, K. J. (2003). Why social dominance theory has been falsified. *British Journal of Social Psychology, 42,* 199–206.

van Knippenberg, D., & Hogg, M. A. (2003). A social identity model of leadership in organizations. In: R. M. Kramer & B. M. Staw (Eds), *Research in organizational behavior,* (Vol. 25, pp. 243–295). Greenwich, CT: JAI Press.

van Knippenberg, D., van Knippenberg, B., De Cremer, D., & Hogg, M. A. (2004). Leadership, self, and identity: A review and research agenda. *The Leadership Quarterly, 15,* 825–856.

Wilson, M. S., & Liu, J. H. (2003). Social dominance orientation and gender: The moderating role of gender identity. *British Journal of Social Psychology, 42,* 187–198.

Wundt, W. (1916). *Elements of folk psychology: Outlines of a psychological history of the development of mankind.* London: Allen & Unwin (German original 1912).

Yzerbyt, V., Castano, E., Leyens, J.-P., & Paladino, M.-P. (2000). The primacy of the ingroup: The interplay of entitativity and identification. *European Review of Social Psychology, 11,* 257–295.

SOCIAL IDENTITIES AND SOCIAL CONTEXT: SOCIAL ATTITUDES AND PERSONAL WELL-BEING

John F. Dovidio, Samuel L. Gaertner, Adam R. Pearson and Blake M. Riek

ABSTRACT

In this chapter, we consider the fundamental importance of social identity both in terms of how people think about others and for personal well-being. The chapter reviews how social categorization and social identity impact people's responses to others and, drawing on our own work on the Common Ingroup Identity Model, examines how identity processes can be shaped to improve intergroup relations. This model describes how factors that alter the perceptions of the memberships of separate groups to conceive of themselves as members of a single, more inclusive, superordinate group can reduce intergroup bias. The present chapter focuses on four developments in the model: (1) recognizing that multiple social identities can be activated simultaneously (e.g., a dual identity); (2) acknowledging that the meaning of different identities varies for different groups (e.g., racial or ethnic groups); (3) describing how the impact of different social identities can vary as a function of social context and social and personal values; and (4) outlining how these processes can influence not

Social Identification in Groups
Advances in Group Processes, Volume 22, 231–260
ISSN: 0882-6145/doi:10.1016/S0882-6145(05)22009-X

only intergroup attitudes but also personal well-being, interms of both mental and physical health.

Personal identity has long been identified within psychology as critical to an individual's functioning, feelings of well-being, and actual accomplishment. Stage models of personal identity development, such as those of Freud, Erickson, and Maslow (Schultz & Schultz, 2001), have traditionally held a central place in personality and clinical psychology. However, more recently, social psychologists have also begun to recognize the significance for social behavior and intergroup relations of collective identities, such as those related to ethnic (Phinney, 2003) and racial group membership (Cross, 1991; Helms, 1990; Sellers, Rowley, Chavous, Shelton, & Smith, 1997) as well as to other important reference groups (Luhtanen & Crocker, 1991). Indeed, among the most significant developments in social psychology over the past 35 years has been the recognition that individuals have many different self-concepts and identities, rooted in personal experiences and aspirations (Markus & Nurius, 1986) and in the social groups to which they belong (Brewer, 2001; Tajfel & Turner, 1979).

In this chapter, we consider the fundamental importance of social identity both in terms of how people think about others and for personal well-being. We begin by discussing the psychological foundation of social identity, the role of social categorization in human perception and action, and briefly review theories of social identity processes. Next, we examine how social identity impacts people's responses to others and how identity processes can be shaped to improve intergroup relations. Our own program of research, guided by the Common Ingroup Identity Model, has focused on how factors that alter the perceptions of the memberships of separate groups to conceive of themselves as members of a single, more inclusive, superordinate group reduce intergroup bias and conflict. We then explore how the simultaneous activation of multiple identities, particularly the experience of a dual identity in which superordinate and subgroup identities are both salient, can in some cases produce more favorable intergroup responses and in other instances promote more negative reactions. We propose a framework to help understand and conceptually integrate these seemingly contradictory findings. Finally, we consider outcomes beyond intergroup attitudes, such as psychological and physical well-being, that may be significantly influenced by these social identity processes.

We begin our discussion by examining one of the fundamental processes underlying group identification effects, the social categorization process.

SOCIAL CATEGORIZATION

Social categorization forms an essential basis for human perception, cognition, and functioning. Because of the adaptive significance of intellect in human survival, people have a fundamental need to understand their environment. To cope with the enormous complexity of the world, people abstract meaning from their perceptions and develop heuristics and other simplifying principles for thinking about important elements in their environment. Categorization is one of the most basic processes in the abstraction of meaning from complex environments.

Categorization enables people to make decisions quickly about incoming information. The instant an object is categorized, it is assigned the properties shared by other category members (Biernat & Dovidio, 2000). Time-consuming consideration of each new experience is forfeited because it is usually wasteful and unnecessary. Categorization often occurs spontaneously on the basis of physical similarity, proximity, or shared fate. In this respect, people may be characterized as "cognitive misers"who compromise total accuracy for efficiency (Fiske & Taylor, 1991).

When people or objects are categorized into groups, actual differences between members of the same category tend to be perceptually minimized (Tajfel, 1969) and often ignored in making decisions or forming impressions. Members of the same category appear to be more similar than they actually are, and more similar than they were before they were categorized together. In addition, although members of a social category may be different in some ways from members of other categories, these differences tend to become exaggerated and overgeneralized. Thus, categorization enhances perceptions of similarities within groups and differences between groups – emphasizing social difference and group distinctiveness.

Because humans are social animals, relying on select others for interdependent activity and cooperation can have important short- and long-term consequences for individuals' fitness and survival. Group membership is a key element in the maintenance of social bonds. Psychologically, expectations of cooperation and security promote positive attraction toward other ingroup members and motivate adherence to ingroup norms that assure that one will be recognized as a good or legitimate ingroup member. In this context, group identity becomes essential to a secure self-concept. Once group identification has been established, maintaining a sense of inclusion and cohesiveness becomes tantamount to protecting one's own existence. Within this context, culture serves to regulate social behavior both within and between groups so as to maintain group cohesion and boundaries. The reciprocal relationship between group identification and group culture makes intragroup coordination, trust, and cooperation possible. These same processes, however, can also give rise to intergroup differences and distrust that may seed and sustain conflict.

A universal perceptual process that is essential for efficient functioning is the ability to sort people, spontaneously and with minimum effort or awareness, into a smaller number of meaningful categories, social groups (Brewer, 1988; see also Fiske, Lin, & Neuberg, 1999). In the process of categorizing people into groups, people commonly classify themselves *into* one social category and *out of* others. Because of the centrality of the self in social perception (Dovidio & Gaertner, 1993), social categorization fundamentally involves a distinction between the group containing the self (the ingroup) and other groups (the outgroups) – between the "we's" and the "they's."

This distinction can have a profound influence on evaluations, cognitions, and behavior. The insertion of the self into the social categorization process increases the emotional significance of group differences and thus leads to further perceptual distortion and to evaluative biases that reflect favorably on the ingroup (Sumner, 1906), and consequently, on the self (Tajfel & Turner, 1979). Perhaps one reason why ethnocentrism is so prevalent is because these biases operate even when the basis for the categorization is quite trivial, such as when group membership is assigned randomly (Billig & Tajfel, 1973). In the following section, we review two influential theories of group identity: social identity theory and self-categorization theory.

THEORIES OF SOCIAL IDENTITY

The essentially automatic process of distinguishing the group containing the self, the ingroup, from other groups, the outgroups (Dovidio & Gaertner, 1993), represents a foundational principle in some of the most prominent contemporary theories of intergroup behavior, such as social identity theory (Tajfel & Turner, 1979) and self-categorization theory (Turner, 1985; Turner, Hogg, Oakes, Reicher, & Wetherell, 1987).

In social identity theory, Tajfel and Turner (1979) proposed that a person's need for positive self-identity can be satisfied by membership in prestigious social groups. This need motivates social comparisons that favorably differentiate ingroup from outgroup members. This perspective also posits that a person defines the self in one of two ways, as a unique individual with distinct characteristics and personal motives, or as the embodiment of a social collective, reflecting shared characteristics and goals. At the individual level, one's personal welfare and goals are most salient and important. At the collective level, the goals and achievements of the group are merged with one's own, and the group's welfare is paramount. At the level of personal identity, self-interest is represented by the pronoun "I"; at the level of social identity, it is represented by "We." Intergroup relations begin when people in different groups think about themselves as group members rather than as distinct individuals.

Though similar to social identity theory, self-categorization theory (Turner et al., 1987) places greater emphasis on the cognitive processes involved in identification and can be considered a more general theory of inter- and intra-group processes. Self-categorization theory also makes a fundamental distinction between personal and collective identity, though these are seen more as different levels on a continuum rather than as qualitatively distinct and mutually exclusive states. When personal identity is more salient, an individual's needs, standards, beliefs, and motives better predict behavior. In contrast, when social identity is more strongly activated, "people come to perceive themselves more as interchangeable exemplars of a social category than as unique personalities defined by their individual differences from others" (Turner et al., 1987, p. 50). Under these conditions, *collective* needs, goals, and standards are primary. For example, Verkuyten and Hagendoorn (1998) found that when individual identity was made salient, individual differences in authoritarianism were the major predictor of prejudice of Dutch students toward Turkish migrants. In contrast, when social identity (i.e., national identity) was primed, ingroup stereotypes and standards primarily predicted attitudes toward Turkish migrants. Thus, whether a person's personal or collective identity is more salient critically shapes how a person perceives, interprets, evaluates, and responds to situations and to others.

These theories of collective identity do not challenge the validity of instrumental theories of behavior, in which individual and group behavior are viewed as functional for obtaining resources and protecting self- and group interest. Both traditional and contemporary research demonstrates the profound functional advantages of intragroup solidarity and intergroup bias. For example, consistent with realistic conflict theory (Blumer, 1958; Bobo & Huchings, 1996; Esses, Jackson, & Armstrong, 1998), the classic Robber's Cave study (Sherif, Harvey, White, Hood, & Sherif, 1961) illustrated how competition between groups produces prejudice and discrimination. In contrast, intergroup interdependence and cooperative interaction that result in successful outcomes reduce intergroup bias. Nevertheless, social identity theory and self-categorization theory emphasize how identification as a member of a social group is *sufficient* to shape how people respond to others and influence how people perceive themselves.

In the next section of the chapter we consider the ways, in which the recognition of group identity can have a critical impact on how people respond to others and can form the social psychological foundation for prejudice and intergroup bias.

SOCIAL IDENTITY AND RESPONSES TO OTHERS

Viewing oneself as a member of a social group and others as members of other groups has immediate consequences for how people perceive, think about, feel, and act toward others. As we noted earlier, categorization leads people to emphasize similarities within groups and differences between groups in their perceptions and cognitions. For *social* groups, this process is particularly important because social groupings are often assumed to represent natural categories, categories in which membership is determined by some aspect of the member's nature (Yzerbyt, Corneille, & Estrada, 2001). Membership in natural categories is often believed to reflect similarities in the *essence* of group members, and, thus, people are especially likely to generalize characteristics across members (producing strong stereotypes) and to generalize beyond the characteristic that originally differentiated the categories to additional dimensions and traits. As the salience of the social categorization increases, the magnitude of these distortions also tends to increase (Abrams, 1985; Turner, 1985).

Not only does social categorization activate perceptual and cognitive processes that emphasize the differences between ingroup and outgroup members, it also systematically biases the affective and evaluative associations with these groups. People spontaneously experience more positive affect toward other members of the group with which they identify, particularly toward those who are most prototypical of their group (Hogg & Hains, 1996), than toward members of other groups (Otten & Moskowitz, 2000). In addition, cognitive biases emerge in which people retain more information in a more detailed fashion for ingroup members than for outgroup members (Park & Rothbart, 1982), have better memory for information about ways in which ingroup members are similar to (and outgroup members dissimilar to) the self (Wilder, 1981), and remember less positive information about outgroup members (Howard & Rothbart, 1980). These affective and cognitive biases have important behavioral implications.

People are more helpful toward ingroup than toward outgroup members (Dovidio et al., 1997) and work harder for groups identified as ingroups (Worchel, Rothgerber, Day, Hart, & Butemeyer, 1998). In addition, when ingroup–outgroup social categorization is salient, people tend to behave in a more greedy and less trustworthy way toward members of other groups than if they react to each other as individuals (Insko et al., 2001).

Moreover, the extent to which people identify with their ingroup typically (albeit not universally; see Brown & Zagefka, 2005) moderates the level of intergroup bias they exhibit. Bias consists of the separate elements of ingroup favoritism and outgroup derogation (Brewer, 1999), and ingroup identification can, under different circumstances, influence one or both of these components. Although stronger ingroup identification generally relates to more positive feelings and beliefs about the ingroup and its members, it predicts prejudice against outgroups primarily when people think about their group in relation to, and particularly in contrast to, the other group (Mummendey, Klink, & Brown, 2001). Thus, the relationship of ingroup identification to intergroup bias depends on the context in which intergroup relations are observed.

Similarly, social identification, in terms of the particular group with which one identifies and the degree, to which one identifies with the group, is contextually responsive. Social categories are not completely unalterable. People possess multiple social identities (Brewer, 2001), and the relevant social categories are often hierarchically organized, with higher-level categories (e.g., nations) more inclusive of lower level ones (e.g., cities or towns). By modifying a perceiver's goals, motives, perceptions of past experiences, and expectations, as well as factors in the immediate context, one can alter the level of category inclusiveness that is most influential in a given situation (Gaertner & Dovidio, 2000). This malleability in the level at which impressions are formed is important in terms of its implications for altering the way people think about members of ingroups and outgroups, and, consequently, about the nature of intergroup relations.

SOCIAL IDENTITY AND INTERGROUP RELATIONS

Because identification with social groups is a basic process that is fundamental to intergroup bias, social psychologists have targeted this process as a starting point for improving intergroup relations. A variety of different approaches have been employed successfully. For example, decategorization strategies that emphasize the individual qualities of others (Wilder, 1981) or encourage personalized interactions (Miller, 2002) have been used to decrease the salience of social identities. The mutual intergroup differentiation approach, in contrast, attempts to keep group identities salient but to change the perceived relation between groups from competitive to cooperative (Hewstone & Brown, 1986; see also Brown & Hewstone, 2005).

The approach we have employed, the common ingroup identity model (Gaertner & Dovidio, 2000), draws on the theoretical foundations of social identity theory (Tajfel & Turner, 1979) and self-categorization theory (Turner et al., 1987). This strategy emphasizes the process of recategorization, whereby members of different groups are induced to conceive of themselves as a single, more inclusive superordinate group rather than as two completely separate groups. As a consequence, attitudes toward former outgroup members become more positive through processes involving pro-ingroup bias.

The Common Ingroup Identity Model identifies potential antecedents and outcomes of recategorization, as well as mediating processes. Fig. 1 summarizes the general framework and specifies the causes and consequences of a common ingroup identity. Specifically, we hypothesize that different types of intergroup interdependence and cognitive, perceptual, linguistic, affective, and environmental factors, can, either independently or in concert, alter individuals' cognitive representations of the aggregate. For example, a common ingroup identity can be achieved by increasing the salience of existing common superordinate memberships (e.g., a school, a company, a nation, etc.) or by introducing factors (e.g., common goals or fate) perceived to be shared by these memberships. The resulting cognitive representations (i.e., one group, two subgroups within one group, two groups, or separate individuals) are then hypothesized to have specific cognitive, affective and overt behavioral consequences. Thus, the antecedent factors are proposed to influence members' cognitive representations of the memberships that, in turn, mediate the relationship, at least in part, between the antecedent factors and the cognitive, affective, and behavioral consequences.

Decategorization and recategorization strategies were directly examined and contrasted in a laboratory study of intergroup bias (Gaertner, Mann, Murrell, & Dovidio, 1989). In this experiment, members of two separate laboratory-formed groups were induced through various structural interventions (e.g., seating arrangement) either to decategorize themselves (i.e., conceive of themselves as separate individuals) or to recategorize themselves as a superordinate group. Consistent with the notion that altering the level of category inclusiveness can have a positive impact on intergroup

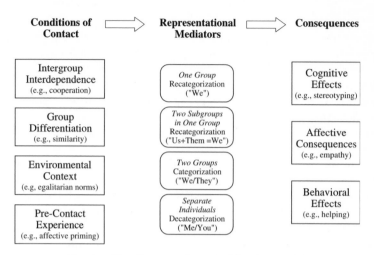

Fig. 1. The Common Ingroup Identity Model.

evaluations, the changes in the perceptions of intergroup boundaries reduced intergroup bias. Furthermore, as expected, these strategies reduced bias in different ways. Decategorizing members of the two groups reduced bias by decreasing the attractiveness of former ingroup members. In contrast, recategorizing ingroup and outgroup members as members of a more inclusive group reduced bias by increasing the attractiveness of the former outgroup members. Consistent with self-categorization theory, "the attractiveness of an individual is not constant, but varies with the ingroup membership" (Turner, 1985, p. 60).

Considerable empirical support has been obtained for the Common Ingroup Identity Model. In particular, people who identify more strongly with a superordinate group have more favorable attitudes toward those formerly seen as members of other groups who have been recategorized within this superordinate group identity. This effect has been obtained in laboratory and field experiments involving temporary and enduring groups, in cross-sectional and longitudinal field studies of the relations between racial and ethnic groups in high schools and colleges, in research on the responses of executives who recently experienced a corporate merger, in longitudinal studies of blended families, and as a consequence of programmatic anti-bias interventions with elementary school students (Banker, et al., 2004; Gaertner, Bachman, Dovidio, & Banker, 2001; Houlette et al., 2004). In addition, emphasizing a common group identity between two groups facilitates forgiveness by members of the victimized group for historical transgressions by the other group and promotes intergroup trust (Wohl & Branscombe, 2005). Moreover, the different strategies that have been used (e.g., decategorization, mutual intergroup differentiation, and recategorization) can operate sequentially over time and in complementary ways (Hewstone, 1996; Pettigrew, 1998). For example, creating a common ingroup identity facilitates more intimate self-disclosure (Dovidio et al., 1997), which in turn can produce more personalized interactions that can further reduce intergroup bias.

Despite the evidence for the effectiveness of achieving a common group identity for improving intergroup relations, it is often difficult to sustain a superordinate group identity in the face of powerful social forces within naturalistic settings that emphasize group differences and reinforce separate group memberships. Hewstone (1996) has argued that, at a practical level, interventions designed to create a common, inclusive identity (such as equal status contact) may not be sufficiently potent to "overcome powerful ethnic and racial categorizations on more than a temporary basis" (p. 351). With respect to the perception of others, when the basis for group membership is highly salient (e.g., physical features) and the social category is culturally important, the impact of interventions that temporarily induce feelings of common identity may quickly fade as the original category membership becomes repeatedly, and often automatically (as with race in the US; Dovidio & Gaertner, 1993) activated. With respect to the experience of one's own social identity, when group identities and their associated cultural values are vital to one's functioning it would be undesirable or impossible for people to relinquish this aspect of their self-concept completely. Indeed, demands to abandon these group identities or to adopt a colorblind ideology would likely arouse strong reactance and result in especially poor intergroup relations.

It is therefore important for practical as well as theoretical reasons to consider more complex forms of social identity, in which more than one identity is salient at a time. Within the context of the Common Ingroup Identity Model, however, the development of a common ingroup identity need not require each group to forsake its less inclusive group identity. In particular, the most recent developments in our work on the Common Ingroup Identity Model have focused on a second form of recategorization, the impact of a *dual identity,* in which the superordinate identity is salient but in conjunction with a salient subgroup identity (a "different groups working together on the same team" representation). In this respect, the Common Ingroup Identity Model is aligned with bidimensional models of acculturation, in which cultural heritage and mainstream identities are relatively independent (Berry, 1997), not with unidimensional models, which posit that cultural identity is necessarily relinquished with adoption of mainstream cultural identity (Gans, 1979). We consider this development in the Common Ingroup Identity Model in the next section.

DUAL IDENTITY

Because individuals frequently belong to several groups simultaneously and possess multiple potential identities, it is possible to activate or introduce a shared identity even while separate group identities are salient. Such a strategy characterizes the crossed categorization approach for reducing intergroup bias (Brewer, Ho, Lee, & Miller, 1987; Deschamps & Doise, 1978). In this approach, group boundaries are restructured such that the newly established boundaries crosscut the original group boundaries, redefining who is an ingroup member and who is an outgroup member. This type of intervention thus changes the pattern of who is "in" and who is "out," or the degree to which participants are ingroup or outgroup members when both subgroup categories are considered simultaneously. That is, some members are ingroup members on one dimension but outgroup members on the other, while others are ingroup or outgroup members on both dimensions. Crossed categorization strategies have proven to be effective at reducing biases toward members of other groups, relative to the original simple group categorization (Mullen, Migdal, & Hewstone, 2001), across a broad range of situations (Crisp, Ensari, Hewstone, & Miller, 2003).

The dual identity approach is a particular form of crossed categorization, in which the original group boundaries are maintained but within a salient superordinate group identity that represents a higher level of inclusiveness. Establishing a common superordinate identity while maintaining the salience of subgroup identities may be effective in reducing bias because it permits the benefits of a common ingroup identity to operate without arousing countervailing motivations to achieve positive intergroup distinctiveness. Moreover, this type of recategorization may be particularly effective when people have strong allegiances to their original groups. In this respect, the benefits of a dual identity may be especially relevant to interracial and interethnic group contexts.

In his classic book, *The souls of Black folk*, DuBois (1938) observed that whereas Whites form a relatively simple and direct form of social consciousness because White culture and dominant American culture are synonymous, Black Americans develop a dual form of consciousness, in which they are sensitive to the values and expectations of the majority culture while also aware of and responsive to the values and expectations of Black culture. In our terms, whereas Whites may generally assume a single, identity, in which White and American identity correspond, minority group members may generally form a dual identity, in which the American superordinate and the racial or ethnic subgroup identity are distinct. Empirical research, 60 years later, supports DuBois' observation: White identity is much more closely aligned with a superordinate American identity than is Black identity (Sidanius, Feshbach, Levin, & Pratto, 1997). However, whereas DuBois argued that "double-consciousness" was debilitating, contemporary research suggests that, under certain conditions, it can be adaptive and constructive.

Berry (1984) offered a framework to help understand the different types of consciousness and identity processes that immigrant groups can experience within the dominant culture of the host society. Specifically, Berry (1984) presented four forms of cultural relations in pluralistic societies that represent the intersection of "yes – no" responses to two fundamental questions: (1) Are the original cultural identity and customs of value to be retained? and (2) Are positive relations with the larger society of value, and to be sought? These combinations reflect four adaptation strategies, identified by Berry, for intergroup relations: (1) integration, when cultural identities are retained and positive relations with the larger society are sought; (2) separatism, when original cultural identities are retained but positive relations with the larger society are not sought; (3) assimilation, when cultural identities are abandoned and positive relations with the larger society are desired; and (4) marginalization, when cultural identities are abandoned and are not replaced by positive identification with the larger society.

Although this framework was originally applied to the ways in which immigrants acclimate to a new society (van Oudenhoven, Prins, & Buunk, 1998), we have adapted it to apply to intergroup relations between majority and minority groups more generally (see Dovidio, Gaertner, & Kafati, 2000). Substituting the separate strengths of the subgroup and subordinate group identities for the answers to Berry's (1984) two questions, the combinations map onto the four main representations considered in the Common Ingroup Identity Model: (1) dual identity (subgroup and superordinate group identities are high, such as feeling like different groups on the same team: which relates to Berry's adaptation strategy of integration); (2) different groups (subgroup identity is high and superordinate identity is low: separatism); (3) one group (subgroup identity is low and superordinate group identity is high: assimilation); and (4) separate individuals (subgroup and superordinate group identities are low relative to individual identity: which relates to Berry's adaptation strategy of marginalization). Within our conceptualization, the processes involved in the formation of a dual identity or one group identity represent recategorization, an emphasis on different group memberships reflects separatism, and perceptions of others as separate individuals rather than as group members represents decategorization.

Consistent with our hypothesis that a dual identity represents a form of recategorization that can facilitate positive intergroup relations for minority group members, Huo, Smith, Tyler, and Lind (1996) found that even when racial or ethnic identity is strong for minority group members, perceptions of a superordinate connection enhance interracial trust and acceptance of authority within an organization. We found converging evidence in a study of students in a multiethnic high school (Gaertner, Rust, Dovidio, Bachman, & Anastasio, 1996). Students who described themselves as *both* American and as a member of their racial or ethnic group showed less bias toward other groups in the school than did those who described themselves only in terms of their subgroup identity. Thus, even when subgroup identity is salient, the simultaneous salience of a common ingroup identity is associated with lower levels of intergroup bias.

Although these findings support the value of developing a dual identity as an alternative to a one-group representation for improving intergroup attitudes and the behavioral orientations of minority group members, we caution that the effectiveness of a dual identity may be substantially moderated by the nature of the intergroup context. In contrast to the consistent, significant effect for the one-group representation across studies of a multiethnic high school (Gaertner et al., 1996), for banking executives who experienced a corporate merger and for stepfamilies (Gaertner et al., 2001), the experience of a dual identity functioned differently, producing different effects across intergroup settings. In particular, a stronger sense of dual identity was related to less bias in the high school study but to more bias in the corporate merger study and more conflict within the stepfamily study (see Gaertner et al., 2001).

One potential factor that might moderate the effectiveness of a dual identity is the "cultural ideal" of the social entity. That is, a dual identity may relate to positive attitudes toward members of other groups within the superordinate identity as well as to indicators of well-being when a dual identity, itself, represents a cultural ideal, as with a pluralistic social value, or as an intermediate stage in movement from separatism to primarily a one-group, superordinate identity (i.e., assimilation). In a national probability sample of Latinos, for example, de la Garza, Falcon, and Garcia (1996) found that ethnic identity was not perceived as competing with an American identity. In fact stronger ethnic identity was related to more positive attitudes toward other groups and personal adjustment because, as the researchers found, "ethnics use ethnicity to create resources such as group solidarity and political organizations to facilitate their full participation in American society" (p. 337).

In contrast, when the simultaneous activation of subgroup and super ordinate group identities is inconsistent with the dominant cultural value (e.g., assimilation) or is perceived to reflect movement away from that cultural value, a dual identity is hypothesized to be negatively related to intergroup attitudes and to feelings of well-being. Our previous findings can be interpreted as consistent with this proposition. Within the context of a corporate merger, in which maintaining strong identification with the subgroup might threaten the primary goal of the merger, and within the context of a blended family, in which bias toward one's former family can be diagnostic of serious problems, a one-group representation would be expected to be – and is – the most important mediator of positive intergroup relations.

In general, then, we propose that the meaning, and thus the impact, of the experience of a dual identity are dynamically determined by the social context. Research on the self, for instance, has conceptualized self-esteem as an interpersonal monitor, a sociometer that "alerts the individual to the possibility of social exclusion" (Leary, Tambor, Terdal, & Downs, 1995, p. 518), and varies as a function of individual differences in personal values and priorities (Crocker & Wolfe, 2001). We hypothesize that cognitive representations of groups (and particularly a dual identity) operate in an analogous way at the collective level. That is, a dual identity can reflect the degree of social inclusion or exclusion of one's group, and thus its meaning can vary as a function of the dominant social values in the context as well as a function of one's motivations, priorities, and perspectives. When the dominant value in a given context is assimilationist (i.e., one group) or if an individual has assimilation as a personal goal, a dual identity may reflect exclusion and be associated with negative attitudes toward other groups. In contrast, when the primary cultural, subcultural, or personal value is pluralistic and integrationist, a dual identity may be more strongly associated with positive intergroup attitudes and orientations. In the next section, we further explore the implications of this framework for understanding intergroup attitudes.

DUAL IDENTITY AND INTERGROUP ATTITUDES

Although achieving a common ingroup identity can have beneficial effects for both majority and minority group members, as our previous research has demonstrated, it is still important to recognize that members of these groups also have different perspectives (Islam & Hewstone, 1993). These different perspectives can shape perceptions of and reactions to the nature of the contact. Whereas minority group members often want to retain their cultural identity, majority group members tend to favor the assimilation of minority groups into one single culture (a traditional "melting pot" orientation) – a process that reaffirms and reinforces the values of the dominant culture. Van Oudenhoven et al. (1998), for instance, found in the Netherlands that Dutch majority group members preferred an assimilation of minority groups, in which minority group identity was abandoned and replaced by identification with the dominant Dutch culture, whereas Turkish and Moroccan immigrants most strongly endorsed integration, in which they would retain their own cultural identity while also valuing the dominant Dutch culture. These orientations, assimilation for the majority group and integration for minority groups, are stronger for majority and minority group members who identify more strongly with their group (Verkuyten & Brug, 2004). Within the US, Whites place primary value on assimilation, whereas minority most strongly value multicultural integration (Plaut & Markus, 2004). In terms of the Common Ingroup Identity Model, we have found that White college students value a one-group (assimilation) orientation most, whereas racial and ethnic minorities most favor a "same team" (pluralistic integration) representation (Dovidio et al., 2000).

One direct consequence of these different values is that attempts to induce or impose a common ingroup identity may be differentially successful for groups that already value a superordinate identity as compared to groups for which a one-group identity can threaten important subgroup identities. Under these conditions of identity threat, manipulations emphasizing common group identity can potentially exacerbate rather than reduce intergroup bias (Hewstone & Brown, 1986).

Furthermore, to the extent to which Whites hold assimilationist cultural values and Blacks possess pluralistic values, one-group and dual-identity representations would be expected to operate differently as mediators of the effect of intergroup contact on intergroup attitudes. Supportive of this hypothesis, we found that perceptions of favorable intergroup contact predicted more favorable intergroup attitudes for both White and minority college students, but they did so in different ways (Dovidio, Gaertner,

Hodson, Houlette, & Johnson, 2004; Dovidio et al., 2000). For White students, more favorable perceptions of intergroup contact predicted stronger one-group representations, which, in turn, primarily mediated more positive attitudes toward minorities. For minority students, it was the strength of the dual identity, not the one-group representation that mediated the relationship between favorable conditions of contact and positive attitudes toward Whites. Paralleling the results of Verkuyten and Brug (2004) who found differences in preference for assimilation and integration by majority and minority group members as a function of group identification in the Netherlands, these relationships that we found were stronger for majority and minority group members who identified more strongly with their racial group.

Complementing these findings for White students and students of color, we have also found that, within a sample of predominantly White students, status moderates the relationship between a dual identity and bias (Johnson, Gaertner, & Dovidio, 2001). Among low and high status university students (i.e., regular students and students in the prestigious Honors Program, respectively), who were expected to perform the same tasks within a superordinate workgroup, the relationship between perceptions of the aggregate as two subgroups within a group (a dual identity) and bias depended upon the status of the group. For low status (regular) students, higher perceptions of a dual identity significantly predicted less bias, whereas for higher status (honors) students, a stronger dual identity predicted greater bias.

Intergroup relations, however, represent more than simply the attitudes of one group toward another; they reflect the fact that groups bring different values to their interactions and have different perspectives on their interactions (Dovidio, Gaertner, Kawakami, & Hodson, 2002; Islam & Hewstone, 1993). As a consequence, the expression of an identity that is valued and functional for a member of one group (e.g., a dual identity for a minority group member) may unintentionally and without full awareness produce a negative reaction from a member of another group holding a different cultural value (e.g., a one-group, assimilationist value held by a majority group member). Piontkowski, Rohmann, and Florack (2002) found that discordance in acculturation values between majority and majority groups was directly related to feelings of intergroup threat. One manifestation of this threat may be negative intergroup attitudes. We illustrated this dynamic in another study.

In this experiment (Dovidio, Gaertner, & Johnson, 1999), White college students from Colgate University first read a campus newspaper article about a Black student who had experienced a serious illness that had caused the student academic difficulties and then viewed a videotape that portrayed the student being interviewed about the situation. The presentation of the Black student, a confederate, was designed to make a positive impression. After the initial presentation of the confederate, an interviewer on the videotape asked, "And how do you see yourself?" The confederate's response was constructed to reflect one of the four representations outlined in the Common Ingroup Identity Model: (1) "I see myself primarily as a Colgate student" (one group), (2) "I see myself primarily as a Black person" (different group), (3) "I see myself primarily as a Black Colgate student (or a Colgate student who is Black)" (dual identity), or (4) "I see myself primarily as a unique individual" (separate individuals). The outcome measure of interest was the attitudes of White participants toward Blacks after observing the Black confederate.

The results of this study provide further evidence that the effectiveness of a dual identity is critically moderated by the social context and cultural values. In this case, the manipulation based on a one-group representation, which was most compatible with an assimilationist ideology, was most effective in inducing more positive attitudes in White college students. Attitudes toward Blacks in general were significantly less prejudiced and more favorable when the Black student described himself or herself solely in terms of common university membership than in the other three conditions. Attitudes in the other three conditions – dual identity, different groups, and separate individuals – did not differ from one another. Indeed, attitudes toward Blacks tended to be the most negative when Black confederates expressed a dual identity. Thus, understanding intergroup relations requires a knowledge not only of the separate attitudes and values held by members of different groups, but also an appreciation of the consequences of bringing together people who hold different values and perspectives and who, thus, may form different impressions of the same interaction (Dovidio et al., 1999).

Increasing the salience of different cultural orientations can systematically influence Whites' responses to Blacks. Participants in a study by Wolsko, Park, Judd, and Wittenbrink (2000) received a message advocating either a colorblind (assimilationist) or multicultural (pluralistic) approach to improving intergroup relations, making either of these social values salient. Participants in a control condition did not receive such a message. Wolsko et al. found that White participants who received the message advocating a multicultural social value had more positive attitudes toward Blacks than did White participants who received the message advocating a colorblind social value. The responses of White participants in the control condition were closely aligned with those in the color-blind condition.

Mummendey and Wenzel (1999) suggest a specific mechanism, relative prototypicality, which may be involved in determining the relative effectiveness of interventions designed to produce one-group or dual identity representations. They propose that when a common, superordinate identity is salient, people tend to overestimate the extent to which their own groups' norms, values, and standards are prototypical of the superordinate category relative to the extent to which other groups' norms, values, and standards are prototypical. When the standards of one's own group are perceived to represent those of the superordinate category, the standards of other groups may be seen as nonnormative and inferior. As a consequence, bias results. It is further possible that a salient subgroup identity, which can increase the strength of projection of beliefs, values, and norms (Mullen, Dovidio, Johnson, & Copper, 1992), can exacerbate the effects of relative protypicality when the superordinate group identity is also salient. Thus, even though strong racial identities, alone or in the form of a dual identity, may be initially beneficial, particularly for minorities, the adoption of a single, inclusive identity might be the primary predictor of reductions in bias over time and across situations. This may be especially true within the context of organizations such as historically White colleges, in which assimilation is the traditional ideal.

Supportive of this reasoning, in a longitudinal study, we investigated the *changes* that occurred in the attitudes of minority college students over an academic year as a function of group representations (Dovidio et al., 2004). In particular, minority students were surveyed first at the beginning of the academic year and then again within 6 weeks before the end of the academic year. Students were asked about their perceptions of the favorability of intergroup contact on campus, their perceptions of racial and ethnic groups on campus (one group, different subgroups on the same team, different groups, and separate individuals), and their attitudes toward Whites on campus.

Perceptions of favorable intergroup contact at the beginning of the year predicted more favorable attitudes toward Whites initially and at the end of the year. In addition, although the dual identity (same team) representation was the primary predictor of positive attitudes toward Whites initially, it was the development of a stronger one-group representation, not a stronger dual identity, that predicted increases in favorable intergroup attitudes over the year. Across this same period, the minority students apparently recognized the dominant institutional value as a one-group representation, and, thus, those who showed greater correspondence with that value had more positive attitudes toward the majority group on campus, Whites.

In summary, whereas our earlier work on intergroup attitudes focused on the value of inducing a common ingroup identity for improving intergroup relations, our more recent work has recognized the importance of a dual identity, simultaneously salient subgroup and superordinate identities, as well. However, the effects for the dual identity representation may appear contradictory, sometimes relating positively and sometimes negatively to intergroup attitudes. We propose however that these seemingly contradictory findings can be reconciled by considering the meaning ascribed to a dual identity, in terms of its "fit" with one's cultural values (e.g., colorblind or multicultural values) and its interpretation as movement toward or away from achieving these values.

IDENTITY AND WELL-BEING

Although the focus in our research on the Common Ingroup Identity Model has been on intergroup attitudes and relations, we believe that the experience of social identity can have far-reaching implications for the well-being of both minority and majority group members. That is, intergroup bias is hypothesized to be symptomatic of more fundamental conflicts and threats that can pervasively influence mental and physical health. To the extent that people identify with a social group, their self-concept will likely be shaped by how others think about, feel about, and treat their group. That is, self-concept develops not only from other people's views of the self (Cooley, 1902; Mead, 1934) but also from others' views of one's social group (Allport, 1954/1979).

Because minority groups are often devalued and discriminated against by the majority group, greater identification with one's minority ingroup might be expected to have adverse effects on mental and physical well-being. Allport (1954/1979), for example, remarked, "Ask yourself what would happen to your own personality if you heard it said over and over again that you were lazy, a simple child of nature, expected to steal, and had inferior blood?...One's reputation, whether false or true, cannot be hammered, hammered, hammered, into one's head without doing something to one's character" (Allport, 1954/1979, p. 142).

Consistent with Allport's speculation, current research on stereotype threat indicates that making one's stigmatized identity salient can promote stereotype-confirming behaviors, even when a person does not endorse the stereotype and the behaviors interfere with achieving desired goals (Steele, 1997). In addition, many stigmatized groups (e.g., White women, over-weight people) have generally lower self-esteem than their nonstigmatized counterparts (see Major, Quinton, & McCoy, 2002). Moreover, because stigmatization not only involves stereotyping and negative attitudes toward one's group but also negative treatment, perceptions of discrimination may produce chronically high levels of stress experienced by minority group members that can negatively impact (both directly and indirectly) mental and physical health (Jackson et al., 1996; Williams, Spencer, & Jackson, 1999). Blacks, for example, exhibit high levels of distrust toward Whites (Dovidio et al., 2002). For both Blacks and Latinos, perceptions of greater racial or ethnic discrimination predict poorer mental health (Stuber, Galea, Ahern, Blaney, & Fuller, 2003). In addition, among Blacks, Williams and Chung (2004) found that experiences of racial discrimination in the previous month were related to subsequently reported health problems. Experiences of racist events are also associated with behaviors that can have long-term adverse consequences for health, such as smoking and drinking, among Black women (Kwate, Valdimarsdottir, Guevarra, & Bovbjerg, 2003).

Awareness of others' negative orientations toward one's group, however, does not always adversely affect members of stigmatized groups. Percep-tions of bias sometimes result in enhanced performance, at least in the short term, as people work especially hard to compensate for the prejudice of others (Miller & Myers, 1998). In addition, inconsistent with Allport's sug-gestion, stigmatized groups do not necessarily exhibit lower self-esteem than nonstigmatized groups. Blacks, for example, show significantly *higher* levels of self-esteem than do Whites (Twenge & Crocker, 2000). Identification with one's group can act as a buffer to the negative attitudes toward, perceptions, and treatment of minority groups.

Prejudice provides an external attribution for negative outcomes, pro-tecting the self-esteem of minority group members (Crocker & Major, 1989). Blacks higher in racial consciousness perceive *external* factors, such as dis-crimination against their group, as more influential for negative outcomes personally, as well as for other Blacks (Brown & Johnson, 1999). In ad-dition, because being the target of prejudice produces stress, responses to the stigmatization of one's group can be conceptualized within frameworks of stress and coping (see Major et al., 2002, for a review). Thus, perceived discrimination may lead to stronger identification with one's group as a way to cope with the stress of being the target of prejudice (Branscombe, Schmitt, & Harvey, 1999; Sanders Thompson, 1999). Greater identification with one's group, in turn, may buffer people against the potentially adverse consequences of perceived discrimination (Branscombe et al., 1999; Fischer & Shaw, 1999).

We acknowledge the validity of each of these various accounts for the effects of stigmatization on different groups, but we also propose that our approach to identity processes within the Common Ingroup Identity Model offers an additional intergroup perspective on the issue of stigmatization and well-being. In particular, much of the previous research on minority group status, group identity, and well-being has focused exclusively on the strength of people's identification with their racial or ethnic group. Moreover, unidimensional models of acculturation emphasize the competitive nature of racial or ethnic and mainstream cultural identities (Gans, 1979). From this perspective, the effects of group identity and well-being would often appear contradictory. Many studies showed that stronger identification with one's racial or ethnic subgroup is associated with greater mental and physical well-being (Branscombe et al., 1989; Miller, 1999), whereas other studies demonstrate that stronger mainstream identity is related to greater personal adjustment and better mental and physical health (Ryder, Alden, & Paulhus, 2000). Our work on intergroup relations demonstrates the importance of considering identification *both* with the subgroup (e.g., one's racial and ethnic group) *and* the superordinate group (e.g., identity as an American), as well as the personal and cultural value of these different cultural representations.

To the extent that members of stigmatized groups identify only with a group that they perceive is marginalized or devalued and do not feel accepted as a member of the larger society, they are likely to experience higher levels of chronic stress and consequent impairment of mental and physical (Williams & Chung, 2004). Thus, minority group members who perceive subgroup identity and superordinate group identity to be in conflict (Ryder et al., 2000; Sidanius et al., 1997) and those who desire inclusion in the larger (American) society but who are excluded may have relatively high levels of stress and low levels of mental and physical well-being. That is, when a separate-group's identity or a dual identity signals the exclusion of a minority group member from full participation in the larger society, minority group members are likely to experience elevated stress levels that can, over time, erode mental and physical health. Thus, our approach acknowledges that experiences of specific acts of discrimination adversely affect mental and physical health, but we further posit that general feelings of exclusion from the larger society represents the fundamental basis of pervasive stress and threat (see MacDonald & Leary, 2005).

Furthermore, from our perspective, although limiting identification to one's racial or ethnic group (i.e., to the exclusion of a larger superordinate American identity) may have some immediate benefits, this can produce disidentification with the larger society that can have long-term detrimental effects. For Blacks, for example, this orientation can lead to lower academic aspiration and achievement (Osborne, 1997). With respect to health, Blacks who more strongly identify with their while rejecting White culture have higher blood pressure (Thompson, Kamarck, & Manuck, 2002) and a distrust that can produce an underutilization of medical, psychological, and social services (e.g., Thompson, Valdimarsdottir, Jandorf, & Redd, 2004).

In contrast, members of minority groups with a dual identity who identify with both their minority group and with the larger society and see these identities as complementary tend to be well-adjusted personally, experience lower levels of stress, and engage in more health-promotive activities (Airhihenbuwa, Kumanyika, TenHave, & Morssink, 2000). A review of the literature by LaFromboise, Coleman, and Gerton (1993) revealed that members of racial and ethnic minority groups who demonstrated stronger bicultural or multicultural identities had better social adjustment, psychological adaptation, and overall well-being. We have also found that minority college students who value and possess dual identities, reflecting identification with both their racial or ethnic group and the greater community, were more satisfied with their educational experience and more motivated to complete their college degree at their institution (Dovidio et al., 2000). Further analysis of that dataset revealed that a dual identity predicted lower feelings of threat and greater intergroup trust among minority students, over and above the effects of ethnic and racial group identification.

Our perspective also draws attention to the relationship between group identity and the mental and physical health of majority group members, something that receives less attention in models of coping with stigmatization. To the extent that identification with one's group corresponds with the superordinate group identity (as with majority group members), individuals may be particularly likely to see their group's attributes and perspectives as prototypical of the superordinate group values (Mummendey & Wenzel, 1999). These perceptions of the value of one's group may eventually become internalized into one's self-concept and reflected by high self-esteem (Leary, 1999) and feelings of self-efficacy (Bandura, 2000), which generally produce better psychological adjustment, higher personal expectations for success, greater resiliency to stressful events, and higher levels of actual accomplishment.

SUMMARY AND CONCLUSIONS

In this chapter, we have examined how social identity relates to intergroup biases and personal well-being in the context of the Common Ingroup Identity Model (Gaertner & Dovidio, 2000). From this perspective, social categorization forms the foundation for social identity and, ultimately, how people respond to others, both to members of the ingroup (e.g., ingroup favoritism) and to members of outgroup (e.g., outgroup derogation). The earliest evidence for the model demonstrated that recategorizing others who were originally viewed in terms of their membership in another group as members of a common superordinate group can redirect the psychological forces of ingroup favoritism to improve attitudes toward these other people and reduce intergroup bias. The current chapter considers four fundamental extensions of the model.

First, in this chapter, we emphasized the importance of recognizing that people belong to many different groups, and these social identities can become activated simultaneously. Thus, to understand more fully the profound influence of social identities, research on intergroup relations and mental and physical well-being as a function of group membership needs to move beyond consideration of the effects of simple categorization to multiple categorization and identities.

Second, we have argued that the meaning of social identities can have different implications for members of different groups. Whereas assimilation is the preferred cultural model for majority group members, integration that values multicultural perspectives is the generally preferred cultural model minority group members. Within the framework of the Common Ingroup Identity Model (Gaertner & Dovidio, 2000), we have found evidence in both laboratory experiments and field studies showing that majority group members prefer a one-group (assimilationist) model, have more positive attitudes toward other groups when then have this representation, and may be threatened by members of other groups who appear to value other representations more highly. Members of minority groups, in contrast, have more favorable attitudes toward Whites and have greater organizational commitment, at least initially, when they have a dual identity, reflecting identification with their racial or ethnic group and with a relevant superordinate group (e.g., a college or nation).

Third, we proposed that the meaning of social identities must be considered in a dynamic context, in relation to perceived social and cultural standards and personal values. For instance, Whites, who value a one-group, assimilationist orientation feel more threatened and have more

negative attitudes toward Blacks who emphasize their separate group identity or a dual identity than toward Blacks who emphasize only their common group membership (Dovidio et al., 1999). Also, when a separate-
group's identity or a dual identity signals the exclusion of a minority group
member from full participation in the larger society, minority group members may respond with feelings of threat and negative attitudes toward the
majority group. In contrast, when racial or ethnic and superordinate identities are perceived to be complementary and the combination is jointly
valued, a dual identity predicts more positive intergroup attitudes. In general, the more concordant a person's social identity is with what they perceive to be the dominant or desired cultural model (Berry, 1997), the more
positive are their intergroup attitudes (Dovidio et al., 2004; see also
Piontkowski et al., 2002).

Fourth, and finally, in the present chapter we consider the implications of
the Common Ingroup Identity Model and its extensions beyond intergroup
attitudes to issues of mental and physical well-being. That is, whereas our
previous research has focused on the effects of different social identities and
representations on intergroup attitudes, discrimination, and relations, we
propose that these may be symptomatic of underlying feelings of threat and
stress that can have a range of consequences for personal well-being, including mental and physical health. Thus, the study of social identities within the
Common Ingroup Identity Model can help integrate previously separate literatures on the topics of prejudice, intergroup relations, acculturation, dis-
parities in mental and physical health, and deviance and offer an intergroup
perspective to complement models of personal identity development.

REFERENCES

Abrams, D. (1985). Focus of attention in minimal intergroup discrimination. *British Journal of Social Psychology, 24*, 65–74.
Airhihenbuwa, C. O., Kumanyika, S. K., TenHave, T. R., & Morssink, C. B. (2000). Cultural identity and health lifestyles among African Americans: A new direction for health intervention research. *Ethnicity and Disease, 10*, 148–164.
Allport, G. W. (1954/1979). *The nature of prejudice*. Cambridge, MA: Perseus Books.
Bandura, A. (2000). Social cognitive theory: An agentic perspective. *Annual Review of Psychology, 52*, 1–26.
Banker, B. S., Gaertner, S. L., Dovidio, J. F., Houlette, M., Johnson, K. H., & Riek, B. M. (2004). Reducing stepfamily conflict: The importance of an inclusive social identity. In:

M. Bennett & F. Sani (Eds), *The development of the social self* (pp. 267–288). Philadelphia, PA: Psychology Press.

Berry, J. W. (1984). Cultural relations in plural societies. In: N. Miller & M. B. Brewer (Eds), *Groups in contact: The psychology of desegregation* (pp. 11–27). Orlando, FL: Academic Press.

Berry, J. W. (1997). Immigration, acculturation, and adaptation. *Applied Psychology: An International Review, 46,* 5–68.

Biernat, M., & Dovidio, J. F. (2000). Stigma and stereotypes. In: T. F. Heatherton, R. E. Kleck, M. R. Hebl & J. G. Hull (Eds), *The social psychology of stigma* (pp. 88–125). New York: Guilford.

Billig, M., & Tajfel, H. (1973). Social categorization and similarity in intergroup behaviour. *European Journal of Social Psychology, 3,* 27–52.

Blumer, H. (1958). Race prejudice as a sense of group position. *Pacific Sociological Review, 1,* 3–7.

Bobo, L., & Huchings, V. L. (1996). Perceptions of racial group competition: Extending Blumer's theory of group position to a multiracial context. *American Sociological Review, 61,* 951–972.

Branscombe, N. R., Schmitt, M. T., & Harvey, R. D. (1999). Perceiving pervasive discrimination among African Americans: Implications for group identification and well-being. *Journal of Personality and Social Psychology, 77,* 135–149.

Brewer, M. B. (1988). A dual process model of impression formation. In: T. S. Srull & R. S. Wyer (Eds), *Advances in social cognition: Vol. I: A dual process model of impression formation* (pp. 1–36). Hillsdale, NJ: Erlbaum.

Brewer, M. B. (1999). The psychology of prejudice: Ingroup love or outgroup hate? *Journal of Social Issues, 55,* 429–444.

Brewer, M. B. (2001). Social identities and social representations: A question of priority? In: K. Deaux & G. Philogène (Eds), *Representations of the social: Bridging theoretical traditions* (pp. 305–311). Malden, MA: Blackwell Publishers.

Brewer, M. B., Ho, H., Lee, J., & Miller, N. (1987). Social identity and social distance among Hong Kong school children. *Personality and Social Psychology Bulletin, 13,* 156–165.

Brown, L. M., & Johnson, S. D. (1999). Ethnic consciousness and its relationship to conservatism and blame among African Americans. *Journal of Applied Social Psychology, 29,* 2465–2480.

Brown, R. J., & Hewstone, M. (2005). An integrative theory of intergroup contact. In: M. P. Zanna (Ed.), *Advances in experimental social psychology.* (in press).

Brown, R. J., & Zagefka, H. (2005). Ingroup affiliations and prejudice. In: J. F. Dovidio, P. Glick. & L. A. Rudman (Eds), *On the nature of prejudice: Fifty years after Allport* (pp. 54–70). Malden, MA: Blackwell.

Cooley, C. H. (1902). *Human nature and the social order.* New York: Schocken.

Crisp, R. J., Ensari, N., Hewstone, M., & Miller, N. (2003). A dual-route model of crossed categorization effects. In: W. Stroebe & M. Hewstone (Eds), *European review of social psychology,* (Vol. 13, pp. 35–74). Philadelphia, PA: Psychology Press.

Crocker, J., & Major, B. (1989). Social stigma and self-esteem: The self-protective properties of stigma. *Psychological Review, 96,* 608–630.

Crocker, J., & Wolfe, C. T. (2001). Contingencies of self-worth. *Psychological Review, 108,* 593–623.

Cross, W. E. (1991). *Shades of Black: Diversity in African American identity.* Philadelphia, PA: Temple University Press.

de la Garza, R. O., Falcon, A., & Garcia, F. C. (1996). Will the real Americans please stand up? Anglo and Mexican-American support of core American political values. *American Journal of Political Science, 40,* 335–351.

Deschamps, J. C., & Doise, W. (1978). Crossed-category membership in intergroup relations. In: H. Tajfel (Ed.), *Differentiation between social groups* (pp. 141–158). London, UK: Academic Press.

Dovidio, J. F., & Gaertner, S. L. (1993). Stereotypes and evaluative intergroup bias. In: D. M. Mackie & D. L. Hamilton (Eds), *Affect, cognition, and stereotyping: Interactive processes in intergroup perception* (pp. 167–193). Orlando, FL: Academic Press.

Dovidio, J. F., Gaertner, S. L., Hodson, G., Houlette, M., & Johnson, K. M. (2004). Social inclusion and exclusion: Recategorization and the perception of intergroup boundaries. In: D. Abrams, J. Marques & M. A. Hogg (Eds), *Social psychology of inclusion and exclusion.* Philadelphia, PA: Psychology Press.

Dovidio, J. F., Gaertner, S. L., & Johnson, J. D. (1999). New directions in prejudice and prejudice reduction: The role of cognitive representations and affect. *Symposium paper presented at the annual meeting of the Society for Experimental Social Psychology,* St. Louis, MO.

Dovidio, J. F., Gaertner, S. L., & Kafati, G. (2000). Group identity and intergroup relations: The common in-group identity model. In: S. R. Thye, E. J. Lawler, M. W. Macy & H. A. Walker (Eds), *Advances in group processes,* (Vol. 17, pp. 1–34). Stamford, CT: JAI Press.

Dovidio, J. F., Gaertner, S. L., Kawakami, K., & Hodson, G. (2002). Why can't we just get along? Interpersonal biases and interracial distrust. *Cultural Diversity & Ethnic Minority Psychology, 8,* 88–102.

Dovidio, J. F., Gaertner, S. L., Validzic, A., Matoka, K., Johnson, B., & Frazier, S. (1997). Extending the benefits of re-categorization: Evaluations self-disclosure and helping. *Journal of Experimental Social Psychology, 33,* 401–420.

DuBois, W. E. B. (1938). *The souls of Black folk. Essays and sketches.* Chicago, IL: A. C. McLurg.

Esses, V. M., Jackson, L. M., & Armstrong, T. L. (1998). Intergroup competition and attitudes toward immigrants and immigration: An instrumental model of group conflict. *Journal of Social Issues, 54,* 699–724.

Fischer, A. R., & Shaw, C. M. (1999). African Americans' mental health and perceptions of racial discrimination. *The effects of racial socialization experiences and self-esteem. Journal of Counseling Psychology, 46,* 395–407.

Fiske, S. T., Lin, M., & Neuberg, S. L. (1999). The continuum model: Ten years later. In: S. Chaiken & Y. Trope (Eds), *Dual process theories in social psychology* (pp. 231–254). New York: Guilford.

Fiske, S. T., & Taylor, S. E. (1991). *Social cognition* (2nd ed.). New York: McGraw-Hill.

Gaertner, S. L., Bachman, B. A., Dovidio, J. D., & Banker, B. S. (2001). Corporate mergers and stepfamily marriages: Identity, harmony, and commitment. In: M. A. Hogg & D. Terry (Eds), *Social identity processes in organizations* (pp. 265–282). Philadelphia, PA: Psychology Press.

Gaertner, S. L., & Dovidio, J. F. (2000). *Reducing intergroup bias: The common ingroup identity model.* Philadelphia, PA: The Psychology Press.

Gaertner, S. L., Mann, J. A., Murrell, A. J., & Dovidio, J. F. (1989). Reduction of intergroup bias: The benefits of recategorization. *Journal of Personality and Social Psychology, 57*, 239–249.

Gaertner, S. L., Rust, M. C., Dovidio, J. F., Bachman, B. A., & Anastasio, P. A. (1996). The contact hypothesis: The role of a common ingroup identity on reducing intergroup bias among majority and minority group members. In: J. L. Nye & A. M. Brower (Eds), *What's social about social cognition?* (pp. 230–360). Newbury Park, CA: Sage.

Gans, H. (1979). Symbolic ethnicity: The future of ethnic groups and culture in America. *Ethnic and Racial Studies, 2*, 1–20.

Helms, J. E. (Ed.) (1990). *Black and White racial identity: Theory, research, and practice.* New York: Greenwood Press.

Hewstone, M. (1996). Contact and categorization: Social psychological interventions to change intergroup relations. In: C. N. Macrae, M. Hewstone & C. Stangor (Eds), *Foundations of stereotypes and stereotyping* (pp. 323–368). New York: Guilford.

Hewstone, M., & Brown, R. J. (1986). Contact is not enough: An intergroup perspective on the "contact hypothesis". In: M. Hewstone & R. Brown (Eds), *Contact and conflict in intergroup encounters* (pp. 1–44). Oxford: Basil Blackwell.

Hogg, M. A., & Hains, S. C. (1996). Intergroup relations and group solidarity: Effects of group identification and social beliefs on depersonalized attraction. *Journal of Personality and Social Psychology, 70*, 295–309.

Houlette, M., Gaertner, S. L., Johnson, K. M., Banker, B. S., Riek, B. M., & Dovidio, J. F. (2004). Developing a more inclusive social identity: An elementary school intervention. *Journal of Social Issues, 60*, 35–56.

Howard, J. M., & Rothbart, M. (1980). Social categorization for in-group and out-group behavior. *Journal of Personality and Social Psychology, 38*, 301–310.

Huo, Y. J., Smith, H. H., Tyler, T. R., & Lind, A. E. (1996). Superordinate identification, subgroup identification, and justice concerns: Is separatism the problem. Is assimilation the answer? *Psychological Science, 7*, 40–45.

Insko, C. A., Schopler, J., Gaertner, L., Wildschut, T., Kozar, R., Pinter, B., Finkel, E. J., Brazil, D. M., Cecil, C. L., & Montoya, M. R. (2001). Interindividual–intergroup discontinuity reduction through the anticipation of future interaction. *Journal of Personality and Social Psychology, 80*, 95–111.

Islam, M. R., & Hewstone, M. (1993). Dimensions of contact as predictors of intergroup anxiety, perceived outgroup variability and outgroup attitude: An integrative model. *Personality and Social Psychology Bulletin, 19*, 700–710.

Jackson, J., Brown, T. N., Williams, D. R., Torres, M., Sellers, S. L., & Brown, K. (1996). Racism and the physical and mental health status of African Americans: A thirteen year panel study. *Ethnicity and Disease, 6*, 132–147.

Johnson, K. M., Gaertner, S. L., & Dovidio, J. F. (2001). *The effect of equality of job assignment on ingroup identity and bias for low and high status groups.* Unpublished data, Department of Psychology, University of Delaware, Newark, DE.

Kwate, N. A., Valdimarsdottir, H. B., Guevarra, J. S., & Bovbjerg, D. H. (2003). Experiences of racist events are associated with negative health consquences for African American women. *Journal of the National Medical Association, 95*, 450–460.

LaFromboise, T., Coleman, H. L. K., & Gerton, J. (1993). Psychological impact of biculturalism: Evidence and theory. *Psychological Bulletin, 114*, 395–412.

Leary, M. R. (1999). Making sense of self-esteem. *Current Directions in Psychological Science, 8,* 32–35.

Leary, M. R., Tambor, E. S., Terdal, S. K., & Downs, D. L. (1995). Self-esteem as interpersonal monitor: The sociometer hypothesis. *Journal of Personality and Social Psychology, 68,* 518–530.

Luhtanen, R., & Crocker, J. (1991). Self-esteem and intergroup comparisons: Toward a theory of collective self-esteem. In: J. Suls & T. A. Wills (Eds), *Social comparison: Contemporary theory and research* (pp. 211–234). Hillsdale, NJ: Erlbaum.

MacDonald, G., & Leary, M. R. (2005). Why does social exclusion hurt? The relationship between social and physical pain. *Psychological Bulletin, 131,* 202–223.

Major, B., Quinton, W. J., & McCoy, S. K. (2002). Antecedents and consequences of attributions to discrimination: Theoretical and empirical advances. In: M. P. Zanna (Ed.), *Advances in experimental social psychology,* (Vol. 34, pp. 251–330). San Diego, CA: Academic Press.

Markus, H., & Nurius, P. (1986). Possible selves. *American Psychologist, 41,* 954–969.

Mead, G. H. (1934). *Mind, self, and society.* Chicago, IL: University of Chicago Press.

Miller, C. T., & Myers, A. M. (1998). Compensating for prejudice: How heavyweight people (and others) control outcomes despite prejudice. In: J. K. Swim & C. Stangor (Eds), *Prejudice: The target's perspective* (pp. 191–218). San Diego, CA: Academic Press.

Miller, D. B. (1999). Racial socialization and racial identity: Can they promote resiliency for African American adolescents? *Adolescence, 34,* 493–501.

Miller, N. (2002). Personalization and the promise of contact theory. *Journal of Social Issues, 58,* 387–410.

Mullen, B., Dovidio, J. F., Johnson, C., & Copper, C. (1992). Ingroup–outgroup differences in social projection. *Journal of Experimental Social Psychology, 28,* 422–440.

Mummendey, A., Klink, A., & Brown, R. (2001). Nationalism and patriotism. *British Journal of Social Psychology, 40,* 159–171.

Mummendey, A., & Wenzel, M. (1999). Social discrimination and tolerance in intergroup relations: Reactions to intergroup difference. *Personality and Social Psychology Review, 3,* 158–174.

Osborne, J. W. (1997). Race and academic disidentification. *Journal of Educational Psychology, 89,* 728–735.

Otten, S., & Moskowitz, G. B. (2000). Evidence for implicit evaluative in-group bias: Affect-biased spontaneous trait inference in a minimal group paradigm. *Journal of Experimental Social Psychology, 36,* 77–89.

Park, B., & Rothbart, M. (1982). Perception of out-group homogeneity and levels of social categorization: Memory for the subordinate attributes of in-group and out-group members. *Journal of Personality and Social Psychology, 42,* 1051–1068.

Pettigrew, T. F. (1998). Intergroup contact theory. *Annual Review of Psychology, 49,* 65–85.

Phinney, J. S. (2003). Ethnic identity and acculturation. In: K. M. Chun & P. Balls Organista (Eds), *Acculturation: Advances in theory, measurement, and applied research* (pp. 63–81). Washington, DC: American Psychological Association.

Piontkowski, U., Rohmann, A., & Florack, A. (2002). Concordance of acculturation attitudes and perceived threat. *Group Processes and Intergroup Relations, 5,* 221–232.

Plaut, V. C., & Markus, H. R. (2004). *Sociocultural models of diversity in America: The dilemma of difference.* Unpublished manuscript, Department of Psychology, Stanford University, Stanford, CA.

Ryder, A. G., Alden, L. E., & Paulhus, D. L. (2000). Is acculturation unidimensional or bidimensional? A head-to-head comparison in the prediction of personality, self-construal, and adjustment. *Journal of Personality and Social Psychology, 79*, 49–65.

Sanders Thompson, V. L. (1999). Variables affecting racial identity salience among African Americans. *Journal of Social Psychology, 139*, 748–761.

Schultz, D. P., & Schultz, S. E. (2001). *Theories of personality* (7th ed.). Belmont, CA: Wadsworth/Thompson Learning.

Sellers, R. M., Rowley, S. A., Chavous, T. M., Shelton, J. N., & Smith, M. A. (1997). Multidimensional inventory of Black identity: A preliminary investigation of reliability and construct validity. *Journal of Personality and Social Psychology, 73*(4), 805–815.

Sherif, M., Harvey, O. J., White, B. J., Hood, W. R., & Sherif, C. W. (1961). *Intergroup conflict and cooperation. The Robbers Cave experiment.* Norman, OK: University of Oklahoma Book Exchange.

Sidanius, J., Feshbach, S., Levin, S., & Pratto, F. (1997). The interface between ethnic and national attachment: Ethnic pluralism or ethnic dominance? *Public Opinion Quarterly, 61*, 103–133.

Steele, C. M. (1997). A threat in the air: How stereotypes shape intellectual identity and performance. *American Psychologist, 52*, 613–629.

Stuber, J., Galea, S., Ahern, J., Blaney, S., & Fuller, C. (2003). The association between multiple domains of discrimination and self-assessed health: A multilevel analysis of Latinos and Blacks in four low-income New York City neighborhoods. *Health Services Research, 38*, 1735–1759.

Sumner, W. G. (1906). *Folkways.* New York: Ginn.

Tajfel, H. (1969). Cognitive aspects of prejudice. *Journal of Social Issues, 25*(4), 79–97.

Tajfel, H., & Turner, J. C. (1979). An integrative theory of intergroup conflict. In: W. G. Austin & S. Worchel (Eds), *The social psychology of intergroup relations* (pp. 33–48). Monterey, CA: Brooks/Cole.

Thompson, H. S., Kamarck, T. W., & Manuck, S. B. (2002). The association between racial identity and hypertension in African American adults: Elevated resting and ambulatory blood pressure outcomes. *Ethnicity and Disease, 12*, 20–28.

Thompson, H. S., Valdimarsdottir, H. B., Jandorf, L., & Redd, W. (2004). The group-based medical mistrust scale: Psychometric properties and association with breast cancer screening. *Preventive Medicine: An International Journal Devoted to Practice & Theory, 38*, 209–218.

Turner, J. C. (1985). Social categorization and the self-concept: A social cognitive theory of group behavior. In: E. J. Lawler (Ed.), *Advances in group processes*, (Vol. 2, pp. 77–122). Greenwich, CT: JAI Press.

Turner, J. C., Hogg, M. A., Oakes, P. J., Reicher, S. D., & Wetherell, M. S. (1987). *Rediscovering the social group: A self-categorization theory.* Oxford, England: Basil Blackwell.

Twenge, J. M., & Crocker, J. (2000). Race and self-esteem: Meta-analyses comparing Whites, Blacks, Hispanics, Asians, and American Indians and comment on Gray-Little and Hafdahl (2000). *Psychological Bulletin, 128*, 371–408.

van Oudenhoven, J. P., Prins, K. S., & Buunk, B. (1998). Attitudes of minority and majority members towards adaptation of immigrants. *European Journal of Social Psychology, 28*, 995–1013.

Verkuyten, M., & Brug, P. (2004). Multiculturalism and group status: The role of ethnic identification, group essentialism and protestant ethic. *European Journal of Social Psychology*, *34*, 647–661.

Verkuyten, M., & Hagendoorn, L. (1998). Prejudice and self-categorization: The variable role of authoritarianism and in-group stereotypes. *Personality and Social Psychology Bulletin*, *24*, 99–110.

Wilder, D. A. (1981). Perceiving persons as a group: Categorization and intergroup relations. In: D. L. Hamilton (Ed.), *Cognitive processes in stereotyping and intergroup behavior* (pp. 213–257). Hillsdale, NJ: Erlbaum.

Williams, D. R., & Chung, A. M. (2004). Racism and health. In: R. Gibson, & J. S. Jackson (Eds), *Health in Black America*. Thousand Oaks, CA: Sage (in press).

Williams, D. R., Spencer, M. S., & Jackson, J. S. (1999). Race, stress, and physical health: The role of group identity. In: J. Contrada & R. Ashmore (Eds), *Self, social identity, and physical health* (pp. 71–100). New York: Oxford University Press.

Wohl, M., & Branscombe, N. (2005). Forgiveness and collective guilt assignment to historical perpetrator groups depends on level of social category inclusiveness. *Journal of Personality and Social Psychology*, *88*, 288–303.

Wolsko, C., Park, B., Judd, C. M., & Wittenbrink, B. (2000). Framing interethnic ideology: Effects of multicultural and color-blind perspectives on judgments of groups and individuals. *Journal of Personality and Social Psychology*, *78*, 635–654.

Worchel, S., Rothgerber, H., Day, E. A., Hart, D., & Butemeyer, J. (1998). Social identity and individual productivity with groups. *British Journal of Social Psychology*, *37*, 389–413.

Yzerbyt, V., Corneille, O., & Estrada, C. (2001). The interplay of subjective essentialism and entitativity in the formation of stereotypes. *Personality and Social Psychology Review*, *5*, 141–155.

SET UP A CONTINUATION ORDER TODAY!

Did you know that you can set up a continuation order on all Elsevier-JAI series and have each new volume sent directly to you upon publication? For details on how to set up a **continuation order**, contact your nearest regional sales office listed below.

To view related series in Business & Management, please visit:

www.elsevier.com/businessandmanagement

30% Discount for Authors on All Books!